TRAILBLAZERS

TRAILBLAZERS

THE UNMATCHED STORY OF
WOMEN'S TENNIS

BILLIE JEAN KING
WITH CYNTHIA STARR

Andrews McMeel
PUBLISHING®

A NOTE TO THE READER

Each generation looks back and sees history through new eyes and in new ways. Events we once clearly understood might seem confusing years later. A bygone status quo might cause alarm, while injustice once unchallenged might cry out for repair. We could be surprised to learn of an exciting development that was barely celebrated when it happened. And so it is fitting that, on the fiftieth anniversary of the founding of the Women's Tennis Association, we offer a refreshed and updated accounting of *We HAVE Come a Long Way: The Story of Women's Tennis*, published in 1988.

Margaret Osborne duPont was one of many great champions I had the privilege of knowing. Here she is with the 1962 Wightman Cup team, which she captained. From left, Karen Hantze, Margaret Varner, Margaret duPont, Darlene Hard, me, and Nancy Richey.

Page 2:

Top row, from left: Dorothea Douglass Lambert Chambers holds the Wightman Cup in 1925; Billie Jean King serving at the 1974 U.S. Open; Althea Gibson, a reluctant but unforgettable pioneer, had reason to smile after winning the 1957 U.S. women's singles championship.

Middle row, from left: Stefanie Graf following her 1993 victory in the Virginia Slims Championships at Madison Square Garden; Chrissie Evert, right, congratulates Martina Navratilova, who has just won their 1978 Wimbledon singles final; Esther Mary Vergeer, champion and ambassador of wheelchair tennis.

Bottom row, from left: Louise Brough, winner of four Wimbledon singles titles; Serena and Venus Williams, three-time Olympic gold medalists in women's doubles, shown here in 2012; Angela Mortimer, left, and Christine Truman after Angela won their 1961 Wimbledon final.

So much has happened since the start of the WTA, an association that empowers women tennis professionals and allows us to speak with one voice. New waves of champions have been crowned, while many memorable figures have passed away. Other important figures have finally received the recognition they always deserved. And like a steady drumbeat throughout these past years, opportunities for women tennis players have grown steadily around the globe.

In 1970, three years before the founding of the WTA, nine brave women—myself included—broke with the tennis establishment and signed $1 contracts with Gladys Heldman to launch our own professional tournament in Houston. We are remembered today as the Original 9, and what we did was the most important thing that has ever happened in women's sports. Within three months, we had enough financial support to stage our first professional tour, the Virginia Slims tour. Our generation took a chance, and we transformed the game of tennis.

When we took these first steps in a journey that would benefit future generations of women, we had three primary goals. With great satisfaction, I note that all three have been achieved. Our first goal was to see a day when any girl or woman in the world, if she were good enough, would have a place to compete. Not play, but *compete*. Second, we wanted her to be appreciated for her accomplishments, not just her looks. And third, we wanted her to be able to make a living with her craft—to have a chance to make her greatest skill a vocation. We achieved these three goals—proof that clarity of vision and commitment can effect great change—and, in the process, women's tennis became the most lucrative women's professional sport in the world.

A tennis player has been the world's highest-paid woman athlete ever since *Forbes* magazine began publishing its rankings in 1990. For the year ending June 2021, Naomi Osaka earned a record $60 million in prize money and endorsements. As *Forbes* columnist Kurt Badenhausen wrote: "Tennis is the one pro sport where paydays for men and women are even in the same zip code and is the only sport with female athletes represented on the annual ranking [of The World's 100 Highest-Paid Athletes]. In basketball, NBA players often make 100 times what their counterparts in the WNBA do."

But women in other professional sports are catching up, and women's tennis has helped model what is possible. In 2022, the U.S. Soccer Federation agreed to equalize pay for the men's and women's national teams in all competitions, including the World Cup.

Today, I find myself in a better position than ever to tell the story I have wanted to read ever since I was a child playing tennis on the public courts in Long Beach, California. I have relished my own place in tennis history, of course. But because I have always loved history, I have been able to meet—and even play against—many of the great players. In every instance, I listened to what they had to say.

When I was a kid, I had a chance to speak with Elizabeth Ryan, whose nineteen Wimbledon titles between 1914 and 1934 I eventually equaled and then surpassed. I was coached by Alice Marble, the last important champion before World War II. I hit with Maureen Connolly, whose short, spectacular career included, in 1953, the first Grand Slam by a woman. I visited with Sarah Palfrey, who won the 1945 U.S. singles title as the mother of a two-year-old daughter. As a young teenager, I watched Althea Gibson play on the grandstand court at the Los Angeles Tennis Club and found out what No. 1 looks like. And I knew Louise Brough, who dominated women's doubles with Margaret Osborne duPont in the 1940s and 1950s. I had the privilege of playing Wightman Cup when Margaret duPont was captain. She is the one who sat down next to me and taught me in one word the secret to winning on clay: "patience." Indeed, a long parade of history-making women overlapped with my own career.

I helped Ted Tinling celebrate his birthday in the early 1970s.

Opposite page: Here I am with Alice Marble, center, and Carole Caldwell. Carole and I were teammates at Los Angeles State College (now California State University, Los Angeles).

And when I didn't have a chance to meet these terrific people who accomplished so much, I learned about them from elder tennis statesmen like Ted Tinling, the boundary-breaking tennis official, fashion designer, and astute observer of our sport.

As a youngster, I had difficulty finding books about the sport I loved best. My library had only two, *How to Use Your Head in Tennis* by Bob Harman and Keith Monroe and *Tennis with Hart* by Doris Hart, the tennis star of the 1940s and 1950s. I acquired my own copies of Doris Hart's book and Althea Gibson's autobiography, *I Always Wanted To Be Somebody,* and I actually slept with these books. But I wanted to read more—especially about history. It would have meant so much to me if I could have read about all the great women champions I admired so much.

By the 1970s and 1980s, libraries and stores were offering many books about women's tennis, but most were autobiographical or instructional. The history books usually dealt with only the most famous female Wimbledon champions and typically devoted the majority of their pages to the men's game. I decided that if I wanted to see a complete history of women's tennis in print, I would have to do it myself.

The history of women's tennis, of course, is not only the story of individual champions. It is also the story of an enormous struggle for equality. My coauthor, Cynthia Starr, and I seek to tell this story here in broad brushstrokes and historic photographs. We seek to give credit where credit is due—not only to the players but also to the sponsors, promoters, media, and fans whose contributions are vital to the success of any professional sport. Truth, we know, is often elusive. Memories frequently prove inadequate, and accounts of some historic events differ vastly. We have done our utmost throughout to be accurate and fair.

We believe this is a book for everyone who loves tennis. It is also a book for anyone who enjoys reading about people who made a difference in their vocation and in the world beyond.

When Chrissie Evert burst upon the tennis scene, an ingenue in Tretorns and hair ribbons, she was making a difference for thousands of girls who, overnight, decided to take up a sport. When the U.S. Open crowd thundered its approval for a defeated and tearful Martina Navratilova, a gay athlete who did not fit the stereotype of the traditionally feminine, Martina was making a difference for the LGBTQ community throughout the world. When Jana Novotná finally won her precious Wimbledon championship five years after her excruciating collapse in the 1993 final, she was making a difference for anyone who had ever tried and failed and tried again. When Serena Williams won title after title with an unprecedented combination of power and aggressiveness, she was making a difference for anyone who aspired to live as the person they were born to be. And when Naomi Osaka walked onto stadium courts in proud support of Black Lives Matter, she was making a difference for any person of color who had ever felt the sting of prejudice or oppression.

I hope you draw encouragement and inspiration from these women and many others whose stories are shared here. More than just heroes for those who love tennis, they are heroes for all.

**— Billie Jean King
April 2023**

For Billie Jean
my gratitude for a talented pupil
and a special friend Fondly Alice
Alice Marble
1962

CHAPTER ONE

ORIGINS

1874
1914

TO

DECADES before they could vote, run for office, or hold a credit card in their own name, women played tennis. On this timeless playground, they always had a foothold. Our sport's female pioneers took to the courts right alongside their male counterparts—albeit less comfortably. They wore skirts that nearly brushed the ground, petticoats that flounced around their ankles, and steel-boned corsets that pressed in on their ribcages. Their shirt collars came up to their chins, and their sleeves were buttoned tightly at their wrists.

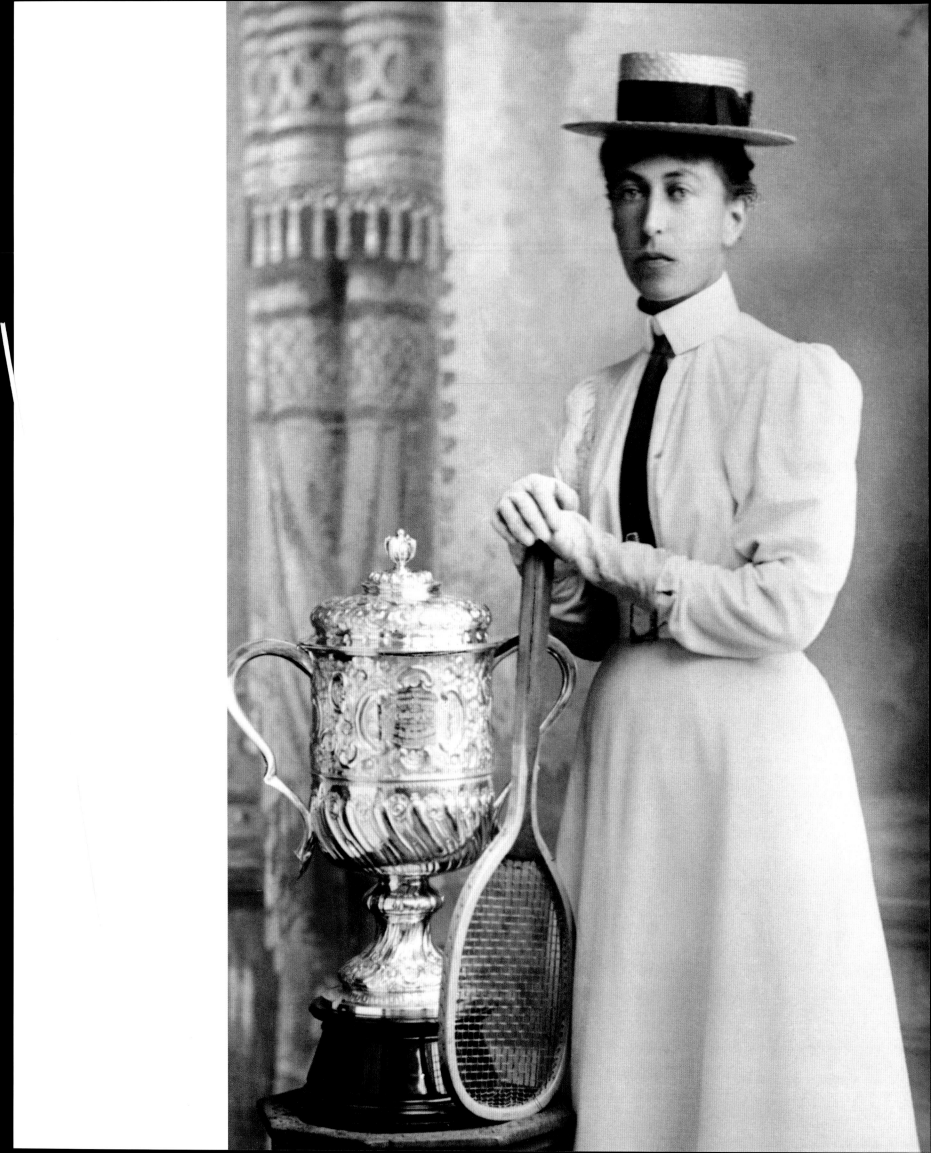

How they could breathe—let alone run—escapes me. Nor could they have struck the ball hard with the heavy, loosely strung rackets of that era. They were our first generation—pioneers who coped with the dress and norms of their culture—and they are vitally important in the history of our game. They started a passionate love affair with tennis that has lasted for nearly 150 years.

The first women who competed in tennis would be stunned by the level of play today. A sport that began as a kind of garden party and once offered only a title and silver cup to the champion is today a major-league entertainment business played by laser-focused professionals who earn millions in prize money and endorsements.

Nonetheless, if the best women players of the past could be united with the best of the present, they would discover many parallels in their lives. Each generation of champions felt stress, ambition, and elation. Each suffered disappointment and defeat. Each forged new paths and cleared new hurdles. Each had advantages that the preceding generation did not have. Each generation got even better than the last. Each generation, in its own way, came a long way.

Exactly when a woman first picked up a racket is impossible to determine. Yet we do know that women appear to have played with rackets and balls from the time that such objects came into existence. For centuries, women played court tennis (also known as real tennis and royal tennis), a net-and-racket sport played in an enclosed area. A few dozen of these courts are still in use today in Britain, Australia, the United States, and France. Court tennis had its origins in twelfth-century France, where sportsmen first played *Jeu de Paume*, French for "game of the hand." As the game evolved, players donned a glove to protect their hand—the balls were very hard—and then used short-handled rackets. The earliest-known reference to a woman playing court tennis, dated 1427, describes a woman named Margot, who came to Paris from Hainault,

HOW THEY COULD BREATHE—LET ALONE RUN—ESCAPES ME. NOR COULD THEY HAVE STRUCK THE BALL HARD WITH THE HEAVY, LOOSELY STRUNG RACKETS OF THAT ERA.

Page 10: Lillian Upshur Morehead of Pittsburgh, Pennsylvania, showcased the fashion of the day during competition in the Chevy Chase Club tennis tournament in 1913 in Chevy Chase, Maryland.

Page 13: Dorothea Douglass Lambert Chambers, winner of seven Wimbledon singles titles between 1903 and 1914, is shown here during an exhibition match that benefited soldiers wounded in World War I.

Opposite page: Blanche Bingley Hillyard won six Wimbledon titles between 1886 and 1900. She won her final championship at age thirty-six and remains the second-oldest winner of the Ladies' Singles in Wimbledon history. The oldest was Charlotte Cooper Sterry, who won the 1907 championship at age thirty-seven.

Above: Charlotte Cooper of Great Britain won the first Olympic gold medal in women's singles at the 1900 Olympics in Paris. In 1901, as Charlotte Cooper Sterry, she won her fourth of five Wimbledon singles titles by defeating six opponents, more than any previous women's champion. Charlotte won three of her Wimbledon titles after losing all of her hearing at age twenty-six. She was inducted into the International Tennis Hall of Fame in 2013.

Opposite page, top: Members of New York's Staten Island Cricket Club in 1888.

Opposite page, bottom: An advertisement for tennis rackets with handles made from California redwood.

a town north of Paris, and "played better at hand-ball than any man had seen and played very strongly both forehanded and backhanded, very cleverly as any man could, and there were few men whom she did not beat, except the very best players."

Court tennis continued to be played into the seventeenth century—in England, Spain, Switzerland, Sweden, the German States, and the Austro-Hungarian Empire—though primarily by royalty and members of the royal court. The popularity of court tennis had declined by the mid- to late eighteenth century, however, and new forms of racket games were being played outdoors on the expansive lawns of England's well-to-do. In a watershed event, Major Walter Clopton Wingfield was awarded a patent for his portable lawn tennis sets in 1874. The manufacturing process began, and tennis became accessible to thousands of people. Women took to the game immediately.

Wingfield, a handsome man with a full, bushy beard, was a gentleman-at-arms in the court of Queen Victoria. He certainly intended for women to play his game, which he called *Sphairistikè,* Greek for "ball and stick." His *The Book of the Game,* a rule book that accompanied his first equipment sets, shows a game of mixed doubles played on a court shaped like an hourglass. On his price list for equipment, he included not only "Full-sized Sphairistikè Bats," but also lighter "Ladies' Bats." Indeed, lawn tennis proved to be an ideal pastime for women in this genteel, Victorian era. A well-bred English lady could dress up for a garden party in all her ruffles and then bustle right out onto the court.

Tennis spread rapidly throughout the British Empire and to other parts of the world, as enthusiasts took their love of the game wherever they traveled. Tennis came to Scotland, Ireland, Bermuda, Australia, South Africa, and China; to Brazil and Argentina; and to Germany, France, Italy, and Sweden. It came to the United States, at least in part, by way of a young woman from Staten Island, New York.

PECK & SNYDER CELEBRATED RACKETS.

THE BEECKMAN.

This new racket is made in the same style and manner as the English Tate rackets that are used by most of the prominent players abroad. Quality guaranteed to be of the best that skill or money can produce. Octagon redwood handle. Price, each, $5 50.

THE FRANKLIN EXPERT.

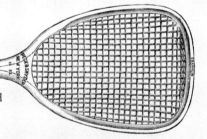

This racket is offered as one of the most popular shapes ever produced, and the style of finish and selection of the frame will recommend it. With California redwood handle and patent concave bevelled frame. Price, $5 50.

TENNIS BALLS.

Mary Ewing Outerbridge, who gave her occupation as "lady," was vacationing in Bermuda in January of 1874 or 1875 when she saw some British officers playing tennis. Mary was so taken with the game that she acquired a net, rackets, and balls from the British regimental supply and took the equipment home with her to New York. The following spring, Mary set up a court in one corner of the Staten Island Cricket and Baseball Club.

Mary's younger sister, Laura C. Outerbridge, described the first game of tennis in a letter she wrote to the United States Lawn Tennis Association more than seventy years later, when she was ninety-five years old. "We laid out the course with white tapes, but soon changed to lime. No white line was used at the top of the net, and we made little colored wool tassels to mark the line, and the effect was very pretty. Miss Krebs, sister of the president of the cricket club . . . coaxed us to give up the long dresses worn at the time, which touched the ground in the back. So we provided ourselves with flannel dresses to the tops of our boots."

We cannot be sure that the Outerbridge court was truly the first in America. Frederick Sears and James Dwight claimed an American first for their court, near Boston, at about the same time as the Outerbridge court. There is also evidence of a tennis set in San Francisco as early as 1874. Whether first or not, we do know this: Mary Ewing Outerbridge introduced tennis to New York and helped Staten Island become one of the first prominent tennis centers in the United States.

For women, joining the garden party scene was the easiest part of their trek through tennis history. The more difficult second step—to the competitive arena—was blocked for several years by prevailing social norms. The thought of women competing (and perspiring!) in a public arena was more than many men back then could bear. To Herbert Chipp, the first secretary of

Above: In this 1914 photograph, Elizabeth Ryan is on her way to winning her first of nineteen doubles titles at Wimbledon. She won twelve in women's doubles and seven in mixed doubles, the last of them in 1934. Her record stood until I won my twentieth in 1979. Elizabeth, a Californian who lived most of her life in England, won twenty-six major doubles titles overall and was inducted into the International Tennis Hall of Fame in 1972.

England's Lawn Tennis Association, it was "unalloyed heathenism."

The Irish and the Bermudians, less inhibited than the English, got us going. The first tennis competition for women was played in 1876 in conjunction with the Irish Championships for men; it had a draw of two, with a Miss W. Casey defeating a Miss Vance for the title. The Bermudians also staged a women's tournament in 1876. This one had four entries, and the winner was Mary G. Gray. The 1879 Irish Championships, with a draw of eight, resembled a real tournament, and fourteen-year-old May Langrishe, a serious player (and future Wimbledon runner-up), took the prize.

The Irish also figured out that white clothing was an excellent concealer of sweat, according to Ted Tinling, the legendary fashion designer and tennis historian. "In fact, the 'all-white' tradition in women's tennis attire derived and was perpetuated from this problem," Tinling wrote, in *The Story of Women's Tennis Fashion.*

Also in 1879, a forward-thinking man we know only as Mr. Hora stepped up and proposed that a ladies' singles tournament be staged by the All England Croquet and Lawn Tennis Club (the words Croquet and Lawn Tennis were later reversed), an increasingly powerful tennis organization based in the town of Wimbledon. Two years earlier, in 1877, the club had begun a gentlemen's championship. But Mr. Hora's proposal was swiftly struck down during a meeting of the All England Club Committee. "At present," the minutes read, "it is not desirable to have a ladies' tennis cup for lady members of the club under any circumstances."

By this time, however, women were competing in small tournaments that had sprung up in England and the eastern United States, and they were becoming more and more skillful. They were playing so well, in fact, that the tennis world had begun debating whether, in mixed

California's Hazel Hotchkiss entertains a crowd around 1910.

doubles, the man should serve his hardest to the woman. Some favored the genteel approach; others argued that this was unfair to men, as women were returning the powder-puff serves with force and direction. It's a debate that has continued among everyday players ever since. In a "friendly" game of mixed doubles on your neighborhood tennis court, a man who is determined to win might balance that desire against the consequences of blasting serves at his wife's best friend. But at the highest level of mixed doubles competition, men will rifle the ball at women if they think it increases their chances of winning the point.

In 1884, five years after Mr. Hora's initial proposal, Wimbledon opened its arms to women. The All England Club Committee was roused into action after it learned that the London Athletic Club was about to take the step. The first ladies' field featured thirteen players and offered an elegant first prize: a silver flower basket, valued at twenty guineas. Second prize was a silver-and-glass hand mirror and a silver brush, worth ten guineas. The ladies' prizes, though pretty, were not equal to those awarded to the men. The gentlemen's champion, in addition to winning a more expensive prize, also had the honor of temporarily possessing a handsome and valuable silver challenge trophy, a trophy owned by the All England Club and passed along from winner to winner, beginning with the first Wimbledon in 1877. It would take 123 years for women's prizes to equal the men's at Wimbledon.

The tournament was played at the All England Club's original site on Worple Road. The Centre Court, which could seat at least 2,500, had permanently covered stands for the first time. Major Wingfield's hourglass court had long since been abandoned in favor of the conventional rectangular court; the height of the net, which had been dropping steadily over the years, was 3 foot 6 at the posts, just as it is today. Spectators were formally dressed, the men in suits and hats, the women in long pastel dresses. The ladies' singles event—it is called the "Ladies' Singles" to this day—was held during the second week of July, the week after the gentlemen's singles, along with another new event, the gentlemen's doubles. Tennis fans found the women well worth watching, with an estimated four to five hundred taking in the ladies' singles final.

The winner of that inaugural title was Maud Watson, a nineteen-year-old Englishwoman who had not lost a match

MAUD WATSON

First Champion of "Garden Party" Tennis

•

Maud Watson, seated, is shown here in 1884 with Ernest Renshaw, also seated, and with her sister, Lilian, and Herbert Lawford. Renshaw and Lawford were top players of the day.

Maud Watson, the first ladies' singles champion at Wimbledon, grew up in Berkswell, a small village near Coventry, where her father was rector and a prominent mathematician. Maud honed her game on the rectory grounds with her older siblings and frequently practiced with the male mathematics students who visited her father. Maud reportedly had an even temper, excellent concentration, and a solid forehand and backhand. She often rushed the net, and, unlike many of her female contemporaries, she served overhand instead of underhand. Clearly, she was comfortable striking the ball over her head, and this likely gave her a competitive advantage. She was a favorite mixed doubles partner among the top male players, including William Renshaw, a seven-time Wimbledon champion. Today, the winner of the annual tournament at Maud Watson's tennis club, the Edgbaston Priory Club in Birmingham, is awarded the Maud Watson trophy. Maud won the same silver cup here in the 1880s, and it is more than just a beautiful antique. It is a link to the first real champion of women's tennis. I loved winning the trophy in the early 1980s, even though I was allowed to hold it for only a moment. The cup reminded me of what Maud Watson's tennis world must have been like: small, social, and relaxed, like a garden party. People walked or rode their bicycles to the courts. During the matches, they stood around with parasols or sat down and had tea. I could hear them saying "jolly good shot" and "jolly good try" to the runner-up. It was a much slower game in every way.

CHARLOTTE "LOTTIE" DOD

Privileged but still corseted

•

Charlotte "Lottie" Dod, the daughter of a wealthy retired cotton broker, grew up in Bebington, Cheshire, on a sprawling estate with two tennis courts, one grass and the other crushed stone. Playing tennis with her older siblings, she developed a powerful forehand drive and solid backhand, an excellent volley, a fine overhead smash, and an underhand serve that she used throughout her career. The underhand serve, a remnant of the more genteel garden-party scene, was still widely used in the 1880s and 1890s. (There was no rule stating how the serve should be delivered.) Charlotte, whose serve was deep, hard, and well placed, declared that the overhead serve was no more effective against good players than the underhand and was simply an unnecessary exertion. She was undoubtedly correct, because most women could not possibly have hit strong overhead serves. Women were smaller in those days, and their wooden rackets were cumbersome, weighing as much as fourteen and a half ounces and lacking leather grips. Compared with today's carbon fiber rackets, which weigh as little as ten and a half ounces, those relics must have felt heavy as lead. And how could a woman have executed an effective overhead serve while wearing a tight-fitting dress and corset? I put on one of those outfits for a television special, and I could hardly breathe.

in three years. Intense and unflappable, she wielded a handmade wooden racket with an oblong head, wore an ankle-length white dress, and stroked the ball with expertise. She also started the timeless discussion: could she beat a good male player? One observer there said she could defeat one-third of the men entered in the championship that year, but another argued that "the worst of them" could give her a 30–love lead in every game and still win.

The status of women at Wimbledon rose another notch in 1886 with two changes: The defending ladies' champion, like the defending gentleman's champion, would not need to play through the entire competition bracket, or draw. She would instead play a single match—the challenge round—against the winner of all the previous rounds, known as the all-comer's tournament. The second change was the arrival of the ladies' own challenge trophy. Unlike the men's trophy—a traditional cup—the women's trophy was a beautiful silver salver, or rosewater dish, partially overlaid with gold. The word "salver," or serving tray, derives from the French noun *salve,* a tray for presenting food to the king, and from the Spanish verb *salva,* to taste food to detect poison. Rosewater dishes were used in England up until the 1700s, before forks caught on, to catch water poured over the hands of diners following their meals. The rosewater dish later became a prized household possession and a symbol of high status.

The Wimbledon salver, which was made by Elkington & Co. of Birmingham, England, is an imitation of an antique in the Louvre. It is nearly 19 inches in diameter and is still presented to the winner today. Also referred to as the Venus Rosewater Dish, it is ornately decorated with mythological figures. The central figure is Temperance, seated, with a lamp in her right hand. Depicted at the base of the salver are Venus, Jupiter, Mercury, and a water goddess. Embossed around the rim are Minerva and figures representing the seven liberal arts: astronomy, geometry, arithmetic, music, rhetoric, logic, and grammar. The salver is inscribed with the names of the winners from 1884 until the present. The interior of the plate has been filled entirely, and the names of recent champions appear on the exterior.

Some people have raised the question as to whether this unique trophy was a sexist choice because it was a serving tray or rosewater dish. Frankly, I don't care whether it was a serving dish. I think it is one of the most beautiful, iconic trophies in the history of sports. The workmanship is stunning. I also like the trophy because it's a circle, a symbol of totality and timelessness that, to me, also conveys equality and inclusion.

Maud Watson won fifty-four straight matches before her streak was snapped by young Charlotte "Lottie" Dod, the first great woman athlete in tennis. Charlotte was dubbed the "Little Wonder" when she emerged as a threat at age thirteen.

SHE ALSO STARTED THE TIMELESS DISCUSSION: COULD SHE BEAT A GOOD MALE PLAYER?

She won her first Wimbledon in 1887 at fifteen years and 285 days and remains the youngest champion to this day. Charlotte (she preferred her formal name) went on to win four more Wimbledon titles before leaving competitive tennis at age twenty-one and turning her attention to other sports. "The great joy of games," she once said, "is the hard work entailed in learning them."

In 1904, she won the British national golf championship for women at Troon, Scotland, and was co-medalist in qualifying for the U.S. women's amateur golf championship before losing in the first round. She captured the silver medal for archery in the 1908 London Olympic Games and twice played for England in field hockey competition against Ireland.

Charlotte Dod was more than a champion: she was a progressive thinker with whom I feel a kinship. She was, first and foremost, a strong advocate of exercise for women, and she set an example with her approach to sports. "She uses her shoulders with a freedom we have not noticed in any other lady," wrote one observer. Charlotte herself said: "Ladies should learn to run and run their hardest, too, not merely stride."

In 1888, Charlotte successfully defended her Wimbledon title and later, in a rare exhibition match, played in tennis's first battle of the sexes. Her opponent was none other than Ernest Renshaw, the reigning men's Wimbledon champion! Charlotte, never afraid to display her athleticism and ambition, relished the challenge of playing a man in his prime who was, of course, faster and stronger

Above:

A young Franklin D. Roosevelt leans on his grandfather Warren Delano Jr.'s wheelchair, with his relatives surrounding them on a family tennis court.

than she was. As an enthusiastic crowd looked on, Ernest gave her a 30–love lead in every game and barely won, 2–6, 7–5, 7–5.

After Great Britain, women's tennis developed most quickly in the United States. The game made strong inroads among upper-class women in the East, particularly on Staten Island, where the Outerbridge family had introduced the game, and in Philadelphia, which had several private athletic clubs. Women's tennis also thrived in Boston, Pittsburgh, Atlanta, Cincinnati, New Orleans, and Chicago, and in the West. Not all of the tennis was played at private clubs: public courts appeared in Manhattan, Brooklyn, Philadelphia, and Boston in the 1880s, and private courts sprang up on many a home lawn. Ellen and Grace Roosevelt, two early champions and first cousins of Franklin D. Roosevelt, the future president of the United States, played on a private court with lines gouged into the earth. "There was never any doubt if a ball was out," Grace Roosevelt Clark said many years later. "As soon as it struck a sideline it was dead." Ellen Hansell, the first national women's tennis champion, played on a court with a clothesline for a net.

Despite the growing interest in tennis among women, the United States National Lawn Tennis Association (USNLTA) ignored women for many years. The U.S. Championships, inaugurated at Newport Casino, Rhode Island, in 1881, were for men only. I sometimes wonder whether Mary Ewing Outerbridge had ever tried to persuade her brother Eugenius, one of the USNLTA founders, to stage a women's championship along with the men's.

Several years later, a handful of Philadelphia women took the matter of a women's championship into their own hands. They included four accomplished players, known as the "Big Four," from the Belmont Cricket Club: Bertha "Birdie" Townsend, Margarette Ballard, Louise Allderdice, and Ellen "Nellie" Hansell. They played with squared-off rackets, hit wristy ground strokes with plenty of slice, and served with a sidearm motion.

The Big Four of Philadelphia's Belmont Cricket Club were, from left, Bertha Townsend, Margarette Ballard, Louise Allderdice, and Ellen Hansell.

Opposite page: The Philadelphia Cricket Club, site of the first U.S. national championships for women. In 1887, Ellen Hansell won the first championship that would be granted national status; Bertha Townsend triumphed in 1888 and 1889.

The Big Four were part of the upper class but not necessarily the Philadelphia elite. Ellen Hansell, daughter of an upholstery manufacturer, later recalled that the cost of special tennis shoes and annual $10 dues "surely hurt" her father's pocketbook. To keep expenses to a minimum, Ellen walked a mile and a half to the club instead of paying the five-cent horsecar fare.

With the backing of these enthusiastic women, a forerunner of the women's national championships was held in 1886 on the velvety lawns of the Philadelphia Cricket Club in the exclusive neighborhood of Wissahickon Heights. The tournament was staged by the Chestnut Hill Tennis Club, which rented the courts from the cricket club. Only five women entered the singles competition, but fourteen entered the doubles events. The singles winner was seventeen-year-old Birdie Townsend.

The 1886 tournament was so successful that a year later a challenge trophy honoring "the female champion of the United States" was offered by proprietors of the Wissahickon Inn, whose grounds were adjacent to those of the Philadelphia Cricket Club. By 1890 the tournament was attracting a thousand spectators a day.

Americans were beginning to admire healthy, athletic women. This "new woman" of the 1890s was typified by the "Gibson Girl" in a series of drawings by the artist Charles Gibson in *Life* magazine. The Gibson Girl was dressed simply and was frequently shown engaging in tennis, golf, or bicycling. Attention was also being focused on women politically. Throughout the world, the fight for women's suffrage—the right to vote—was gaining momentum. In 1890, America's competing suffrage organizations merged as the National American Woman Suffrage Association (NAWSA), and in 1893—a dramatic first—New Zealand became the first self-governing colony to allow all women to vote.

The Olympic Games, held in Ancient Greece from the eighth century BC to the fourth century AD, were revived in Athens in 1896 and included tennis, though only men's singles and doubles. Women's singles became part of the 1900 Paris Games, with Charlotte Cooper of Great Britain defeating Helene Prévost of France for the gold medal. Mixed doubles was also included in 1900, and women's doubles was added in 1920. Tennis vanished from the Olympics after the 1924 Paris Games because of a rift

Opposite page: Californian May Sutton, physically strong and mentally tough, brought a new look to tennis. She pushed up her sleeves, shortened her skirts, and attacked the ball with a Western forehand grip.

between the Olympic Committee and the International Lawn Tennis Federation. Not until 1988—sixty-four years later—would it return as an official Olympic sport.

In 1904, women from the East Coast saw the arrival of a new kind of tennis champion. May Sutton, a seventeen-year-old from Pasadena, California, came from the less inhibited and more adventurous West, where women had begun winning the right to vote and holding elective office decades before the Nineteenth Amendment's ratification in 1920. (In 1869, women in the Wyoming Territory became the first to win suffrage; California women would win suffrage in 1911.)

May, unlike her eastern counterparts, dressed for the game, not the show. Her dresses hung just above her ankles, and the sleeves of her oversize shirts (some thought they belonged to her father) were pushed up above the elbows to allow her freedom of movement. Although by then most women were wearing only loose-fitting corsets, it is questionable whether May wore any kind of corset at all.

May did not look like the former champions, and she did not play like them. Instead of slicing the ball on her forehand side with an open racket face that was tilted upward, May pounded it, imparting topspin with a slightly closed racket face that was tilted downward. She also held her racket in a new way. While her Eastern and British counterparts hit their forehands with a Continental grip, with the palm of the hand at or near the top of the beveled racket handle, May used a Western grip, with the palm turned clockwise and resting under the handle. (A hundred years later, the Western forehand grip would become the predominant choice among the world's leading players.) Along with power and topspin drives that leaped up off the court, May brought something else: a fierceness that was reflected in her unsmiling eyes and square jaw. The eastern women were not prepared to play this attacking style of tennis, and May won the national tournament, losing only ten games in five matches.

After running away with the national title in 1904, May decided she wanted to move on to Wimbledon, the most prestigious tournament of all. Only one other American woman, Marion Jones, of Santa Monica, California, had played at Wimbledon, but an ever-increasing number of foreign contestants was making Wimbledon a truly international event. Friends of the Sutton family helped raise the money May needed to make the trip, and at age eighteen she set off alone on the six-thousand-mile journey.

MAY SUTTON BUNDY

From California, something very new

•

May Godfray Sutton was born in 1887 in Plymouth, England, the daughter of a British naval officer. The Sutton family moved from Plymouth to Pasadena, California, when May was six. They eventually settled on a ten-acre ranch, where they built a tennis court. The oldest Sutton sister, Adele, had played tennis in England, and the four other sisters—Ethel, Florence, Violet, and May—developed an even keener interest in the game. Because May was such a chubby little girl, her older sisters refused to play tennis with her. Angered, May shook her fist and said, "Someday I'll beat you all." It was a vow she kept.

May learned her booming, topspin forehand on the family's clay court, which allowed for higher, truer bounces than the slick grass courts in the East. The four Sutton sisters began dominating Southern California tennis in the late 1890s and accounted for every singles title in the Southern California Championships between 1899 and 1915. Their unrivaled skill gave rise to the saying "It takes a Sutton to beat a Sutton."

May won her first of nine Southern California Championships in 1900 at age thirteen. She won the U.S. singles title in 1904 at age seventeen and remained the youngest women's champion until sixteen-year-old Tracy Austin won in 1979. May did not play the nationals again for many years, but she won numerous titles in California, Chicago, and Cincinnati. Her fame transcended tennis: in 1908, she became the first sports celebrity to become queen of Pasadena's Tournament of Roses Parade.

May won the U.S. Clay Court title in Pittsburgh in 1912, the year she married Thomas Bundy, a U.S. doubles champion and member of the U.S. Davis Cup team. As she began raising a family, she put her tennis career on hold. In 1921—by then the mother of four children—May Sutton Bundy returned to the U.S. Championships and reached the semifinals. In 1938, her daughter, Dorothy "Dodo" Bundy Cheney, became the first American to win the Australian singles title.

May Sutton, background, became the first overseas champion at Wimbledon in 1905 with her victory over Dorothea Douglass, foreground. May won again in 1907.

Opposite page: May Sutton played tennis throughout her long life. Here she is, serving, around 1930.

THEIR UNRIVALED SKILL GAVE RISE TO THE SAYING "IT TAKES A SUTTON TO BEAT A SUTTON."

BEST-OF-FIVE SETS, HERE AND GONE

Five-set matches were common among women between 1891 and 1901, as most women's tournaments in America adopted the best-of-five format for the final rounds. (At Wimbledon, women have always played best-of-three.) Juliette Atkinson of Brooklyn, New York, holds the distinction of never having lost a five-set match. Her victory over Marion Jones in 1898, by the score of 6–3, 5–7, 6–4, 2–6, 7–5, remains the longest women's singles final, in games played, in the U.S. Championships. Five-set matches for women became an issue within the all-male USNLTA after Elisabeth Moore, the first American woman to win four national singles titles, played two of them in two days in 1901. Elisabeth was still standing after playing 105 games of singles in forty-eight hours, but several months later, the men within the USNLTA shortened the women's matches to the best-of-three sets. Elisabeth was among the women who criticized the USNLTA's decision. "I do not think any such change should have been made without first canvassing the wishes of the women players," she wrote in a letter to the USNLTA's official publication, *Lawn Tennis.* "I venture to say that if this were done today, a very large majority would be found to be against the change. Lawn tennis is a game not alone of skill but of endurance as well, and I fail to see why such a radical change should be made to satisfy a few players who do not take the time or have not the inclination to get themselves in proper condition for playing." Not until 1984 – in the season-ending WTA Finals – did women play another best-of-five-set match. For men, the best-of-five format has continued throughout history at the major tournaments.

At Wimbledon in 1905, May created an immediate stir, not only with her booming forehand but also with her attire. Dorothea Douglass, the two-time defending champion, later wrote, "One of our players was so horrified that she made Miss Sutton let down her skirt a bit before playing on the Centre Court!"

May advanced to the challenge round without the loss of a set, yet she found the British women generally much better than the Americans—not surprising, because women's tennis in England had a ten-year head start. Awaiting May Sutton in the challenge round was Dorothea Douglass, destined to become the greatest British woman player before World War I. Dorothea, a vicar's daughter, won more than two hundred titles during her career and was unbeaten in five different years. She won seven Wimbledon singles titles between 1903 and 1914, a record that was not broken until twenty-four years later, when Helen Wills Moody won her eighth. Dorothea won two of her Wimbledon titles after the birth of her first child, and she won two more after the birth of her second.

The Douglass-Sutton match was, perhaps, the first real showdown in women's tennis. It generated interest throughout London, and four thousand spectators jammed the stands. Dorothea, who had injured her right wrist several months earlier and had not competed since, put up a good fight. But she was not strong enough to cope with May's deep and penetrating shots, which brought the crowd to its feet. May won the match in straight sets, and the first overseas champion of Wimbledon was crowned. "Miss Sutton is a phenomenon," Dorothea said afterward.

May Sutton returned to Wimbledon to defend her title in 1906, again playing before a packed stadium. But this time, Dorothea, now Mrs. Lambert Chambers, was the victor. In 1907, the result was reversed again, with May defeating Dorothea in the challenge round. Here I note that in each of the three meetings, the defending champion lost. In theory, the defending champion had the "advantage" of sitting out during the all-comers tournament and then playing only one match, against the all-comers champion. In fact, the champion had the distinct *disadvantage* of having to walk out on Centre Court before thousands of people without the benefit of any tune-up matches. As Dorothea later wrote: "I always felt that my opponent must be playing at the top of her form to have reached the challenge round, and that she must have got so used to the court and the crowds to feel quite at home there, while I was only making my debut of the year." This sentiment, almost universal among players, led to the abolition of the challenge round at the women's U.S. Championships in 1919 and at Wimbledon in 1922.

One of May Sutton's keenest California rivals was Hazel Hotchkiss, who years later as Hazel Hotchkiss Wightman founded the Wightman Cup. Hazel, who grew up in Berkeley, became interested in tennis at the relatively advanced age of sixteen, as she watched a match between May and another of the Sutton sisters. Hazel became even more interested when she saw the rapid-fire volleying of a men's doubles match. Hazel began playing tennis with her brothers on Berkeley's only court at that time, on the University of California campus. Because girls were not allowed on the court after 8 a.m., Hazel arrived daily at 6.

She soon established herself as the best woman player in Northern California, and her matches with May, the best woman in Southern California, generated widespread interest. One of their meetings, an exhibition match arranged by the Pacific Lawn Tennis Association in 1910, drew three thousand spectators and several "moving-picture photographers."

Hazel Hotchkiss was capable of challenging May while other women were not, because she did not stay in the backcourt and allow May to dominate the match with her forehand. Hazel was the first American woman to attack the net consistently in singles, and she scored many points against May by hitting to her weaker backhand and then rushing in to the net to put the ball away. We would see much more of this attacking style of play in the years ahead.

The years before World War I were restless times for women. In England, as in the United States, suffragettes were demanding the right to vote, and, to make themselves heard, some members of the British movement set fires on private properties. Twice the suffragettes invaded Wimbledon in an effort to burn down the grandstands. One woman was caught and jailed for two months. Among the incriminating evidence was a notice left behind: "No peace until women have the vote."

At the same time, new tennis stars were emerging throughout Europe. Marguerite Broquedis of France won the

TWICE THE SUFFRAGETTES INVADED WIMBLEDON IN AN EFFORT TO BURN DOWN THE GRANDSTANDS. ONE WOMAN WAS CAUGHT AND JAILED FOR TWO MONTHS.

Above: Marguerite Broquedis of France won
the gold medal in women's singles at the 1912
Olympic Games in Stockholm. She won the French
National Championship in 1913 and 1914, when
the tournament was open to French players only.
The tournament welcomed players from all
nations beginning in 1920.

gold medal for women's singles at the 1912 Olympic Games in Stockholm, and she won the French Championships twice. Dora Köring of Germany won the silver medal at Stockholm, and Molla Bjurstedt of Norway won the bronze. Tennis was also flourishing in Russia, Czechoslovakia, and Hungary.

But an era was rapidly coming to an end. On June 28, 1914, in the middle of the Wimbledon Fortnight, Archduke Francis Ferdinand of Austria-Hungary was assassinated in Sarajevo, Yugoslavia, an event that set off World War I.

For a few short weeks, all seemed well enough. Dorothea Lambert Chambers won her seventh Wimbledon singles title, and Elizabeth Ryan, a wealthy Californian living in England, won the first of her nineteen Wimbledon doubles titles. Elizabeth, whose record stood until I won my twentieth in 1979, then proceeded to St. Petersburg for the Russian Championships. She and Henrich Kleinschroth, the German men's champion, had been invited to compete, and they enjoyed royal treatment from the Russians. At courtside, they were given tennis balls on a silver platter. Unaware that a war was looming, they traveled to Moscow for another tournament. When they finally departed, apparently in late July, they were on the last train to leave Russia for Germany. Elizabeth, in turn, boarded the last train from Berlin to Belgium. Austria-Hungary declared war on Serbia on July 28, 1914, and by early August the war had spread to Russia, Germany, France, and Britain.

For four years, Wimbledon and other important European tournaments were abandoned. Women everywhere went to work, in offices, factories, and hospitals. Maud Watson became commanding officer of the Berkswell Rectory Auxiliary Hospital, a convalescent hospital administered by the British Red Cross. Charlotte Dod served as a home nurse and was later honored with the Red Cross gold medal. When championship tennis resumed in 1919, the world had changed, and the women who played tennis had changed with it.

CHICAGO PRAIRIE TENNIS CLUB

Competitive tennis in America was segregated until after World War II. But no amount of segregation could keep Black women from playing tennis. They played a leading role in developing the sport in New York and Chicago and were celebrated in Black news publications. In 1912, four women — Mrs. Maude Lawrence, Madelyn Baptist McCall, Ruth Shockey, and Mrs. C.O. "Mother" Seames — cofounded the Chicago Prairie Tennis Club. They were motivated by their love of tennis and the belief that "athletic competition and good sportsmanship are prerequisites for building personalities and character." Located first at 37th and Prairie on Chicago's South Side, the club featured four dirt-and-clay courts. Several years later, Mother Seames and her husband moved the club to 32nd and Vernon, thus establishing the first Black tennis club on privately owned grounds. The Chicago Prairie Tennis Club continues today, more than one hundred years after its founding. It has helped develop numerous young Black players, including Katrina Adams, who went on to win twenty professional women's doubles titles and become president of the United States Tennis Association.

CHAPTER TWO

THE INCOMPARABLE YEARS

1915
1940

TO

THE YEARS following World War I are one of the most colorful eras ever in women's tennis. Women said goodbye to corsets and—eventually—stockings, flexed their very real muscles, and ran with all their might. They played with skill and power, and their rivalries could be fierce. Women's voices also began to be heard as they stepped forward to challenge the unfairness and hypocrisy of amateurism. And in one of the biggest leaps of all, they became professional tennis players—trying bravely to convert their exceptional skill into a vocation.

Page 36: Californian Helen Wills Moody won nineteen major singles titles, including eight at Wimbledon.

Page 39: Suzanne Lenglen, our sport's first superstar, enchanted audiences with her athleticism and grace.

Above: An international lineup of stars poses before a 1920s Wimbledon. From left, Elizabeth Ryan (United States), Suzanne Lenglen (France), Julie "Diddie" Vlasto (France), Dorothea Lambert Chambers (England), Joan Fry (England), Lilí de Álvarez (Spain), and Kitty McKane Godfree (England).

These women did more than break new ground in women's tennis; they were vital to *tennis*, period. And they focused the spotlight on the potential of women everywhere.

Competitive tennis was still mostly a game for people with money. But our sport also began to see stars from everyday backgrounds who had access to public courts and coaching that was affordable—and sometimes even free. Interest in the game exploded beyond the private clubs. Thousands of people—aristocrats, working-class folks, and laborers—watched the women stars compete, while the media treated the biggest matches like world heavyweight prizefights.

At the same time, another expansion was quietly occurring. Black Americans, denied access to white-run tennis clubs and their sanctioned tournaments, continued to create their own clubs and tournaments. In 1916, they established the American Tennis Association (ATA), the first all-Black national organization in any sport. And in 1917, the first ATA National Championships were held at Druid Hill Park in Baltimore.

Our sport's first superstar, Suzanne Lenglen, hailed from France. She was dominating on the court and fascinating off it, the first woman to create as much interest as the leading men. She was theatrical, controversial, and glamorous—I can just imagine her repairing her makeup between sets—and she proved that show business and tennis could go hand in hand. She wore lovely, filmy tennis dresses—practical but also sexy—and in the process shattered the old rules for women's attire. Elizabeth Ryan, an American who lived much of her life in England, said that "all women tennis players should go on their knees in thankfulness to Suzanne for delivering them from the tyranny of corsets." Suzanne also set new standards for athleticism, excellence, and training, and her glorious, balletic style captivated galleries everywhere she went. She showed the world just how good a woman could become if she devoted her life to tennis.

For years, we have heard the lament—from male players and promoters—that people come to tennis matches to see the men, not the women. But that was never true. And Suzanne was our first proof positive that it wasn't true. At Wimbledon, fans came by the thousands to see her in all her glory. They formed long lines that were called the "Leng-len Trail a-Winding," a play on the words of a popular World War I song. Her popularity was so great that Wimbledon officials had no choice but to abandon the Worple Road site for larger grounds.

The new Wimbledon, located on Church Road and opened in 1922 by King George V, featured a

THESE WOMEN DID MORE THAN BREAK NEW GROUND IN WOMEN'S TENNIS; THEY WERE VITAL TO TENNIS, PERIOD.

Suzanne Lenglen could hit the ball hard when she wanted to but usually did not. Her game was based on control. She could hit every shot with precision, including the difficult backhand down the line, and she came to the net whenever she had an opening.

SUZANNE LENGLEN

"The Goddess" of Tennis

●

- **8 major singles titles**
    - **2 French (1925, 1926)**
    - **6 Wimbledon (1919–1923, 1925)**
- **8 major women's doubles titles**
- **5 major mixed doubles titles**
- **Olympics: 1920 Antwerp (gold medals, singles, mixed doubles; bronze, women's doubles)**
- **Year-end No. 1 in the world: 1921, 1925, 1926**
- **International Tennis Hall of Fame inductee, 1978**

NOTEWORTHY STATISTIC

- **Won all six of her Wimbledon women's doubles titles with Elizabeth Ryan.**

Suzanne Lenglen was born into a family of some financial privilege in the village of Compiègne in the north of France. Fortunately for women's tennis, her parents also had a winter home in the south. Located in Nice, on the Riviera, the Lenglens' second home gave them a close-up look at the world's great players, who flocked to this Mediterranean paradise to practice and compete during the winter months. Suzanne's father, Charles, liked the game and gave Suzanne a racket when she was eleven. It didn't take long for him to realize that she had talent, and he was soon coaching her. Thus began the first in a long line of famous father-daughter partnerships (think Jimmy and Chris Evert; Peter and Steffi Graf; Richard, Venus, and Serena Williams; and Leonard Francois and Naomi Osaka). Charles Lenglen made Suzanne swim; jump rope; run hurdles; and practice, practice, practice. He was a taskmaster, but an unconventional one: Suzanne was high-strung, and if she seemed to falter during competition, he tossed her brandy-soaked sugar cubes to help settle her nerves. With or without this eyebrow-raising crutch, Suzanne's balletic style was mesmerizing. She was called "the Diana of Tennis," "Lenglen the Magnificent," "the Goddess," or simply "incomparable."

"She reminds you of the movement of fire over prairie grass," one writer declared. Grantland Rice, the famous sports journalist, wrote that the court "seemed entirely too small" for her. "She is all over it in a brace of agile leaps, which proclaim her a combination sprinter, hurdler and high jumper any time she cares to abandon her chosen sport and seek another field for conquest."

At age 15, Suzanne Lenglen was already signing autographs. Natural grace, exhaustive work, and calculation made her a champion. She was the talk of Europe, the pride of France.

MOLLA MALLORY

"Hitting with all my might"

- **8 major singles titles**
  U.S. (1915–1918, 1920–1922, 1926)
- **2 major women's doubles titles**
- **3 major mixed doubles titles**
- **Olympics: 1912 Stockholm (bronze medal, singles)**
- **Wightman Cup: 5–5 in singles, 1–1 in doubles**
- **Best year-end world ranking: No. 2 (1921)**
- **International Tennis Hall of Fame inductee, 1958**

Anna Margarethe "Molla" Bjurstedt Mallory, the daughter of an army officer, grew up in Norway and became the first woman to represent Norway in the Olympics. She visited America in 1914 and liked it so much that she stayed, making New York City her home. She was a thunderous backcourt player who hit the ball on the rise, before it had reached the top of its bounce, and aimed it low over the net and toward the lines. "I find that the girls generally do not hit the ball as hard as they should," Molla once said. "I believe in always hitting the ball with all my might, but there seems to be a disposition to 'just get it over' in many girls whom I have played. I do not call this tennis." Former USLTA president Robert (Bob) Kelleher, who served as a ball boy during Molla's era, remembered Molla as "a nice lady," but an intimidating one. "She looked and acted tough when she was on the court hitting tennis balls. She walked around in a manner that said you'd better look out or she'd deck you. She was an indomitable scrambler and runner. She was a fighter."

twelve-sided stadium with seating for fourteen thousand spectators. Other tournaments also gained financially from Suzanne, and the financial inequity of amateurism began to rear its head. Suzanne was one of the first to rail against the injustice of a system in which amateur players—both women and men— played before paying crowds without being fairly compensated. "If we amateurs are to contribute a life's work to learning to play for nothing," she asked, "why isn't there an amateur gallery which can look on for nothing?" Not that Suzanne went away empty-handed. She was treated like a princess during her amateur years; she dressed expensively and lived well. But by condemning the amateur status quo, she was way ahead of her time.

Suzanne's emergence coincided with an international focus on women, whose important contributions during World War I raised their status and visibility. So it was no surprise that women's tennis was taking off globally. In 1921, a showdown between Suzanne and the reigning American champion, Molla Mallory, drew a sellout crowd of eight thousand to the West Side Tennis Club in Forest Hills, New York. It also sparked a cross-Atlantic controversy.

These were the days before seeding—the deliberate spacing of the best players throughout the draw—and officials drew Suzanne's and Molla's names so close together that the two champions met in the second round.

Left: Anita Lizana of Chile was the first Latin American player to win a major singles championship. She won the 1937 U.S. singles title and finished the year ranked No. 1 in the world.

Right: Dorothy Round was the last Englishwoman to win Wimbledon twice. She won her titles in 1934, the year she ranked No. 1 in the world, and 1937.

Although Suzanne had expressed some reservations about her health shortly after her arrival, she looked well and appeared to be supremely confident when she walked into the large horseshoe stadium. From the beginning, however, she played tentatively, while Molla, advised by her friend Bill Tilden to "hit the cover off the ball," attacked with a vengeance. The British sportswriter A. Wallis Myers wrote that Molla "was like a tigress finally let loose in a pen with her victim."

Suzanne was trailing, 0–2, love–40 in the first set, when she began to cough. She looked up toward her mother in the stands, but it did no good. Molla won the first set, 6–2, and Suzanne continued to cough. She served the first game of the second set, fell behind, love–30, double-faulted, and did not play another point. Suzanne had learned many things from her papa, but she had never learned how to lose. She approached the umpire's chair, shaking her head. She was ill and could not go on. Then she walked off the court, weeping and coughing.

Molla Mallory went on to win the U.S. title with a victory over Mary K. Browne in the final. Suzanne, still ailing, canceled her exhibition tour for the benefit of devastated France and went home.

For months afterward, the debate raged in France and the United States: was Suzanne really ill, or had she simply "coughed and quit"? Suzanne was quoted as saying, "I thought I could stay the course, but I just couldn't. My chest felt like nothing on earth; I could scarcely breathe; I wonder I went on for nine games. In France my parents would not have allowed me to play at all." Suzanne also admitted that she had underestimated Molla Mallory.

Other new stars included Lilí de Álvarez of Spain, Simonne Mathieu of France, Cecilia "Cilly" Aussem and Hilde Krahwinkel of Germany, Jadwiga Jędrzejowska of Poland, Anita Lizana of Chile, and Dorothy Round and Betty Nuthall of England. Australian women also were beginning to enter the international scene.

The Australians held their first national championships for women in 1922, seventeen years after their inaugural championships for men, and Daphne Akhurst and Nancye Wynne Bolton emerged as Australia's first notable female stars. Daphne won fourteen national titles, including five singles championships, between 1924 and 1931. Nancye won twenty Australian titles, including six singles, between 1937 and 1951. The European tennis circuit was a distant luxury for Australians, and Daphne made the trip

THE SKETCH

Registered as a Newspaper for Transmission in the United Kingdom and to Canada and Newfoundland by Magazine Post.

No. 1589.—Vol. CXXIII.　　　WEDNESDAY, JULY 11, 1923.　　　ONE SHILLING.

THE GREATEST GATE-NAME IN LAWN-TENNIS : MLLE. SUZANNE LENGLEN, WOMAN WORLD'S CHAMPION.

Suzanne Lenglen is not only the greatest girl player known to lawn-tennis history, but the most certain "draw" so far as a big "gate" is concerned. English crowds love to see her rhythmic movements, and to admire the calm certainty with which she strikes the ball, and | Suzanne is said to be, in fact, even more popular with the spectators in this country than in her own. She is playing as well as ever this year, and, in spite of Miss McKane's excellent play, the French girl beat her in the final.

Photograph by Harris Picture Agency.

FAMOUS FASHIONISTAS

Suzanne Lenglen made waves on the tennis court and also in fashion. She came to Wimbledon in 1920 dressed in the fabulous creations of French couturier Jean Patou. Silky, flowing, and unrestricting, her tennis dresses were a clear break from tradition and were quite revealing for their time. No doubt they did much to accentuate Suzanne's figure and grace. Further dash came from her brightly colored cardigans and matching turbans or bandeaus, often featuring a diamond pin. She always wore white stockings, each twisted into place just above the knee with a small French coin. And over everything, in a gesture meant to signify royalty, she walked onto the court wearing a costly fur.

Helen Wills, rather than revealing more, revealed less. Her white eyeshade, or visor, not only kept the sun out of her eyes but also helped conceal her emotions. Visors were popular in California at the time, but Helen is the one who made them famous.

Not nearly as famous but not to be forgotten: Billie Tapscott, a South African, in 1929 became the first woman to play without stockings on a back court at Wimbledon, and Joan Lycett, of England, in 1931 became the first woman to walk bare-legged onto the Centre Court.

KITTY MCKANE GODFREE

Kitty McKane—later Kitty Godfree—was a natural athlete who never had the advantage of coaching. She said the only advice she ever received was from family members who instructed her, as a child, to use her right hand "because tennis is played with the right hand." Kitty complied, even though—like Maureen Connolly and Margaret Court who came after her—she was left-handed. She became a capable volleyer in the mold of Suzanne Lenglen. Her game, one critic said, was characterized by "speed, speed, speed." Kitty was also a fighter. Helen Wills said that Kitty was 25 percent better on Centre Court than anywhere else. In her most memorable match, in 1924, Kitty rallied from a 4–6, 1–4 deficit against Helen Wills to win her first of two Wimbledon singles titles. Decades later, she recalled the third set as "a ding-dong battle." The partisan crowd, hoping to see its first Englishwoman champion since before the war, apparently unsettled Helen. It was the only time Helen ever lost a singles match at Wimbledon.

Opposite page: In a match between two of the world's most famous players, England's Kitty McKane Godfree lost to America's Helen Wills before a capacity crowd at the Kent Championships at Beckenham, England, in June 1927.

KITTY WAS ALSO A FIGHTER. HELEN WILLS SAID THAT KITTY WAS 25 PERCENT BETTER ON CENTRE COURT THAN ANYWHERE ELSE.

only twice, Nancye only three times. Tragically, Daphne died from an ectopic pregnancy, in 1933, when she was only twenty-nine years old. The next year, the Australian Championships named the women's singles trophy in her memory.

Succeeding Molla as U.S. champion and joining Suzanne as a bona fide international celebrity was Helen Wills. Helen, who won many of her titles as Helen Wills Moody, captivated the tennis world with her beautiful, chiseled features and her athleticism and poise. Her concentration was rock-solid, and her uncanny anticipation meant that she nearly always arrived at the ball on time. The fact that she hardly ever missed made her almost unbeatable. Her eight Wimbledon singles titles was a record that stood unmatched for nearly half a century.

Nothing illustrated women's power in tennis more than the match that took place in February 1926. That's when America's champion, Helen Wills, took a semester off from her studies at the University of California and traveled to the French Riviera, where Suzanne Lenglen was competing. Although Helen said she was making the trip to study art, everyone on the Riviera knew that what she really wanted was to compare the art of Suzanne's tennis with her own. The boldness of Helen's challenge—"cheeky," Suzanne called it—gave the showdown the drama of a prizefight. In fact, the buzz was building even before the women knew which tournament they might play each other in. Helen was greeted by a

Above: Suzanne Lenglen and Helen Wills met only once in their storied careers, at Cannes, France, in 1926. This aerial view shows the scene at the Carlton Club, where fans packed the stands and watched from neighboring rooftops.

Above: When Suzanne Lenglen signed a $50,000 contract with the American entrepreneur Charles C. Pyle, she became the first woman tennis player to turn professional.

Below: Announcing their professional tennis tour, from left, Vincent Richards, Suzanne Lenglen, entrepreneur Charles C. Pyle, and Mary K. Browne.

HELEN WILLS MOODY

The Renaissance woman who rarely missed

•

Helen Wills Moody was a Renaissance woman. In addition to being an all-time great in tennis, she was an accomplished painter and an excellent student who earned a Phi Beta Kappa key while attending the University of California. Her father, a prominent physician, gave her a tennis racket when she was thirteen and a year later gave her a membership in the prestigious Berkeley Tennis Club, where William "Pop" Fuller was the teaching professional. That same year, Hazel Wightman, while making her annual pilgrimage to the West Coast, spotted Helen and spent six weeks working with her. Three years later, Helen was the top player in America. From 1927 until 1933, she won every set she played and at least 158 consecutive matches. A consummate baseliner, she rarely missed. She was strong and fit, the result of practicing with men nearly every day, year-round—a strategy top women have followed ever since.

An aura of mystery surrounded her. On the court, she rarely smiled or showed emotion. Grantland Rice, the famous American sportswriter, nicknamed her "Little Miss Poker Face" early in her career. She was still called "Miss Poker Face" long after the "Little" was dropped. Helen won nineteen major singles titles during her career, despite missing major tournaments because of illness or injury in 1926 and 1934 and willingly passing up many others. Her record is among the first to remind us that a player's total victories in major events must not be the only yardstick by which we measure champions.

- 19 major singles titles
    - 4 French (1928–1930, 1932)
    - 8 Wimbledon (1927–1930, 1932, 1933, 1935, 1938)
    - 7 U.S. (1923–1925, 1927–1929, 1931)
- 8 major women's doubles titles
- 3 major mixed doubles titles
- Olympics: 1924 Paris (gold medals, singles and doubles)
- Wightman Cup: 18–2 in singles, 2–7 in doubles
- Year-end No. 1 in the world (1927–1933, 1935, 1938)
- International Tennis Hall of Fame inductee, 1969

Above: Helen Wills Moody at Wimbledon in 1935.

Below: Helen with some of her drawings at her first exhibition at the Grand Central Art Galleries.

Opposite page: Helen visits with Queen Victoria of Spain at a tennis party in Highgate, London, in 1938 after winning her eighth Ladies' Singles title at Wimbledon.

Above: A crowd of thirteen thousand watches Suzanne Lenglen play Mary K. Browne when their 1926 tour opens at Madison Square Garden.

Opposite page: Helen Wills Moody demonstrates how she gripped her racket. Imagine holding on to that wooden handle in hot weather!

crowd of sportswriters when she arrived, and reporters came from as far away as Norway and South America to cover a match that was not even a certainty. Helen wrote: "No tennis game deserved the attention that this one was getting." That might have been true, but it was the Roaring Twenties, an era of sports stars and spare time. A showdown between the two glamorous champions was irresistible.

Helen Wills, wrote Larry Engelmann in *The Goddess and the American Girl*, had been "transformed by the American press from a mere national tennis champion into an ideal and the perfect symbol of young America. Everything she did now was newsworthy and described in glowing, near-mythic terms."

The match took place at the Carlton Club in Cannes, and by the time Suzanne and Helen had reached the final, the event no longer looked anything like an amateur tournament. An American motion picture company reportedly offered $100,000 for the rights to film the proceedings; promoters generated an estimated 600,000 francs from ticket sales, fabulous sums in the 1920s. After taxes and expenses, perhaps 400,000 francs remained. Where it went—and how much might have found its way to Suzanne and Helen—is impossible to know.

A crowd of four thousand jammed the bleachers, most of which were erected especially for this match. Those who couldn't get a seat watched from hotel windows and rooftops. Men standing outside the fences used periscopes. It was entertainment fit for royalty. Those in attendance included the former King Manuel of Portugal, the former Grand Duke Michael of Russia, and Prince George of Greece. The extravaganza seems remarkably similar to the one that preceded my battle of the sexes with Bobby Riggs in 1973—unnatural and unreal. I can only imagine the players' nervousness as the day drew near.

The match lived up to everyone's expectations, proving once again that women's tennis was terrific entertainment. It was close and tense, with Suzanne prevailing, 6–3, 8–6. Having survived the greatest tennis challenge of her life, Suzanne collapsed on a bench and wept as photographers pressed around her and well-wishers arrived with flower arrangements six feet high. Helen, as cool and detached as always, watched the scene in awe and then left the court with a handsome young man—Frederick Moody—whom she had met on the Riviera and would marry three years later. "There will be other tennis matches," she told news reporters. "Other years are coming."

The excitement was not yet over, however. Suzanne was led into the small clubhouse, and when she saw what was inside—thousands of francs from the ticket sales—she became hysterical. Was she laughing because much of the money would be hers, or was she crying because she was to get so little? One cannot discount the possibility that the club owners paid her well for allowing them to stage the match. But my friend Ted Tinling, who umpired many of her matches on the Riviera, believed that was not the case. "It has often occurred to me that the sight of the piles of money, when she was making so much for everybody else and so little for herself, may have unconsciously set off her hysterics," he said.

The tennis world eagerly awaited a rematch, but the two champions never played each other again. Suzanne closed out her amateur career at Wimbledon, an unsatisfactory conclusion that resulted in controversy over her late arrival for a match and her ultimate withdrawal from the tournament. A month later, in another historic break with tradition, she accepted a $50,000 offer to turn professional from the American entrepreneur Charles C. Pyle. In doing so, she became the first woman to accept payment for playing the game. The second woman to sign with Pyle was Mary K. Browne, who had been ranked sixth in the United States in 1925. Four men also signed: Vincent Richards, who would have been ranked first in the United States in 1926; Howard Kinsey, the U.S. doubles champion; Paul Féret, a leading French player; and Harvey Snodgrass, a former top American player who had become a teaching professional.

The tennis establishment, having lost an important revenue stream, did not respond kindly to Suzanne's decision to turn pro. The All England Club revoked her honorary membership. At the same time, Suzanne was supported by many members of the media, particularly in the United States, where professional golf and football were becoming ever more popular. Mary K. Browne, who had been an amateur for twenty years, said she had felt "contaminated" just thinking about Pyle's offer, which she said was for something less than the published figure of $30,000. But Mary was practical enough not to feel contaminated for too long. "There were many things to consider," she wrote at the time. "The money was one. I am still Miss Browne and therefore obliged to take a husbandly view of opportunities."

Above, left: Australian champion Daphne Akhurst, who died from an ectopic pregnancy when she was only twenty-nine years old.

Above, right: The South African women's tennis team arrives at Waterloo Station in London in 1938. From left, Bobbie Heine Miller, Margaret Morphew, Olive Craze, and Sheila Piercey.

HAZEL HOTCHKISS WIGHTMAN

"Queen Mother of Tennis"

•

Hazel Hotchkiss Wightman's name is woven into the tapestry of women's tennis like a shining golden thread that stretched from the 1900s through the 1920s, 1930s, 1940s, 1950s, and 1960s. Champion, patron, coach, and founder of the famed Wightman Cup team championships, she devoted her life to teaching, encouraging, sheltering, and enlightening aspiring young tennis stars.

From 1909 through 1911, Hazel won the three U.S. triple crowns—the singles, doubles, and mixed doubles titles—at the Philadelphia Cricket Club. In the years that followed, she married George W. Wightman of Boston and began raising a family of five children. She won her fourth and last national singles title in 1919.

The on-court achievements, however, were just so many small baubles in the crown of the "Queen Mother of Tennis," as she came to be known. In 1919, she urged tennis officials to stage an international team championship for women along the lines of the men's Davis Cup, initiated in 1900. Hazel wanted the championship to include Great Britain, the United States, France, and all other nations with prominent women players. One of her major objectives was to bring the spectacular Frenchwoman Suzanne Lenglen to America. Hazel backed up her idea with her pocketbook. She walked into a Boston jewelry store, N.G. Wood, and plunked down $300—about $5,000 in 2022 dollars—for a tall, slender silver cup. "I wasn't very crazy about it, but it was the most appropriate thing they had, and I'm a purchaser, not a shopper," Hazel told the *Boston Globe* many years later. "I gave it to the USLTA with the idea that a competition would be started."

UNFORTUNATELY, TENNIS WAS NOT YET READY FOR A FEMALE VERSION OF THE DAVIS CUP.

Unfortunately, tennis was not yet ready for a female version of the Davis Cup. For four years, the trophy sat. Then, in 1923, USLTA officials decided they should do something special to celebrate the opening of the new tennis stadium at the West Side Tennis Club in Forest Hills, New York. Several British players were in town for the nationals, and the USLTA officials thought a team match between the British and American women would be appropriate. Finally, Mrs. Wightie's trophy was put to use. Inscribed on the trophy are the words "Ladies International Lawn Tennis Challenge Trophy," but it was always known by its unofficial name, the Wightman Cup.

The annual team match, played alternately in the United States and England, helped generate tremendous interest in the women's game. It was most popular in Britain, where for years it preceded Wimbledon. The queen of England honored Mrs. Wightman in 1973 by making her an honorary commander of the Order of the British Empire.

In 1940, Mrs. Wightman was divorced from her husband and moved to a new home in Chestnut Hill, Massachusetts, not far from the Longwood Cricket Club, which had a rich tradition in tennis. At Longwood, Hazel conducted clinics and numerous tournaments. During tournament weeks, her three-story home became a kind of sorority house for aspiring young girls and women from all over the world. Guests slept everywhere, from the basement to the solarium, coexisting peacefully with Mrs. Wightie's cats, which came and went as they pleased through the open windows.

Above: Alice Marble's famous friends included the actor Clark Gable and his wife, actress Carole Lombard. They are shown here with producer Felix Young.

In fact, the amateur system was nothing short of predatory. Its "purity" involved profit for the sport's promoters and administrators while leaving many players to pay their bills as best they could. Helen Wills was able to earn money by contributing to periodicals and newspapers and by selling sketches of tennis players. England's Kitty Godfree, a two-time Wimbledon champion, saved up prize vouchers that could be exchanged at a high-end jewelry store. She eventually exchanged the vouchers for a diamond ring, sold the ring to a friend, and then used the money to buy what she really wanted—a car.

Suzanne had no difficulty making the decision to turn pro. Her family's fortune had withered away, and she needed money. She was also sick and tired of filling promoters' pockets instead of her own. Turning professional, she once said, was "an escape from bondage and slavery." In an article that appeared in her tour's program, Suzanne wrote, "In the twelve years I have been champion I have earned literally millions of francs for tennis and have paid thousands of francs in entrance fees to be allowed to do so. . . . I have worked as hard at my career as any man or woman has worked at any career. And in my whole lifetime I have not earned $5,000—not one cent of that by my specialty, my life study—tennis. . . . I am 27 and not wealthy—should I embark on any other career and leave the one for which I have what people call genius? Or should I smile at the prospect of actual poverty and continue to earn fortune—for whom?"

ORA WASHINGTON

Her greatest loss in tennis was also her sport's

●

One could argue that the most athletic tennis player of the 1930s was one who never played at Wimbledon or even in a single USLTA tournament. Her name was Ora Belle Washington, and segregationist policies meant she could only play in all-Black tournaments. Nevertheless, Ora was a star—first in tennis and then in professional women's basketball. She won eight singles titles in the American Tennis Association Championships along with fifteen women's doubles and mixed doubles titles. I know Ora would have loved to compete in the major all-white tournaments, and it is shameful that she was denied a chance to prove herself and further develop her game. It is said that she wanted to play Helen Wills Moody but that Helen declined to schedule a match. It's impossible to put Ora's talents into context, but we do know that when she was in her late forties, she and George Stewart defeated Dr. Robert Walter Johnson and Althea Gibson in the 1947 ATA Championship mixed doubles final. This was ten years before Althea won her first Wimbledon and U.S. titles, so Althea was still very far from her prime. Ora spent her earliest years on her family's farm in Virginia and later moved with her family to Philadelphia. She came to tennis late, picking up the game after her twentieth birthday. At the same time she was dominating her peers in tennis, she was also starring in basketball, leading the Philadelphia Tribune women's semiprofessional team to eleven straight all-Black world championships (1932–1942). The team's sponsor, the *Philadelphia Tribune,* was a leading Black newspaper. Ora competed well into her forties but retired before the USLTA opened up its tournaments to Black players in 1948. She worked as a housekeeper following her athletic career and was inducted into the Women's Basketball Hall of Fame in 2009, nearly four decades after her death.

Above: Ora Washington, right, defeated Dorothy Morgan in the final to win the 1939 Pennsylvania Open.

HELEN JACOBS

- 5 major singles titles
    1 Wimbledon (1936)
    4 U.S. (1932–1935)
- 3 major women's doubles titles
- 1 major mixed doubles title
- Wightman Cup: 14–8 in singles, 5–3 in doubles
- Year-end No. 1 in the world (1936)
- International Tennis Hall of Fame inductee, 1962

She had "lots and lots of stomach muscles"

Of all the notable women who competed in the 1920s and 1930s, the strongest challenger to Helen Wills was her very own neighbor, Helen Jacobs. The daughter of a mining executive, Helen was born in Arizona but moved to California with her family and eventually into the very home in Berkeley where Helen Wills had lived. Like Wills, Jacobs learned the game at the Berkeley Tennis Club, took lessons from Pop Fuller, attended the University of California, and started a fashion trend of her own in 1933 when she became the first woman to wear shorts at Wimbledon. But in personality, Jacobs was nothing like Wills. She was outgoing, friendly, and popular among players and fans. Whenever she played Wills, she was the crowd's favorite. Unfortunately for "Little Helen," as she was called, she had the misfortune to spend the peak of her career in the shadow of "Queen Helen." For ten years, Jacobs ranked second in the United States. Although Jacobs did not have the talent that Wills had, she is a memorable champion—and holds a special place in my heart—because she never, ever gave up. George Lott, a top American doubles player in the 1930s, said Helen Jacobs was one of his favorites. "I always thought she got the furthest with the leastest," he wrote. "She had a forehand chop, a sound backhand, and lots and lots of stomach muscles. She was buffeted from pillar to post by Helen Wills and still came back for more." My admiration for Helen Jacobs, who was Jewish, continues to grow as I learn more about her. She was a commander in U.S. Navy intelligence during World War II; she was a writer of books, both fiction and nonfiction; and she was a lesbian who did not hide her sexual orientation. She was survived at her death, at age eighty-eight, by her life partner, Virginia Gurnee. In 2015, Helen was inducted into the National Gay and Lesbian Sports Hall of Fame.

Above: Helen Jacobs, the defending champion, during first-round play at the U.S. Championships at Forest Hills, New York, in 1933.

Suzanne's criticism of tennis went beyond self-serving arguments. She saw how the amateur system hurt others, too. "Under these absurd and antiquated amateur rulings, only a wealthy person can compete, and the fact of the matter is that only wealthy people do compete," she complained. "Is that fair? Does it advance the sport? Does it make tennis more popular—or does it tend to suppress and hinder an enormous amount of tennis talent lying dormant in the bodies of young men and women whose names are not in the social register?" Thus, Suzanne Lenglen was an early leader in the fight against the establishment's stranglehold on tennis—a battle that took players another forty years to win.

For four months, Suzanne and her troupe toured the United States, Canada, Cuba, and Mexico. The tour was profitable—Suzanne reportedly received an extra $25,000 beyond her guarantee—and there were some exciting moments. A crowd of thirteen thousand was on hand for the tour's opening night at Madison Square Garden in New York City. But most stops were much less successful. Why? Because the men who owned the tour made a mistake that future promoters would continue to make again and again: they paired one of the top women of the day against someone who wasn't nearly as good. People didn't pay simply to see the glamorous Suzanne leap around in her bandeau and designer tennis outfit; they also wanted to see *competition*. They wanted to see exciting tennis, not a blowout. But in nearly forty matches with Mary, Suzanne lost only two sets. Imagine for a moment that Suzanne had been paired with Helen Wills. Now *that* would have had the makings of a successful tennis tour!

In 1930, the USLTA made a bid to open up some tournaments to professionals, but the move was nixed by the International Lawn Tennis Federation (ILTF), the sport's international governing body. Confronted with the ILTF roadblock, the USLTA in 1935 took a step backward and tried to enforce true amateurism. The USLTA adopted

"UNDER THESE ABSURD AND ANTIQUATED AMATEUR RULINGS, ONLY A WEALTHY PERSON CAN COMPETE, AND THE FACT OF THE MATTER IS THAT ONLY WEALTHY PEOPLE DO COMPETE."

TENNIS CRITICS AGREED THAT ALICE HAD SET A NEW STANDARD OF EXCELLENCE.

the "eight weeks rule," which stated that amateurs could accept expense money for only eight weeks during the year; during the other weeks, they had to pay their own expenses. In her memoir, the American champion Helen Jacobs called the rule, which favored wealthy amateurs over the less well-to-do, "intrinsically unfair."

Despite the tension between players and the establishment, tennis flourished throughout the 1930s. It survived the Great Depression; it persisted through increasing political unrest in Europe; it was celebrated within America's Black community, which in 1936 staged its twentieth annual ATA National Championships; it embraced the magic of the Grand Slam in 1938 when Don Budge won all four majors (the Australian, French, Wimbledon, and U.S. Championships); and it provided a showcase for Alice Marble, the first member of a new generation of women who played real power tennis. Other women had played well at the net before Alice, but none had put together a complete attacking game along the lines of the best men. Alice had everything it took to do it. She was tall and lithe at 5 foot 7 and 140 pounds, and she was quick, strong, consistent, and fearless. She also had the first exceptional serve in the women's game. Alice was one of my mentors and early coaches, and in my mind's eye I can still see her beautiful serve. I can see her bending, stretching, uncoiling, and unleashing herself into the ball with total abandon. No woman had done that before Alice Marble.

At Wimbledon in 1939, tennis critics agreed that Alice had set a new standard of excellence. She won her semifinal and final matches with the loss of only two games. No woman since Suzanne Lenglen had routed the field like that. At the Wimbledon ball, Alice enchanted everyone there with her lovely contralto voice. But the outside world was not singing with her. While Alice and her peers were celebrating tennis, London and the rest of Europe were preparing air raid shelters, organizing hospitals, and recruiting volunteers to give blood. Two months later, England and France declared war on Nazi Germany.

Alice Marble never returned to Wimbledon. She won a second straight U.S. singles title in 1940 and then turned pro. Promoters guaranteed her $25,000 for a tour of five American cities with Mary Hardwick, Bill Tilden, and Don Budge. Like Suzanne Lenglen's tour, it was doomed for lack of drama. Alice was too good for Mary, Budge too good for Tilden. Thus, the groundbreaking prewar era in women's tennis faded quietly away. But Alice Marble's explosive style wasn't about to die. Women's power tennis had only begun. Nevertheless, in the realm of economic and racial equality, we still had much to do. Women stars could not yet earn a living doing what they did best, and Black players could not even gain entry into the primary American tennis circuit. These important issues awaited leaders who were willing to show up, speak up, and fight for them.

ALICE MARBLE

"The fastest tennis ever played"

- 5 major singles titles
    1 Wimbledon (1939)
    4 U.S. (1936, 1938–1940)
- 6 major women's doubles titles
- 7 major mixed doubles titles
- Wightman Cup: 5–1 in singles, 3–1 in doubles
- Year-end No. 1 in the world (1939)
- International Tennis Hall of Fame inductee, 1964

Alice Marble was among the tennis stars who made it with the help of public infrastructure. She learned to play on the public courts at Golden Gate Park under the watchful eye of Howard Kinsey, the top San Francisco professional at that time. At age eighteen, ranked seventh in the United States, she came under the guidance of a teacher who would change her life: Eleanor "Teach" Tennant. Eleanor, who had ranked third among American women in 1920, was a highly regarded professional in Los Angeles who was often called "Hollywood's best-known coach." Over the years, her pupils ranged from actors and actresses like Clark Gable and Carole Lombard to champions like Bobby Riggs and Maureen Connolly. Teach and another coach, Harwood White, helped Alice develop her twisting serve and powerful drives. Teach also made Alice train, believing that "five sets of singles in practice are equal to three in a match." In 1933, Alice made the world take notice of a new kind of women's tennis. At the Essex County Club Invitation in Manchester, Massachusetts, she raced through her quarterfinal in sixteen minutes, in one stretch ripping off twenty-eight straight points. The Associated Press called it "the fastest tennis ever played" in the tournament's nine-year history. Alice never achieved the records of players like Helen Wills Moody and Suzanne Lenglen, in part because her career was pinched at both ends—by illness early in her career and by World War II just as she had reached her peak at age twenty-five. Even so, Alice left her mark as our first real power player. Years later, she would help shatter the racial barrier in our sport with a public condemnation of racial discrimination that led up to Althea Gibson's historic appearance in the U.S. Championships at Forest Hills.

Above: Californian Alice Marble and England's Kay Stammers walk onto Centre Court for the 1939 Wimbledon final. Alice won the match with the loss of only two games. She would never have a chance to play at Wimbledon again.

CHAPTER THREE

THE WAR YEARS

1940

TO

1950

LIKE WOMEN everywhere, female tennis players stepped up and did their part during World War II. Among the stars of the prewar era, Simonne Mathieu served in the French Resistance. Helen Jacobs joined the WAVES, the women's reserve of the U.S. Navy. Alice Marble sang for servicemen at hospitals and military camps. And Mary K. Browne served with the Red Cross in Australia.

Those in the midst of their tennis careers also supported the Allied war effort. Margaret Osborne, who would win thirty-seven major singles and doubles titles—later to become known as Grand Slam titles—without ever competing in Australia, worked as a clerk eight hours a day, six days a week, at a ship-building factory. She brought a brown-bag lunch, then rode a bus to the California Tennis Club for practice after work. Margaret and her doubles partner, Louise Brough, entertained American soldiers by playing singles matches at more than fifty military bases. And, in her role as secretary-treasurer of the Northern California Tennis Association, Margaret helped compile rankings behind blackout curtains, the dark household draperies used throughout homes in all American coastal cities to prevent enemy aircraft crews from being able to spot potential targets.

From 1940 through 1945, most of the world's tournaments could not be played. The Wimbledon and French Championships were stopped in 1940, the Australian Championships a year later. Only in the United States did tennis continue at a high level. Now just imagine if we were to "lose" five years of Grand Slam tournaments today. Imagine if you were the best player in the world and—like Californian Pauline Betz—got to play Wimbledon only once! In 2020, we bitterly lamented the loss of competition when the coronavirus pandemic brought sports to a screeching halt. But this absolutely paled compared with the ruin caused by World War II. As Australian tennis star

Page 68: Pauline Betz won four U.S. Championships between 1942 and 1946. She won Wimbledon in 1946, the only year she played there.

Page 71: Australian champion Nancye Wynne Bolton cracks an overhead.

Above: Helen Jacobs was a commander in U.S. Navy intelligence during World War II. She is shown here with boxing champion Jack Dempsey.

Captain Simonne Mathieu, the French women's champion, served in the Resistance and, pictured here with Henri Cochet and Yvon Petra, served as chair umpire of an exhibition that marked the reopening of Stade Roland Garros following the liberation of Paris in 1944. The beautiful stadium, located in Paris's 16th arrondissement, had opened in 1928. It was named after a heroic World War I aviator.

Thelma Coyne Long noted, "In 1938, I was the youngest member of an Australian women's team that went to Europe and America. Then came World War II, and the next time I had the opportunity to travel overseas was in 1949, eleven years later."

Wimbledon was transformed during the war. The Red Cross and the National Fire Service took over the club's grounds; soldiers drilled on the walkway outside the clubhouse; and the famed Centre Court was opened for special guests, including members of the Australian, British, and U.S. armed forces. The club's expansive parking lots were converted into a working farm that provided desperately needed rations—vegetables and protein—for civilians and soldiers. Norah Gordon Cleather, the club's acting secretary, became an expert in animal husbandry, managing pigs, horses, chickens, geese, and rabbits.

The borough of Wimbledon, located less than ten miles from London, housed factories that produced machine guns, spark plugs, and antiaircraft batteries. As a result, the borough suffered intense bombing during the war, and thousands of homes were destroyed. On October 11, 1940, a five-hundred-pound bomb crashed through Centre Court's partial roof.

Stade Roland Garros in Paris also was profoundly changed, and in a way that seems almost unfathomable to me. During a ten-month period beginning in September 1939, the French government—bracing for war and distrustful of foreigners—used the beautiful tennis facility as a holding area for political dissidents and foreign nationals who were living in France at that time. Arthur Koestler, a Hungarian Jewish author and antifascist who for years had divided his time between London and Paris, described his ten-day internment at Roland Garros in his autobiographical book, *Scum of the Earth*, which he wrote in early 1941.

"The Stadium had been converted into a provisional camp for the detention of 'undesirable aliens,'" he wrote.

"There were about five hundred of us, and we were housed in queer sorts of grottos, under the great stand of the central tennis court." Prisoners slept packed together on straw spread over a concrete floor and were granted two hours of exercise on court No. 3, Koestler wrote. Soldiers who guarded the camp also used the courts—for football. (Koestler was transported from Roland Garros to Camp du Vernet, a concentration camp in Le Vernet, France; England secured his release three months later.)

Roland Garros was emptied of its prisoners in June 1940, following Germany's invasion of France. Paul Gittings of CNN reported in 2011 that French authorities set the prisoners free after "verifying their activities" and apparently deeming them not to be a threat.

It also seems that Roland Garros was more valuable to Nazi-occupied Paris as a tennis venue. The author Henry D. Fetter has written that tournament play actually continued during the war, although for French players only. "The courts at Roland Garros were busy even throughout the 'dark years' of defeat and occupation," he wrote in the *Atlantic* in May 2014. "In July 1942, the national junior championship was played out on its red clay courts while thousands of Jews were being rounded up and held in the infamous Velodrome d'Hiver just across the Seine. Two years later, in August 1944, [Yvon] Petra was defending his French singles title before large crowds even as Allied and German armies battled in Normandy less than 150 miles from Paris."

Roland Garros's official reopening took place on September 7, 1944, two weeks after the liberation of Paris. The international French Championships did not resume until 1946.

Many tournaments were put on hold in America, but with the blessing of President Franklin D. Roosevelt, the national championships continued at Forest Hills throughout the war. The matches were more than morale boosters; they became part of the war effort. Beneath the stadium at Forest Hills, Mary Hardwick, a former British Wightman Cup player who had moved to the United States, collected clothing and other supplies for Bundles for Britain, a nationwide war relief agency founded by Natalie Wales Latham, a wealthy New York socialite. Pauline Betz, Sarah Palfrey, and Alice Marble joined prominent male players at the Red Cross Victory Exhibitions at Forest Hills in June 1945.

Tennis was not alone in supporting the Allies. Allison Danzig, tennis reporter for the *New York Times*, chaired the Red Cross Sports Committee, which included representatives from fifteen different American sports—including baseball, basketball, golf, dog shows, and squash—in its quest to raise $500,000 for the Red Cross in 1945. That same year, professional baseball teams were asked to lead the way in

THE MATCHES WERE MORE THAN MORALE BOOSTERS; THEY BECAME PART OF THE WAR EFFORT.

Above: World War II transformed Wimbledon in ways that are difficult for me to imagine. Above, Nora Cleather attends to the All England Club's temporary guests.

Wimbledon's Centre Court was bombed in 1940. It could not be completely repaired until 1949.

America's effort to raise trillions of dollars by selling $25 "E" bonds to small purchasers who attended sporting events. Horseshoes from Seabiscuit, the legendary American racehorse, became good-luck charms that were shipped to bomber pilots overseas.

The American women tennis players who starred during this period reflected the times. They were strong-willed and independent. They held jobs at some point in their lives, and most married relatively late. They wore basic, functional clothing, and their tennis shoes were resoled over and over again because the military's need for rubber (for everything from tanks to battleships) took precedence. They played aggressively, and most of them liked to attack the net.

At the U.S. Championships, the women also took center stage. Because many of America's young male players had enlisted and were no longer competing, tournament directors often had no choice but to put women's matches on the spectator courts. "The women did not mind too much," wrote Doris Hart, one of the leading players. "For once, we

were the feature attractions and played on the front courts instead of being relegated to the 'pasture!'"

In 1945, the U.S. women's singles final was played before a crowd of ten thousand on September 2—V-J Day— several hours after the Japanese formally surrendered to the Allies on the USS *Missouri*. The match pitted three-time defending champion Pauline Betz against Bostonian Sarah Palfrey Cooke, the mother of a two-year-old daughter who had won in 1941 and was making a rather improbable comeback. Sarah had been away from the competitive circuit for most of the previous three years. But while she and her husband, Elwood, a 1939 Wimbledon finalist, were stationed in Pensacola, Florida, she had practiced until the eighth month of her pregnancy. Later, in La Jolla, California, she practiced with tennis great Bill Tilden and gave exhibitions for the Red Cross. Her wartime tennis experience, though unconventional, had primed her for her big moment. Allison Danzig wrote that Sarah's three-set victory had spectators "in a state of almost breathless excitement with the outcome in doubt to the last stroke." The Associated Press described

SARAH PALFREY

An "exquisite" tigress

●

- 2 Grand Slam singles titles
  U.S. (1941, 1945)
- 11 Grand Slam women's doubles titles
- 5 Grand Slam mixed doubles titles
- Wightman Cup: 7–4 in singles, 7–3 in doubles
- Best year-end world ranking: No. 4 (1934)
  (There were no world rankings from 1940 through 1945.)
- International Tennis Hall of Fame inductee, 1963

Sarah Palfrey was a Boston blueblood who made the most of her social privileges and diminutive size. Her father was a Harvard graduate and eminent lawyer; her mother graduated from Smith College, where she was a member of the fledgling golf and tennis teams. Sarah and her five sisters played on their private clay court on the family farm and later polished their games at the Longwood Cricket Club under the watchful eye of Hazel Hotchkiss Wightman. Every one of the Palfrey girls won at least one national junior title. Sarah, only 5 foot 3, moved with the unconscious grace of a dancer. Sportswriters marveled at her "exquisite daintiness" and her "eternal femininity." But she used her racket like a rapier at the net. "I felt like a tiger out there," she said. One of my favorite stories about Sarah was how she upstaged the great Ellsworth Vines, the reigning male Wimbledon champ, in a mixed doubles final at the Longwood Cricket Club. During one point, Vines hit a screaming overhead smash right at Sarah, while her partner, Fred Perry, stood by. Sarah, who had wisely backed up a few paces, caught the missile on her forehand side and whacked it back for a clean winner.

Sarah Palfrey Cooke with her three-year-old daughter, Diana, in 1946 at Forest Hills. Busy with child-rearing and new business interests, she did not defend her U.S. singles title.

FOR WOMEN WHO HAD DREAMED OF WIMBLEDON FOR MOST OF THEIR LIVES, THE INCONVENIENCES OF POSTWAR LIFE WERE MINOR.

it as "a match marked by long rallies and spectacular retrieves that brought admiring shouts" from the crowd. On September 3, a historic day dominated by news of the war's end, the *Boston Globe* still reported the hometown champion's victory on page one.

With the exception of 1943, the all-Black American Tennis Association (ATA) held its national championships throughout the war and saw the emergence of a rising star who years later would help shatter racial barriers in tennis. Althea Gibson won the ATA girls' championship in 1944, and in 1947 she won the first of ten straight ATA national women's singles titles.

The year 1944 was also notable for a historic exhibition match. In a tentative early step toward racial equality in tennis, touring professionals Alice Marble and Mary Hardwick played an exhibition at the ATA national tournament at the interracial Cosmopolitan Club in Harlem. Alice and Mary then played against each other in doubles while partnering with leading ATA players. In the women's doubles exhibition, Alice teamed with Frances Gittens to defeat Mary and Lillian Van Buren, and in the mixed doubles, Alice and Robert Ryland defeated Mary and Dr. Reginald Weir. (Four years later, Dr. Weir became the first Black American to compete in a national USLTA event, the 1948 U.S. National Indoor Championships.)

When the Americans returned to Wimbledon for the Wightman Cup competition in 1946, they found an England scarred by war. The bomb that hit the Centre Court had demolished 1,200 seats; the area would be patched in 1947, but building restrictions would make repairs impossible to complete until 1949. Food was another challenge. Meat, eggs, and sweets were impossible to find, and the word "chicken" on a restaurant menu usually meant pigeon. Bernard Destremau, a French men's tennis champion, wrote in his memoirs that "the first big tournaments post-war were played in conditions that one cannot imagine. We struggled to find clothes to wear, and to get enough to eat, and there were times when we had to make do with some outlandish outfits. Most of the players were still undernourished and underweight." With famine a genuine threat in war-devastated countries, the United States had stepped up to export more than sixteen million long tons of food in the year that ended in June 1946.

For women who had dreamed of Wimbledon for most of their lives, the inconveniences of postwar life were minor. For them, the sight of the All England Club could not have been more moving. "I was awestruck," Margaret Osborne duPont recalled. "It was hard to believe you finally were there."

Britain's top players, Kay Stammers and Jean Bostock, thought they had a chance to beat the Americans. But they were in for a shock. While the war had devastated much of Europe, it had left America's tennis playgrounds unscathed.

Opposite page, top: Young women pose for a photo before competing in the New York State Negro Tennis Championships at the Cosmopolitan Tennis Club in Harlem.

Opposite page, bottom: A groundbreaking exhibition match during the American Tennis Association's National Championships at the Cosmopolitan Club in 1944 showcased, from left, Lillian Van Buren, Mary Hardwick, Alice Marble, and Frances Gittens.

The disparity—the privilege of not being bombed—was stark. A correspondent for the *Times* of London wrote, "It may be that this team is as good as any ever sent over. . . . Our players know clearly now what standard has to be aimed at."

The gap between the American women and the rest of the world would be felt for several years. The five leading Americans—Pauline Betz, Margaret Osborne, Doris Hart, Louise Brough, and Pat Todd—would win sixty-nine Wightman Cup matches against three losses between 1946 and 1962. They also would win twenty-eight singles titles in the four major championships, a remarkable number in view of the lost opportunities during the war and the fact that not all of them had the opportunity to compete in Australia.

Margaret Osborne, who won her later titles as Margaret Osborne duPont, and Louise Brough were all-court players who reached the singles finals so often that the *Times* of London referred to them as "the inevitable duPont and Brough." They each won six Grand Slam singles titles, and their women's doubles record of twenty Grand Slam titles (twelve U.S., five Wimbledon, three French) stood until Martina Navratilova and Pam Shriver matched it in 1989. Their streak of nine straight U.S. doubles titles, from 1942 to 1950, is

Above: The U.S. Wightman Cup team traveled to England in 1946 for the first time since 1939. Pictured from left (at the West Side Tennis Club in New York) are Patricia Canning Todd, Louise Brough, Pauline Betz, Captain Hazel Hotchkiss Wightman, Margaret Osborne, and Doris Hart.

unmatched in any Grand Slam event. They won three more U.S. doubles titles (1955–1957) after Margaret returned to competition following the 1952 birth of her son, William III. In Margaret and Louise's most memorable singles meeting, Margaret prevailed, 4–6, 6–4, 15–13, in the final of the 1948 U.S. Championships. It was the longest women's final ever at Forest Hills.

Through it all, tennis continued to be inaccessible for many. It was still primarily a closed, upper-crust affair. With the exception of the major events, tournaments typically took place at private clubs and before small country club crowds. But the leading women were hardly invisible. Pauline Betz recalled that, in England, the Americans were showered with attention by the British media and fans. "You were a celebrity over there," she said. In September 1946, for the third time in twenty years, *Time* magazine placed a woman tennis player— "California's Pauline Betz"—on its cover. (Helen Wills was the first, in 1926 and 1929.) Pauline had won Wimbledon on her first (and only) try with the loss of only twenty games and would soon capture her fourth U.S. singles title.

In later years, some observers called Pauline Betz one of the best of all time. But she did not earn that praise during her career, and her name has since faded into history, largely because she did not rack up enough of the major titles that currently obsess fans and the media. Unlike today, when the top players compete in every major, Pauline (and so many others) missed tons of them—not only because of wars but also because there was no financial incentive to keep playing them.

I have no doubt that Pauline would have added to her accomplishments had she not turned professional while still in her prime, which made her ineligible for the amateur tournaments overseen by the national tennis federations. Pauline had planned to make one more appearance at Wimbledon and Forest Hills in 1947, but the amateurism protectors intervened. When the United States Lawn Tennis Association (USLTA) discovered that Sarah Palfrey Cooke's husband was making inquiries about a professional tour for the two women, it suspended Pauline from further amateur competition.

Of course, I would have been furious. But Pauline took the disappointment in stride. Many years later, she explained: "I'm sure I could have been reinstated if I had said, no, I wasn't going to turn pro. But by that time, I didn't want to play any more amateur tennis. I wasn't bitter, because I felt it was time to do something else." Then she added with a smile, "But if there had been open tennis, *that* would have been marvelous. We all wanted it. But the USLTA had a stranglehold on tennis."

By now, women had more than proven themselves in the working world. After all, the image of a muscular and super-confident Rosie the Riveter had become a universal symbol of female competence and assertiveness in the workplace. So of course Sarah and Pauline wanted to earn a living with their

Margaret Osborne, left, and Louise Brough share the cover of *El Gráfico*, an Argentine sports publication. For four straight years (1947 to 1950), they were the top two women tennis players in the world.

"INEVITABLE" CHAMPIONS—AND INSEPARABLE

Margaret Osborne duPont and Louise Brough were friends and champions who are almost impossible to separate in history. Their scrapbooks contained few pictures of one without the other. They roomed together on the road, and a typical finals day found them practicing together, having lunch together, and then competing together, in both singles and doubles.

So much alike, yet socially they had much different beginnings. Margaret spent her earliest days on a farm in Oregon and later moved with her family to San Francisco, where her father managed a downtown garage. She played tennis on the public courts at Golden Gate Park and didn't have formal lessons until she was seventeen. Her teacher, Howard Kinsey, helped her make ends meet by allowing her to write his articles for *American Lawn Tennis* magazine for a few pennies a word. Louise, in contrast, learned the game on public courts six blocks from her home in Beverly Hills. Although her parents were divorced, her life was devoid of financial worries.

Above: Louise Brough, left, and Margaret Osborne duPont before their 1949 Wimbledon final. Louise won, 10–8, 1–6, 10–8.

Margaret's and Louise's early development also differed in how their mothers approached winning and losing. Margaret's mother drove her to tournaments and was a gentle observer who was not bothered by losses. "You'll get her next time" was her standard response. Louise's mother was an emotional participant who hated to see Louise lose. "She was so supportive," Louise recalled. "But she didn't understand sports at all. She didn't understand that you could lose. She was very unhappy when I lost in junior tournaments. I think that drove me. I didn't want to go through that battle after I lost. It also made me mad, and a couple of times I threatened that I wouldn't play anymore. I don't remember what she said to me. I just remember it was anger. I'm not sure I didn't cry a little."

Midway through her career, Louise Brough began having trouble tossing the ball on her serve. Possibly as a result, she developed a severe case of tennis elbow during her only trip to Australia. "It was windy over there and I was having trouble with my toss," Louise recalled. "I'd throw the ball different places, and they'd call a foot fault on me, and I got tenser and tenser." Looking back, she added, "I just played too long. You win Wimbledon and you don't want to quit. You keep waiting until somebody beats you and then you can quit. It's hard to give up a trip to Wimbledon."

Margaret left her humble economic roots permanently behind in 1947 when she married William duPont, a scion of the Delaware duPont family and a longtime tennis patron. Louise married Alan Clapp, a dentist, and taught tennis for more than twenty years after her tournament career ended. Margaret died in 2012 at the age of ninety-four; Louise died in 2014 at age ninety.

LOUISE BROUGH

- 6 Grand Slam singles titles
    1 Australian (1950)
    4 Wimbledon (1948–1950, 1955)
    1 U.S. (1947)
- 21 Grand Slam women's doubles titles
- 8 Grand Slam mixed doubles titles
- Wightman Cup: 12–0 in singles, 10–0 in doubles
- Year-end No. 1 in the world: 1955
- International Tennis Hall of Fame Inductee, 1967

MARGARET OSBORNE DUPONT

- 6 Grand Slam singles titles
    2 French (1946, 1949)
    1 Wimbledon (1947)
    3 U.S. (1948–1950)
- 21 Grand Slam women's doubles titles
- 10 Grand Slam mixed doubles titles
- Wightman Cup: 10–0 in singles, 9–0 in doubles
- Year-end No. 1 in the world: 1947–1950
- International Tennis Hall of Fame Inductee, 1967

NOTEWORTHY STATISTIC

- 25 U.S. titles, a record (3 singles, 13 doubles, 9 mixed doubles)

Above: Louise Brough at Wimbledon in 1949.

Below: Margaret Osborne duPont during Wightman Cup play in 1948.

hard-earned skills. They preferred to embark on a well-paid nationwide tour in 1947 to making the circuit of amateur championships for $12 a day in expenses. Sarah and Pauline could not remember exactly how much they made as professionals during their one-year tour; they put the figure in the neighborhood of $10,000 each. "I thought that was pretty good," Sarah said. Pauline was not complaining, either.

It was backbreaking work. They played seven days a week and drove from city to city, traveling as much as four hundred miles a night, frequently by themselves. I find it unfortunate that, while the two were well matched and no doubt provided high-quality tennis, they often resorted to gimmickry. "We wanted to give some instruction without putting the audiences to sleep," Pauline said. Pauline, alias "Susie Glutz," would appear on the court dressed in sloppy men's clothes (size 40 shorts) and a rain hat, with a warped racket in her hand. Sarah, the straight woman, would iron out poor Susie Glutz's problems. Comedian Milton Berle once suggested that Pauline blacken her front teeth, but here Pauline drew the line.

The publicity engine went into high gear for women's tennis in 1949, but for an unexpected reason. In a year when "the inevitable" Margaret Osborne duPont and Louise Brough ruled the courts and bored the sports writers, Gertrude "Gorgeous Gussy" Moran of Santa Monica, California, was the most publicized woman tennis player. Of course, this irritates me, because I have always wanted women to be appreciated for their talent and hard work, not their looks. But, OK, let's admit it—Gussy was, in fact, an accomplished player who had ranked as high as No. 4 in the United States. Gladys Heldman, who helped us launch the women's professional tour in 1970, recalled that Gussy was "glorious to watch" on the court. "She was a great athlete. She was very sound technically, and she could hit hard. She was full of personality, a happy spirit. And a helluva doubles player."

Gussy, still in her teens, went to work in an aircraft factory after her older brother was declared missing in action in France, and she did not join the tennis circuit until she was in her early 20s. She peaked in 1949 when she swept the singles, doubles, and mixed doubles titles at the National Indoor Championships. But Gussy was an entertainer first, a tennis player second. And so strategic. On her first trip to Wimbledon, Gussy hired Ted Tinling.

PAULINE BETZ

- 5 Grand Slam singles titles
  1 Wimbledon (1946)
  4 U.S. (1942–1944, 1946)
- Wightman Cup: 2–0 in singles, 1–0 in doubles
- Year-end No. 1 in the world (1946)

Cash-poor but court-rich

•

"You could do it back then," Pauline Betz said. She was one who proved you could make it without a big bank account, provided you had access to good courts. She was born in Dayton, Ohio, but moved to Los Angeles when she was eight. Her mother, a high school physical education teacher, introduced her to tennis, and she slugged balls against the garage door, pretending she was either Helen Wills or Helen Jacobs. At age fifteen, having had no formal training, she used $24 from her dollar-a-week allowance to purchase twelve lessons with Dick Skeen, an excellent teacher. The Betzes never had enough money for Pauline to travel east for the national junior tournaments, but in the long run, Pauline said, it did not matter. "In California they had tournaments all the time, and you always had good competition." After Pauline began traveling to tournaments as a young adult, she and her family practiced a frugality that I can totally appreciate. "Some of the people had plenty of money, but most of us didn't have much," she said. "You could get by with it because some of the tournaments put you up. Once, my mom and I slept on the beach in our sleeping bags. That was the first year I went to Forest Hills. If you got in at two or three o'clock in the morning, you didn't want to pay to stay somewhere all night. So you made it through the night in the car or somewhere, and then you could check in at the hotel in the morning."

> "ONCE, MY MOM AND I SLEPT ON THE BEACH IN OUR SLEEPING BAGS."

Tinling, a 6-foot-5 couturier, had been part of the tennis scene for more than three decades, first as an umpire and player on the Riviera in the days of Suzanne Lenglen. In 1927, he became an official liaison between Wimbledon's tournament committee and the players. Four years later, he launched his career as a designer of women's fashions. In 1947, Joy Gannon, an English player, was the first to wear Tinling's dresses at Wimbledon.

Gussy wrote to Tinling and asked him to make her "something feminine" for her Wimbledon debut. Tinling, for his part, was eager to clothe this striking young woman. "She had a beautifully modulated, laughing voice, and her skin had a lustrous California gleam," Ted wrote in his memoir, *Sixty Years in Tennis*. "I thought of her as a person who actually shimmered."

His creation was a pretty white dress of rayon trimmed in satin. In keeping with the times, the dress hung just a few inches above the knees. When making the panties that went under the dress, Tinling added a ribbon of lace around the edges. "And why shouldn't they be pretty?" he asked. "I never could understand tennis players who wore nice dresses but showed dreary garments underneath."

Surely Tinling was not so naive as to think the panties would go unnoticed. But it is doubtful that he designed them intending to create an international spectacle. Then again, maybe he did.

Of course, the Wimbledon establishment was shocked. Gussy was wearing the equivalent of lingerie on their hallowed courts! But the rest of Britain went wild. People had grown tired of the plain styles worn during the war, when silk and lace were virtually impossible to find. Gussy was inundated with requests. The Marx Brothers called. The London *Daily Express* plastered her on its front page five times in one week. Wimbledon enjoyed its biggest crowds since the war. "Maybe an extra thousand a day," Tinling said, "and all to see Gussy's panties."

CALIFORNIA GIRLS

With the exception of Doris Hart, a Floridian, the entire 1946 U.S. Wightman Cup team was made up of Californians. And no wonder. California was an amazing incubator of champions. You could play tennis year-round, there were tons of tournaments, and players had access to good public courts and coaches. One reason I made it to the top was access. I had great public courts to play on, and I had free instruction. I was so lucky.

Above: From left, Captain Hazel Hotchkiss Wightman, Pauline Betz, Margaret Osborne, Doris Hart, Louise Brough, Patricia Canning Todd, and an unidentified traveler.

Opposite page: Gussy Moran followed up her tennis career by becoming one of the very first women sportscasters. In 1955, she provided commentary on WMGM radio before and after Brooklyn Dodgers baseball games. In this promotional image, she waves her "racket wand" and the men leap— from left, Don Zimmer, Duke Snider, Carl Erskine, and Walt Moryn.

Gussy was soon able to parlay her fame onto a fledgling pro tour. In 1950, Bobby Riggs signed Gussy and Pauline Betz (who by then was Pauline Betz Addie) to tour with Jack Kramer and Pancho Segura. Pauline earned between $500 and $600 a week playing against Gussy, who reportedly earned about $25,000—the equivalent of nearly $300,000 in 2022.

But the Betz-Moran matchup never gained traction for the same reason that the Lenglen-Brown and Marble-Hardwick tours never gained traction: it was a total mismatch. The men who controlled the game thought about sex appeal instead of competition. Gussy wore several varieties of fake fur, including tiger and antelope, and Pauline even tried to upstage her by wearing gold lamé

shorts. But Gussy endured one shellacking after another in her matches with Pauline, proving once again that glamour alone is a guaranteed failure in the sports arena. Because if you've got athletes on the court, people want to see competition. They want to see a close match. They want to see the skills. Everyone thinks that men just want to look. It's not true. That's where I get really irritated, because, for over a century, this is how we've been teed up, because the media is predominantly controlled by men.

The memory of Gussy Moran lasted long after she vanished from the tennis scene without ever having won a major singles title. She followed up her tennis career by becoming one of the very first women sportscasters. In 1955, she provided commentary on WMGM radio

before and after Brooklyn Dodgers baseball games. Dubbed the "Glamour Girl of Sports" who transitioned from "tennis anyone to who's on first," she was credited with "spouting batting averages with the best of them" and drawing new female listeners to the broadcasts and games at Ebbets Field.

Although I think it unfair that more successful players were not as famous as Gussy was, Gussy's notoriety made people take notice of the women's game. The war years had left deep scars on the world, the tennis world included, and people needed time to recover from their loss and grief. They needed diversions, things to smile about. Gussy, with a big assist from Ted Tinling, helped people heal.

Despite severe setbacks from the war, women's tennis forged ahead during this period. We saw champions in Pauline Betz and Margaret Osborne emerge from the middle class. We saw many more fully developed, all-around games. We saw additional steps in the direction of professional tennis. And we saw Pauline land on the cover of *Time*. But still, so much more to do! Real professional tennis was still a dream, and our major tournaments were still all white. The racial barrier *had* to be broken. Fortunately, we had some groundbreaking champions in the wings in 1949, and the spotlight on women's tennis was ready and waiting for them.

Above: You bet they're jumping for joy! They're going to be paid for entertaining thousands of people with their incredible skills. From left, Pauline Betz Addie, Jack Kramer, Gussy Moran, and Pancho Segura.

Opposite page: Gussy Moran, left, and Pauline Betz Addie (in gold lamé shorts), brought glamour to their professional tour, but not enough drama. Pauline was the dominant player, and her matches with Gussy were seldom close.

CHAPTER FOUR

THE ACHIEVERS

1950

1958

TO

TENNIS as a career path in the 1950s was little changed from the 1940s. As before, tournament officials gave competitors token amounts of money to cover their <u>expenses</u>, while awarding some of the biggest stars more generous appearance fees under the table. As Shirley Fry, one of this era's <u>champions</u>, said: "It cost money to play. Trying to make ends meet was an endless job." Shirley said she never broke even. Unless you were <u>financially</u> independent or had the backing of <u>patrons</u> from your community, you probably weren't going to be able to pursue a career in tennis.

Page 92: Angela Buxton of England, shown here at the Surrey Hard Court Championships in London, teamed with Althea Gibson in 1956 to win doubles titles at the French Championships and at Wimbledon. She was a finalist in the Ladies' Singles at Wimbledon that same year.

Page 95: Althea Gibson is laser focused on her way to winning the 1957 Ladies' Singles title at Wimbledon.

Above: Althea Gibson and Louise Brough pose by the scoreboard after the completion of their dramatic second-round match in the 1950 U.S. Championships at the West Side Tennis Club.

At the start of the decade, that was doubly true for Black players, who were denied entry into tournaments held by the all-white United States Lawn Tennis Association (USLTA).

But something big was coming. Some of the leading white players—most notably Alice Marble—condemned the racial discrimination that had kept Black players out of the game. And within the American Tennis Association (ATA), the Black counterpart to the USLTA, one player—Althea Gibson—was becoming too good to hold back.

Althea was a shy trailblazer who was never entirely comfortable in her role as tennis's Jackie Robinson. She kept her frustrations to herself, letting her racket speak for her—loudly from the get-go and more and more eloquently as time went by. The hard road she traveled to reach the pinnacle of women's tennis makes her one of our most memorable champions. I'll never forget seeing her compete in Los Angeles when I was a teenager. She was long, thin, with a great wingspan. She was No. 1 at the time, and I was shocked by how good she was. Seeing Althea was a gift, because if you can see it, you can be it. It was my wake-up call: I wanted to be No. 1, and now I knew what that looked like and how much work it was going to take for *me* to be the best. My parents taught us that every generation has to be better than the last. At the time I remember thinking in wonderment, "I have to be better than *this*!?"

In 1947, Althea captured the women's ATA championship, her first of ten in a row. Despite her clear readiness for a larger stage, Althea claimed that during the 1940s she did not even *dream* of playing at Wimbledon and Forest Hills. She thought she would never have the opportunity. "I wasn't disappointed, because I was learning something every time I struck a ball," she said.

Those were the days when Black people in the South still had to sit in the backs of buses, watch movies from the balconies, and use segregated restrooms. In cities throughout the country, Black families were prevented from buying homes in white neighborhoods. The Supreme Court's landmark 1954 decision in *Brown v. Board of Education,* which prohibited segregation in the public schools, was still several years away.

But if Althea was not dreaming about competing in the great all-white tournaments of the world, others were. In 1948, Dr. Reginald Weir, a veteran player, became the first Black person to compete in a USLTA tournament, the National Indoor Championships. The ATA, encouraged by Weir's breakthrough, wanted Althea to go one giant step further. During the winter of 1949, they urged her to apply to play in the USLTA-sponsored Eastern Indoor Championships in New York. She was accepted and reached the quarterfinals.

ALTHEA WAS A SHY TRAILBLAZER WHO WAS NEVER ENTIRELY COMFORTABLE IN HER ROLE AS TENNIS'S JACKIE ROBINSON.

Above: Althea shows her gratitude in 1951 for the boxer Sugar Ray Robinson, who was a friend and mentor during her teenage years. Sugar Ray paid for Althea's saxophone, which she played in her high school marching band, and he sent her the $15 she needed to pay for her class ring when she graduated in 1949.

The next week, she reached the quarterfinals at the National Indoor Championships. Althea had never before competed in tournaments where she was the only Black player. She and the ATA might have sought to open more doors that year, specifically the summer grass-court tournaments, including the U.S. Championships at Forest Hills. But Althea's ATA backers apparently wanted to give her a little more time to mature and adjust to the new international level of competition. In addition, Althea wanted to pursue a college degree. She had earned a scholarship to Florida A&M University in Tallahassee and was already taking courses during the summer of 1949.

In the winter of 1950, Althea won the Eastern Indoor and was runner-up in the National Indoor. Clearly, she was qualified to compete in the U.S. Championships at Forest Hills. But no—tennis insiders heard rumors that she would not gain entry until she proved herself on grass. If that were true, Althea faced another obstacle. Most of the grass-court events preceding the nationals were invitationals played at white-only country clubs, and Althea was not receiving any invitations.

On July 1, 1950, *American Lawn Tennis* magazine printed a guest editorial by Alice Marble lambasting the tennis community for failing to open its tournaments to Althea. "Miss Gibson is over a very cunningly wrought barrel, and I can only hope to loosen a few of its staves with one lone opinion," Alice wrote. "If tennis is a game for ladies and gentlemen, it's also time we acted a little more like gentlepeople and less like sanctimonious hypocrites. . . . If Althea Gibson represents a challenge to the present crop of women players, it's only fair that they should meet that challenge on the courts." Should Althea not be given the chance to succeed or fail, Alice added, "then there is an ineradicable mark against a game to which I have devoted most of my life, and I would be bitterly ashamed."

Shortly after Alice's passionate indictment appeared, Althea tried to enter the New Jersey State Championships

Above: Alice Marble, who championed Althea's cause, escorts her friend back to the West Side Tennis Club's clubhouse. Althea had just won her historic first-round match in the 1950 U.S. National Championships.

at the Maplewood Country Club. Tournament officials rejected her, Althea said, because they had insufficient information about her qualifications. It was obviously a ludicrous cover for the club's racist attitudes. How could the winner of the Eastern Indoor and runner-up at the National Indoor not be qualified?

Althea finally got a chance to compete on grass in late July when the Orange Lawn Tennis Club in South Orange, New Jersey, accepted her into the 1950 Eastern Grass Court Championships. She won her first-round match on the No. 1 court, and the *New York Times* responded with a top-of-the-page headline in its sports section. (The front page reported President Truman's call for eighty-two thousand National Guard members and thirty-two thousand Marines for wartime service in Korea.) The *Times*'s distinguished tennis reporter, Allison Danzig, wrote: "Today was notable in tennis as marking the first appearance of a Negro player in a grass court tournament under the auspices of the United States Lawn Tennis Association." Danzig also observed that "Miss Gibson has an easy style of stroke production, and her forehand and backhand are soundly wrought. She follows her fast service to the net as do few women, and no other player of her sex hits an overhead more emphatically." He anticipated a promising future once she had "consolidated her game and acquired mastery over the speed she has at her call."

ALTHEA GIBSON

*With help from mentors,
she forged a new path*

•

Althea Gibson, the daughter of sharecroppers and the great-great-granddaughter of a slave, was born in 1927 on a cotton farm in the small town of Silver, South Carolina. When Althea was three years old, her parents abandoned their farm because of the hardships caused by the Great Depression and moved to Harlem in New York City in pursuit of a better life. The walk-up apartment on 143rd Street that Althea shared with her parents and four siblings was only a thirty-minute subway ride from the West Side Tennis Club, an all-white enclave that could not have seemed more remote to Althea had it been located in Siberia.

Her childhood was rocky; she skipped school, stole from street vendors, and was generally aimless. Luckily, there was a safety net, however fragile: Althea lived on a Police Athletic League (PAL) play street that was closed to cars during the day. Paddle tennis was a prime activity, and Althea was the best on the block. In 1940, her PAL supervisor, Buddy Walker, introduced her to the interracial Cosmopolitan Tennis Club, where the members paid for her lessons with Fred Johnson, the club's one-armed professional. Althea won national junior titles in the all-Black American Tennis Association in 1944 and 1945. The next year, eighteen-year-old Althea reached the final of the women's event and caught the eye of two physicians who were also ATA officials: Dr. Robert Walter Johnson and Dr. Hubert Eaton. They thought Althea had a chance to reach the top of tennis, and in an act of generosity that would change tennis history, they came to her aid.

During the winter, Althea lived with the Eatons in Wilmington, North Carolina, where she attended high school for the first time in her life and worked on her game on Dr. Eaton's private court. "His court was a gathering place for all the Negro tennis players of the district, as it had to be," Althea wrote in her memoir. "There were a number of public courts in Wilmington, but no Negro could play on them." During the summer, she stayed with the Johnsons in Lynchburg, Virginia, and traveled the ATA circuit. Together, the two doctors gave Althea the opportunity to change her life. They coached her, taught her tennis etiquette, and, above all, treated her like a daughter. Althea, throughout her life, called both of them "Dad." She graduated from Williston High School in 1949, ranked tenth in her class, when she was twenty-one years old. She earned a degree from Florida A&M University four years later.

- **5 Grand Slam singles titles**
  - **1 French (1956)**
  - **2 Wimbledon (1957, 1958)**
  - **2 U.S. (1957, 1958)**
- **5 Grand Slam women's doubles titles**
- **1 Grand Slam mixed doubles title**
- **Wightman Cup: 3–1 in singles, 2–0 in doubles**
- **10 ATA women's singles titles (1947–1956)**
- **Year-end No. 1 in the world: 1957, 1958**
- **International Tennis Hall of Fame inductee, 1971**

Althea lost decisively in the second round to Helen Pastall Perez, who was ranked fifth in the United States, but she had proved that she belonged. In mid-August, Lawrence Baker, president of the USLTA, announced that "based on her ability," Althea Gibson had been accepted into the U.S. National Championships at the West Side Tennis Club at Forest Hills.

Althea was nervous before her historic first match at Forest Hills but not overwhelmed. "I just wanted to get onto the court and show my talent as a tennis player," she insisted. "I didn't think about the racial issue or anything. I didn't think, 'Here I am, the first Negro.' I was accepted as a tennis player when I walked onto the court. All I thought about was how am I going to play this game and win?"

Althea made her debut on distant court No. 14, where she defeated Barbara Knapp of England in straight sets. (The following summer, in stark contrast, Wimbledon officials honored their first Black contestant by scheduling her opening match on Centre Court.) Althea played her second-round match at Forest Hills on the grandstand court, which was packed. The match was a thriller, as Louise Brough, the reigning Wimbledon champion, barely held on to win, 9–7, in a third set interrupted by rain and completed the next day. Althea Gibson was still a winner, of course. By showing her great skill, she had opened the door for generations of Black tennis players yet to come.

While Althea was making her breakthrough, Maureen Connolly, a precocious California teenager, was toppling her elders with a relentlessly powerful baseline game. Nelson Fisher, a San Diego sportswriter, nicknamed her "Little Mo" in a nod to the World War II battleship *Missouri*. I have no doubt that the adults she thrashed found her as ruthless as "Big Mo's" sixteen-inch guns. Two weeks shy of her seventeenth birthday, Maureen defeated both Doris Hart and Shirley Fry to become the youngest U.S. champion since sixteen-year-old May Sutton in 1904. And at seventeen, she became the youngest Wimbledon

ANGELA BUXTON

Angela Buxton's career was brief but notable. Some of her most satisfying moments occurred at London's Cumberland Lawn Tennis Club, which had denied her a membership because she was Jewish. "I made a point of going back to the Cumberland Club to win their bloody tournament – twice! Just to rub their noses in it," she said. "And they never gave me a cup of tea – not even that." She was an outsider in tennis, and in 1956 she teamed with another outsider – Althea Gibson – to win the French and Wimbledon women's doubles titles. A chronic hand injury forced her to retire from competitive tennis when she was only twenty-two.

Angela Buxton and Althea Gibson teamed up to win doubles titles in 1956 at Roland Garros and Wimbledon. They remained lifelong friends.

winner since Charlotte "Lottie" Dod won back-to-back titles at fifteen and sixteen in 1887 and 1888. Her dominance was so great that she won singles titles in all nine Grand Slam tournaments she played in from 1951 through 1954.

Maureen had a fun-loving side, a glimmer of happy teenage normalcy that prompted designer Ted Tinling to put smiling cats and furry poodles on her tennis dresses. But on the tennis court, Maureen was not as happy as she looked. "I have always believed greatness on a tennis court was my destiny, a dark destiny, at times, where the tennis court became my secret jungle and I, a lonely, fear-stricken hunter," she wrote in her autobiography, *Forehand Drive*. "I was a strange little girl armed with hate, fear, and a Golden Racket."

Maureen's absorption in the game was total, unwavering, and fierce. Her face rarely changed expression, and she rarely smiled. "All I ever see is my opponent," she once said. "You could set off dynamite in the next court and I wouldn't notice."

Little Mo fascinated the tennis public. She charmed many with her cuteness yet alienated others with her cold demeanor and her relentless stream of victories. She maintained a brisk pace, walking quickly between points and serving promptly. A London *Daily Express* correspondent called her "an efficient clockwork machine" and "a subdued tennis robot," while Lance Tingay of the London *Daily Telegraph* wrote, "It is, perhaps, one of the drawbacks of greatness that Miss Connolly's cold efficiency should be regarded as a personal characteristic. Off the court Miss Connolly is a charming youngster. She is remorseless only when she begins to play." Indeed, Maureen sparkled in media interviews. She showed unusual poise for someone so young and enjoyed the star-studded parties that tournaments held in her honor. Shirley Fry recalled that Maureen "loved to party, and she loved to sing."

Had tournament tennis been open to professionals back in the 1950s, Maureen would have become wealthy. Instead, as with so many other talented players before her, she could only protest the system that allowed tournament promoters to pay top amateurs a fraction of their value, and always surreptitiously. Like Suzanne Lenglen, Maureen came to the defense of the "exploited" amateur athlete and urged tennis officials to "drop the mask of hypocrisy" and "pay the players a standard fee."

Although Maureen's rivals believed she was routinely paid, she herself admitted to having received a $400 appearance fee on only two occasions. Players also believed Althea Gibson was paid, but Althea said she was not. "If I was, it probably was peanuts, not thousands of dollars," she said. "Just enough to go in and buy a sandwich."

> # MAUREEN'S ABSORPTION IN THE GAME WAS TOTAL, UNWAVERING, AND FIERCE. HER FACE RARELY CHANGED EXPRESSION, AND SHE RARELY SMILED.

Fashion designer Ted Tinling captured the softer side of Maureen Connolly with sweet outfits like this one.

MAUREEN CONNOLLY

Molded by champion coaches

●

Maureen Connolly, born in San Diego in 1934, became infatuated with tennis at age nine after watching two proficient men playing on the cracked cement courts at the University Heights playground two doors from her home. Maureen was soon picking up balls for the playground coach, Wilbur Folsom, who gave her lessons in return. Folsom was an accomplished player who had lost his left leg as a young man after being struck by an automobile. Undeterred, he continued playing tennis—striding with his good leg and taking short hops on his wooden prosthesis—and built his reputation as "the Architect of Champions," while charging youngsters just 50 cents for hour-long lessons.

Although Maureen was a natural left-hander, Folsom persuaded her to change. In his experience, women who played left-handed did not become champions. (Indeed, a left-handed woman did not win at Wimbledon until Ann Jones triumphed in 1969.) Maureen developed rapidly as a right-hander while practicing three hours a day, five days a week. In 1948, fourteen-year-old Maureen came under the guidance of Teach Tennant, Alice Marble's former mentor.

Teach improved Maureen's game technically and molded her into a fierce competitor by sheltering her and refusing to let her socialize or even practice with the other women players. The tactics worked, but Maureen later blamed Teach for intensifying the hatred that she felt toward her opponents and that consumed and depressed her. In 1952, Maureen and Teach argued over whether Maureen should withdraw from Wimbledon because of an injury that was later found to be inconsequential. Teach wanted Maureen to default; Maureen was determined to play. After winning her first match in twenty-two minutes, Maureen called her own press conference, something no one did in those days, and fired Teach publicly, without having told her first. Ted Tinling later wrote that Teach "never really recovered from the shocks of those few days."

- **9 Grand Slam singles titles**
    - **2 French, 1953–1954**
    - **3 Wimbledon, 1952—1954**
    - **3 U.S., 1951–1953**
    - **1 Australian, 1953**
- **5 Grand Slam women's doubles titles**
- **1 Grand Slam mixed doubles title**
- **Won the Grand Slam, 1953**
- **Wightman Cup: 7–0 in singles, 2–0 in doubles**
- **Year-end No. 1 in the world (1952–1954)**
- **International Tennis Hall of Fame inductee, 1968**

The teenager who people thought was cold and remote grew into a wife and mother who loved sharing her knowledge with young people. Maureen Connolly Brinker coached the British Wightman Cup team on its trips to the United States during the 1960s, and she wrote articles about tennis for the *San Diego Union,* the *London Daily Mail,* and *World Tennis.* In 1968, Maureen and her good friend Nancy Jeffett cofounded the Maureen Connolly Brinker Foundation, which supports junior tournaments—including the yearlong Road to the Little Mo Nationals—and has contributed more than $4 million for player development. Nancy Jeffett served as chair of the U.S. Wightman Cup (1978–1990) and Federation Cup (1981–1990) competitions. In recognition of her administrative and philanthropic contributions to tennis, she was inducted into the International Tennis Hall of Fame in 2015.

MAUREEN CALLED HER OWN PRESS CONFERENCE, SOMETHING NO ONE DID IN THOSE DAYS.

Opposite page: Maureen Connolly defeated Doris Hart to win the 1953 Ladies' Singles at Wimbledon.

Bob Kelleher, chairman of the USLTA's Amateur Rules Committee in the 1950s, told me he did not know of a single dollar that was paid under the table to Maureen or Althea. "But they were part of an era when it was absolutely common knowledge" that players were being paid. "People would look the other way, but everybody knew." The amateur system became so corrupt in the 1950s, he went on, that Jack Kramer, a former champion who by then was a promoter of professional events, complained that the men were making more money as amateurs than he could offer them as professionals.

In 1953, Maureen set her sights on winning all four major championships in a single year, a feat known as a Grand Slam. The term had its origins in bridge, the card game, and was first used in golf in 1930 when Bobby Jones won the four major championships in his sport. Don Budge brought the concept to tennis when he pursued, and won, our sport's first Grand Slam in 1938. Little Mo, who was more than up to the challenge, became the first woman to accomplish it. Her final match was a forty-three-minute rout of Doris Hart at Forest Hills.

In 1954, after winning her second Wimbledon title, Maureen went home to San Diego to rest and engage in one of her favorite pastimes, horseback riding. She and her friends were riding on a narrow side road when a cement truck passed between them. Maureen's horse whirled, and the truck's rear mudguard caught Maureen's right leg, throwing her to the ground. The impact tore the muscles below her knee and broke and exposed the bone. Maureen never played competitive tennis again.

Could she have come back? Some said yes; Maureen and her attorneys said no. Maureen sued the cement company, demanding $265,000 in damages. Maureen testified in court that several attempts at a comeback were thwarted by pains in her leg. She also testified that she had planned to turn professional in October 1954, shortly after the national championships. A jury voted, nine to three, to award her $95,000, the amount she could have expected to earn as a professional.

When Little Mo announced her retirement several months after the accident, she said, "I just don't enjoy tennis anymore." It was a shocking statement that was never fully explained. Perhaps Little Mo had grown disillusioned because of her injury. Perhaps she realized she would never again be the player she once was. I met Little Mo when I was fifteen, and I got goosebumps when I saw the deep and terrible scar in the back of her leg, just below the calf muscle.

RUIA MEREANA MORRISON

Dame Ruia Mereana Morrison was the first New Zealand woman to rise to prominence in international tennis. An indigenous Māori from the Te Arawa and Ngāti Tūwharetoa iwi tribes, she won her first of six New Zealand national singles titles in 1956. In 1957, she became the first New Zealander to play at Wimbledon, where she reached the fourth round. In 1959, she again reached the fourth round at Wimbledon before losing to Maria Bueno. In 1960, she was honored as a Member of the Order of the British Empire.

Maureen continued to play tennis despite her injury. "I still hit with Maureen after the accident," Pancho Gonzales, the men's champion, said. "She didn't move as well, but she hit the ball really well." Maureen also played with a promising ten-year-old named Chrissie Evert, who remembered that "her ground strokes were really hard and crisp and deep."

Maureen's life, like her tennis career, was fulfilling but too short. In 1969, she died of cancer. She was only thirty-four years old.

For Althea, the five years that followed her debut at Forest Hills in 1950 were a mixture of achievement and disappointment. She graduated from Florida A&M University in 1953 and accepted a position teaching physical education at Lincoln University, a historically Black university in Jefferson City, Missouri. In tennis, however, she continued to struggle. She broke into America's top ten at No. 9 in 1952, rose to seventh in 1953, and slid to thirteenth in 1954.

Her confidence flagging, Althea decided to retire from amateur competition in 1955 and join the Women's Army Corps. She explained her decision in her autobiography, *I Always Wanted To Be Somebody*: "I'm just not good enough. I'm probably never going to be. And I'm sick of having people support me, taking up collections for me, buying me clothes and airplane tickets and every damn thing I eat or wear. I want to take care of myself for a change."

Then, that very year, the U.S. State Department invited her to be part of a goodwill tour of Southeast Asia along with three other leading American players: Karol Fageros, Bob Perry, and Ham Richardson. Althea went and won virtually every event she entered, igniting her competitive fires. During the tour, she got to know Angela Buxton, a British player who was competing in the same tournaments as Althea in India. Angela had experienced prejudice herself, having been denied entry into private tennis clubs where she wanted to train because she was Jewish. She and Althea bonded, and in 1956, when Althea was still seeking a doubles partner shortly before the French Championships at Roland Garros, the women teamed up.

Did that new friendship and partnership give Althea an emotional lift? I'm sure it did. At Roland Garros, Althea won her first major title with a 6–0, 12–10 victory over Britain's Angela Mortimer. She also captured the women's doubles with Angela Buxton, and the two friends triumphed again at Wimbledon. Althea Gibson had reached her full potential, and there was no one better. "Behind Althea Gibson," *Time* magazine reported in 1957, "women's tennis curves off into mediocrity."

DORIS HART

*Rising above a physical challenge
with newfound strengths*

●

Doris Hart, born in 1925, was fifteen months old when her family noticed that she was walking with a slight limp, the result of an infection under the right kneecap. She was mistakenly treated for rheumatism, which allowed the infection to spread rapidly, and Doris soon became seriously ill. Three different specialists – fearing gangrene – recommended that the leg be amputated. But Doris's father would not consent until he got an opinion from the Harts' family doctor, David Todd, who was away on a hunting trip. Summoned home, Dr. Todd drained the poisonous fluid from Doris's knee, without anesthesia, while a nurse and Doris's father held her still on the kitchen table.

Doctors believed that Doris would always walk with a limp, but the Hart family never gave up. They moved from St. Louis to Coral Gables, Florida, when Doris was four, and every day Doris's parents took her to the ocean to soak her leg in the salt water. At age ten, Doris underwent surgery for a double hernia. "I was in the hospital so long, not like today," she recalled. "And the hospital was around the corner from where we lived, right next to Henderson Park. My room overlooked the park and the tennis courts. My older brother, Bud, had just started hacking around with tennis. Then, when I got better, the doctor said, 'Why not let Doris try it?'"

Doris received her first racket from Bud, who would become the most profound influence on her career. He later ranked twentieth among American men. He and Doris spent every moment possible on the courts together. Although her right leg bothered her all her life and caused her to shuffle more than run on the court, Doris compensated by becoming a magician with her racket. "I worked hard on the drop shot, which really helped me in my career, and I worked on half volleys, stepping in and taking the ball right after the bounce," she said. "I knew I couldn't stay out there and rally fifty times a point. A lot of those half volleys were at the baseline. I never retreated. When my brother, Bud, and I played sets, he'd mark the court maybe two feet behind the baseline, and if I moved back beyond that line, I'd lose the point. So it made me stay up there and take deep balls on the half volley. People used to say, 'That's such a chancy shot.' But for me, it wasn't. I felt just as confident doing that as someone else would have been when hitting a regular forehand."

Doris played with an effortless grace. Had she been blessed with two normal legs, I think she would have been one of the greatest ever to play the game.

- **6 Grand Slam singles titles**
  - 2 French (1950, 1952)
  - 1 Wimbledon (1951)
  - 2 U.S. (1954, 1955)
  - 1 Australian (1949)
- **14 Grand Slam women's doubles titles**
- **15 Grand Slam mixed doubles titles**
- **Wightman Cup (14–1 singles, 8–1 doubles)**
- **Year-end No. 1 in the world (1951)**
- **International Tennis Hall of Fame inductee, 1969**

Above: The Duchess of Kent presents Doris Hart with the silver salver, also known as the Venus Rosewater Dish, after Doris's victory over Shirley Fry in the 1951 Wimbledon final.

"I tried to play ruthlessly," she said later. "I had the biggest serve in women's tennis. As a matter of fact, somebody wrote, 'Her serve was remarkably like a man's.' Well, it probably felt like that to my opponents. It was hard, and it was well placed."

Despite Althea's many accomplishments and the uniquely difficult challenges she faced, I think she remains one of our most underrated champions. I agree with Angela Mortimer, the 1961 Wimbledon champion, who said that Althea "never received the recognition her powerful tennis and great athleticism deserved."

Few people in the white tennis world really had a chance to know and understand her. Like many champions who came before and after, Althea kept her distance from the rest of the field. She also intimidated her opponents. I sensed that while we were together in the dressing room at the Pacific Southwest Championships in the late 1950s. She was taller than everyone else, which made her imposing to begin with, and she had a swagger that added to that aura.

Althea undoubtedly was under enormous pressure, not only from herself but also from the Black community. "Althea really had a cross to bear," said Darlene Hard, who roomed with Althea for two and a half years on the tour and won the 1957 women's doubles title with her at Wimbledon. "She was trying to be the first Black to succeed in tennis."

As Wimbledon got under way in 1957, Althea knew the No. 1 ranking was within her grasp. After winning her semifinal match, she told reporters, "Praise be, this could be my year." Her instincts were right on target. Althea defeated Darlene Hard in the final, 6–3, 6–2, to become the first Black player, male or female, to win Wimbledon. "At last!" Althea cried, after the final point was played. "At last!" Moments later, Queen Elizabeth II presented the woman from Harlem with the gilded salver. In her autobiography, Althea wrote, "Shaking hands with the Queen of England was a long way from being forced to sit in the colored section of the bus."

The city of New York welcomed Althea home with a ticker-tape parade up Broadway, and the mayor held a luncheon in her honor at the Waldorf-Astoria Hotel.

Two months later, at Forest Hills, Althea soundly defeated thirty-three-year-old Louise Brough to win the 1957 U.S. Championships. Althea received her trophy, filled with white gladioli and red roses, from Vice President Richard M. Nixon. Addressing the crowd, Althea thanked God for her ability and said she hoped she would wear her crown with dignity and humility. "Her remarks," said the *New York Times*, "were followed by the longest demonstration of hand-clapping heard in the stadium in years."

Althea retained her Wimbledon and U.S. titles in 1958 and for the second straight year was named the Associated Press's Female Athlete of the Year. The next year, having won everything she had ever wanted to win, she retired from amateur tennis, bringing a decisive end to a decade of unique events in the women's game. Althea probably would have added to her collection of titles had she remained an amateur, but she had no incentive to do so. "I couldn't eat trophies," she said wistfully.

Althea signed a $100,000 contract with the Harlem Globetrotters for a six-month tour; she would play exhibitions during their halftime intermissions. Her opponent was Floridian Karol Fageros, a gorgeous blonde who—have we heard this story before?—was not nearly as good as Althea. Although the money Althea received for the tour was unprecedented for a woman tennis player at the time, much of it was used for expenses. "That $100,000 had to take care of everybody on our [tennis] part of the tour," Althea explained. "We had to pay salaries out of that to people we traveled with, people who laid out the court, our driver. After it was over I believe I had a little bit left over for myself, enough to get an apartment in New York in those years." The Globetrotters did not renew the contract.

SHIRLEY FRY

The little girl on the bus

●

- 4 Grand Slam singles titles
    - French (1951)
    - Wimbledon (1956)
    - U.S. (1956)
    - Australian (1957)
- 12 Grand Slam women's doubles titles
- 1 Grand Slam mixed doubles title
- Wightman Cup: 4–2 in singles, 6–0 in doubles
- Year-end No. 1 in the world (1956)
- International Tennis Hall of Fame inductee, 1970

Shirley June Fry was born in Akron, Ohio, in 1927, two years before the stock market crash triggered the Great Depression. Akron, the rubber capital of the world, was especially hard hit by the Depression. "No one had that much money, so I was lucky to be able to play tennis," she said. "It wasn't a cheap sport, either, at that time, but my dad believed in sports. We had all the equipment, always."

Shirley learned to play tennis on the white clay courts at the nearby University Club of Akron. Her father, Lester Fry, set up games for her with good male players, and in 1936 when she was only nine, he started her scrapbook and wrote on the first page: "Wimbledon—1945." In 1936, he also tested her courage and independence by sending her by bus to the Cleveland Exposition. Shirley looked over the exhibits and made it back without a hitch. A year later, at age ten, she traveled alone from Akron to Philadelphia, where she competed in a tournament. Shirley's family probably didn't have the resources to send a chaperone with her, and of course, those were different times; you'd never send such a young child off on her own like that now. Shirley recalled having a dollar a day to spend. "I didn't eat breakfast," she said. "I would try to keep seventy cents for the evening meal."

Unlike Floridian Doris Hart and the Californians, who could play tennis year-round, Shirley could play only six months a year while growing up in Ohio. Nor did she have the advantage of expert training. As a result, she was not a classic player but a gritty one who relied on quickness and resolve. She believed her best years overlapped with those of Maureen Connolly, but after taking a break from tennis in 1955, she returned and captured the titles that meant so much to her. After winning her lone Wimbledon title in 1956, she immediately cabled her father: "Worth all the trouble. Love, Shirley." The City of St. Petersburg honored her with a ticker-tape parade and a new car.

SHE WAS NOT A CLASSIC PLAYER BUT A GRITTY ONE WHO RELIED ON QUICKNESS AND RESOLVE.

Shirley Fry, at right, with Doris Hart after their victory over Louise Brough and Maureen Connolly in the 1952 Wimbledon final. Shirley and Doris won eleven major doubles titles together.

Above: Karol Fageros, at right, and Althea Gibson had become good friends during their goodwill tour of Southeast Asia in 1956. Here, they are shown in a promotional picture for their 1959 tour with the Harlem Globetrotters.

In the years that followed, Althea took up golf at the Englewood Golf Club in New Jersey, where Jerry Volpe, the legendary teaching professional, coached her and gave her an honorary membership. In 1963, she became the first Black player on the Ladies Professional Golf Association tour, which thirteen women players had founded three years earlier. Although her success was limited, she drew fans because of her tennis fame and was embraced by her fellow golfers. "At one event, when Althea was forced to change her shoes in the parking lot because she wasn't invited into the clubhouse, all the players changed in their cars in solidarity with her," wrote Steve Eubanks in an article for the LPGA.

Althea taught tennis in New Jersey for several years but experienced bad luck when the clubs at which she worked closed. She served as New Jersey State Athletic Commissioner in the mid-1970s, and in 1977 she ran unsuccessfully in the Democratic primary election for the New Jersey state senate. Althea suffered from poor health in her later years; she suffered two strokes and struggled with the aftereffects. Although she never sought assistance, the tennis community came to her aid. Angela Buxton, her lifelong friend, spearheaded a fundraising campaign that raised $1 million. Althea died in 2003 at the age of seventy-six.

Althea Gibson always expressed satisfaction that the next generations of young women were able to become wealthy playing tennis. "That's beautiful; I'm happy for them," she said. "I just sometimes feel I should have had some of it. But that's the way it goes. I was, would you say, too soon? I'm not mad about it or anything, but I think about it now and then, maybe saying to myself, 'My goodness. Look what I missed!'"

Indeed, for women like Althea Gibson and Maureen Connolly, the professional tennis tour would come twenty years too late.

After Althea Gibson became the first Black tennis player ever to win a Wimbledon championship, New York City welcomed her home with a ticker-tape parade up Broadway. She blew kisses to the adoring crowd.

CHAPTER FIVE

TENNIS SAYS YES! TO THE PROS

1959
TO
1969

THE 1960S

ushered in new champions and <u>explosive</u> change. No longer did Americans rule the major tournaments. The players who learned the game in the years that followed World War II entered their <u>prime</u> during this decade and gave tennis its most global flavor yet. Six women from four <u>continents</u> won Wimbledon: Maria Bueno of Brazil, Margaret Smith Court of Australia, Angela Mortimer and Ann Haydon Jones of England, and Karen Hantze Susman and I of the United States.

Page 118: Darlene Hard was one of the last great amateurs.

Page 121: Margaret Smith benefited from Australia's fitness program.

Above: Maria Bueno of Brazil cracks an overhead.

Meanwhile, the slow march toward professional tennis continued. In July 1960, the progressive thinkers who wanted to abolish the distinction between professionals and amateurs brought the issue to a vote at a meeting of the International Lawn Tennis Federation (ILTF). Consistent with the times, only two women were present—Mme. Garnero-Delubac of Portugal and Miss G. P. Butler of San Marino, Italy. Led by Britain's Lawn Tennis Association (LTA), the United States Lawn Tennis Association (USLTA), and the French and Australian federations, the national federations voted, 134–75, to open up eight major championships to professionals in 1961. Unfortunately, the measure failed to win the necessary two-thirds majority by five votes. The USLTA tried to revive the issue a year later, but the ILTF let the matter slide. For seven more years, amateur tennis went on as before.

Bob Kelleher, president of the USLTA in 1967 and 1968, said he had been "rather violently" in favor of opening the tournaments to pros because he felt sham amateurism was corrupting youth. "We purported to be an amateur game and we had rules that you could not get paid in any way, and actually all the good young kids, especially the Californians, were paid under the table to use a particular tennis racket," he said. "They also were paid to come play in tournaments, in violation of the rules. I felt that it was as crooked as anything could be. The only solution was to have open tennis and let them be pros if they wanted to be and amateurs if not."

Those who sought this change were also alarmed by the drain of talent out of the great amateur tournaments and into the struggling professional sideshows. In an effort to earn a decent living, the top men were leaving the amateur game one by one: Jack Kramer, Pancho Gonzales, Frank Sedgman, Tony Trabert, Rod Laver, Lew Hoad, and Ken Rosewall were among the defectors.

Although only a few women stars had ever turned professional—Pauline Betz and Althea Gibson among them—more women probably would have done so if the male promoters had offered them the opportunity. Some of these women might also have banded together, as Pauline Betz and Sarah Palfrey had, to create their own opportunities. But as Shirley Fry recalled, "We were programmed: get married and have kids."

Thus, the early and middle 1960s—when I came on the scene—were in many ways like the 1940s and 1950s. Men and women played a few great championship matches in front of crowds numbering in the thousands, at Wimbledon, Forest Hills, and Roland Garros, and the rest of our matches took place before small crowds—in the hundreds if we were lucky—at exclusive, mostly white (if not all-white) country clubs. Tournament promoters went on paying the best players under-the-table appearance fees, while lower-ranked players got barely enough to live on.

MARIA BUENO

Grace and style all her own

•

- 7 Grand Slam singles titles
    - 3 Wimbledon (1959, 1960, 1964)
    - 4 U.S. (1959, 1963, 1964, 1966)
- 11 Grand Slam women's doubles titles
- 1 Grand Slam mixed doubles title
- Year-end No. 1 in the world (1959, 1960)
- Associated Press Female Athlete of the Year, 1959
- International Tennis Hall of Fame inductee, 1978

Maria Esther Bueno was introduced to tennis at age five by her father, Pedro Bueno, who bought her a membership at the Clube de Regatas Tietê in São Paulo, a rowing club with swimming pools and tennis courts located across the street from their home. Maria had no formal lessons, adopting instead her own eclectic style. "I would copy anybody I liked to watch, any of the club players," she said. Maria yearned to have a serve like Bill Tilden's. She studied a book that featured several photographs of Tilden's serve and spent hours trying to imitate his majestic motion. She practiced mainly with the best male players at the club, including her brother Pedrinho, and at age fifteen she won the Brazilian women's championship and took a set from Shirley Fry, one of the best women players in the world. At seventeen, Maria began to tour internationally. In 1959, after becoming the first Brazilian ever to win Wimbledon, she returned home to a twenty-one-gun salute and a parade. "Being a girl and by myself, I had gone out to conquer the world," she recalled. "Statues and airmail stamps were made." Regrettably, her body did not hold up well to the demands of her sport, and she was forced to retire while still in her twenties. "I never had two seasons running when I was totally fit," she reflected. "I don't think I played full-time for more than six or seven years. I felt it was very short for me, doing something I wanted to do so much." Maria passed away in 2018 at age seventy-eight but will never be forgotten: the ten-thousand-seat show court at Rio de Janeiro's Olympic Tennis Centre—the tennis venue for the 2016 Summer Olympics—is named the Maria Esther Bueno Court.

"BEING A GIRL AND BY MYSELF, I HAD GONE OUT TO CONQUER THE WORLD."

Maria Bueno wept after winning the
1959 Wimbledon singles title, then
smiled for the photographers.
A headline in the *Observer*, a London
newspaper, hailed the "Mighty Power
in Brazil's Dainty Atom."

Below: Maria Bueno enjoys a hero's welcome home in 1959 after becoming the first Brazilian tennis player to win a Wimbledon title.

Maria Esther Bueno, of São Paulo, Brazil, was among the biggest stars of this era. She was the first great woman player from South America, and she brought more than her heritage to the game. Her natural grace, combined with her imaginative shotmaking, made her wildly popular; her victories, added to these attributes, made her a superstar. "To me, tennis was more of an art than a sport," Maria said. "I was a very natural player. Everything was done by impulse or intuition. I was never satisfied if I did not play beautifully. I was always going for perfection and the impossible shots."

"*La Bueno,*" as she was affectionately called, heightened global awareness of women's tennis and was the first woman tennis player since Suzanne Lenglen to captivate Continental Europe. The Europeans had never much enjoyed watching women play tennis. The Italians were notorious for scheduling women's matches on back courts and at unpopular hours. Rino Tommasi, an Italian radio sportscaster, remembered watching the final of the women's Italian Championships in the mid-1960s. At that time, the women's and men's tournaments were held simultaneously at the beautiful Foro Italico in Rome. "Margaret Smith was playing Lesley Turner on Court 6 and there were six spectators," Tommasi said. "The center court was packed to watch a doubles match with an Italian player. I felt sorry for the girls. I felt sorry also for Italy, because it was terrible."

Maria Bueno helped change that. The Italians, like the rest of the Europeans, embraced *La Bueno*, placing her on a pedestal and center court. "The Italians somehow always thought women's tennis was very boring," she reflected. "But when I first played there at Foro Italico, they had most of my matches on center court, which was never done for the women. Even when I played the Italian players in Italy, one of the things everybody dislikes doing the most, I never had any trouble. I was very lucky and was able to communicate well with the crowds. So I had them on my side most of the time."

Above: Ann Haydon Jones, a former table tennis champion who grew up in Birmingham, England, advanced to the Wimbledon semifinals for the eighth time in her career in 1969. She beat Margaret Smith Court to reach the final, and then—with the crowd pulling mightily for her–she beat me. She never again played at Wimbledon, but she did not retire from tennis. She was destined to be an important part of the new era that would soon begin.

The couturier Ted Tinling enhanced Maria's star quality by dressing her in beautiful swirling dresses. Ted, who was a celebrity by this time, thanks in part to Gussy Moran's lace panties, did not hesitate to go out on a fashion limb for Maria, who was one of his most glamorous clients. The dress that created the greatest stir was unveiled during the 1962 Wimbledon championships. It was white except for the lining below the waste, which was shocking pink. "Every time I served, it would show," Maria said, laughing. "This caused a great deal of commotion."

Commotion? As I recall, the whole Centre Court crowd was shocked. The British gasped (or perhaps sighed) every time Maria's dress flew up, but I remember thinking the dress was wonderful. After that, color started catching on everywhere, though not at Wimbledon, which remained committed to the tradition of all-white clothing that had begun in the dawn of lawn tennis in the late nineteenth century. Maria's fashion splash passed like a meteor, and the next year Wimbledon officials ruled that players must dress predominantly in white. Years later, "predominantly white" reverted again to "all-white" clothing, described as "a great leveler" on Wimbledon's website in the 2020s. "If a player wants to get noticed," the website stated, "they must do so through their play."

The global success of women's tennis was punctuated in 1963 with the beginning of the Federation Cup team championships. At the time, our only major team competition was the Wightman Cup, which was restricted to a team of competitors from Britain vying against a team from the United States. Mrs. Wightman's dream of seeing a team championship for women from *many* nations was revived as early as the 1950s, when four women began lobbying vigorously to open up the Wightman Cup to all countries: Margaret duPont, a longtime cup captain, and three Australians: Thelma Coyne Long, the Australian champion in 1952 and 1954; Nell Hopman, a former touring player who was then a Victorian Tennis Association official; and Floris Conway, an administrator within the New South Wales Tennis Association. The Australians were especially eager to have an international team competition. At that time, they boasted five top women—Lesley Turner, Jan Lehane, Robin Ebbern, Mary Carter, and Margaret Smith. (I should point out that the men's international team championship—the Davis Cup—had expanded to include multiple nations in 1904!)

When England's Lawn Tennis Association steadfastly refused to open up the Wightman Cup competition, Australia's Thelma Long had a brainstorm. In 1960, she began urging Margaret duPont and two key USLTA officials, President Ed Turville and Committee Member Mary Hardwick Hare, to establish an international team championship entirely separate from the Wightman Cup.

Above: In 1963, Darlene Hard and I led the United States to a 2–1 victory over Australia in the inaugural Federation Cup team competition, which was held in London. In the decisive doubles match, Darlene and I fought off a match point against Lesley Turner and Margaret Smith before winning. Pictured here, from left, myself, Carole Caldwell, Darlene, and International Lawn Tennis Federation president George de Stefani.

THE EVENT'S NAME EVENTUALLY DREW CRITICISM FOR BEING OUTDATED AND DULL, AND IT WAS SHORTENED TO FED CUP IN 1995.

Once the USLTA embraced this concept—women's tennis was clearly on the rise internationally—enthusiasm for the women's team championship mounted.

Margaret duPont stepped forward and offered to donate a cup to be awarded to the winning team. She and Thelma Long were actually in the process of drawing up rules for the team championship to present to the ILTF when they were preempted by Mary Hardwick Hare, a British resident of the United States who had played for the British Wightman Cup team in the 1930s and toured as a professional with Alice Marble in 1941. Mary, armed with a report that demonstrated strong support for a women's international team competition, proposed the championship at an ILTF meeting in Paris in 1962. The ILTF passed the proposal without argument and announced that the first Federation Cup matches—it named the event after itself—would feature sixteen teams and be held in June 1963 in London, in conjunction with the ILTF's fiftieth anniversary. The event's name eventually drew criticism for being outdated and dull, and it was shortened to Fed Cup in 1995. It was rebranded as the Billie Jean King Cup in 2020. (I'll talk more about that in a later chapter!)

The United States and Australia dominated the early years of the Federation Cup, but as the number of nations participating increased and their players grew stronger, this hegemony was challenged—especially by the Czech Republic, Russia, and Spain. Today's Billie Jean King Cup—our world cup of women's tennis—features more than a hundred nations competing throughout the world for millions of dollars in prize money.

The year 1963 marked the arrival of Margaret Smith—later Margaret Smith Court—as one of giants of the game. Many of her records probably never will be touched. Between 1960 and 1975, despite two separate yearlong absences from the tour, she won sixty-two Grand Slam titles in singles, doubles, and mixed doubles, including twenty-four Grand Slam singles titles. It would be a generation before Serena Williams came within reach of that Grand Slam singles record.

Margaret, who won the Australian Championships eleven times at various venues, had two distinct advantages: she played her nation's championship year in and year out during a time when many players could not afford to travel to Australia, and the tournament was played on grass, a surface on which she had honed her aggressive, serve-and-volley game but which presented difficulties to others who grew up playing on hard courts. Even without all those Australian victories, her record would be remarkable. In 1970, she achieved one of her greatest ambitions. She became the second woman after Maureen Connolly to win the Grand Slam—all four major championships in a calendar year.

MARGARET SMITH COURT

Her first racket was a piece of wood

•

Margaret Smith, born in 1942, grew up in a small, modest house on the out-skirts of Albury, New South Wales, where her father worked as a foreman in a cheese- and butter-processing plant. Her first "racket" was a piece of wood she had found. A neighbor saw Margaret playing in the streets with her piece of wood and gave her an old racket. Judging from Margaret's descrip-tion, the racket must have predated the days of Helen Wills. The head was squared off at the bottom, and the thick wooden handle had no leather grip. Margaret soon began playing tennis, on the sly, at the Albury Tennis Club, a private club with twenty-five courts near her home. Eight-year-old Margaret would creep under the fence with her neighborhood friends (all boys) and play until they were spotted and told to leave. Finally, the club professional, Wal Rutter, softened his stance and began holding clinics for the children on weekends. Margaret won her first tournament before she was ten, still using her ancient racket. Like Maureen Connolly, Margaret was a natural left-hander who learned to play tennis with her right hand. "I think probably I would have had a better serve if I had played as a lefty," Margaret said. "It probably would have been more natural to me. But I don't regret it because at that time I didn't know any better. There were no women players in the world who were known as left-handed." Margaret quit school and left home when she was fifteen to train with Keith Rogers and Frank Sedgman, the former Australian champion, in Melbourne. She lived with the Sedgmans and earned money working at Frank's office. Robert Mitchell, a wealthy Melbourne busi-nessman, paid for her lessons. In 1960, at age seventeen, Margaret won her first Australian women's singles championship. In 1963, she fulfilled a lifetime dream by becoming the first Australian woman to win Wimbledon.

- 24 Grand Slam singles titles
    - 11 Australian (1960–1966, 1969–1971, 1973)
    - 5 French (1962, 1964, 1969, 1970, 1973)
    - 3 Wimbledon (1963, 1965, 1970)
    - 5 U.S. (1962, 1965, 1969, 1970, 1973)
- Won the Grand Slam, 1970
- 19 Grand Slam women's doubles titles
- 21 Grand Slam mixed doubles titles
- Year-end No. 1 in the world (1962–1965, 1969, 1970, 1973)
- Federation Cup: 20–0 in singles, 15–5 in doubles
- International Tennis Hall of Fame inductee, 1979

NOTEWORTHY STATISTICS

- 1,180 match victories and 192 singles titles, both records
- Won two calendar year Grand Slams in mixed doubles (1963, 1965)
- Won three Grand Slam titles in 1973 as a mother

HER FIRST "RACKET" WAS A PIECE OF WOOD SHE HAD FOUND.

The fitness regimen established by the Australian Lawn Tennis Association helped mold Margaret Smith Court into one of the greatest champions of all time.

Signing with George MacCall's National Tennis League in 1968 was a milestone moment that guaranteed us a steady income. From left, Ann Haydon Jones, Françoise Dürr, George MacCall, Rosie Casals, and me.

Margaret was the first in women's tennis to adopt a rigorous fitness regimen, although this was neither widely publicized nor adopted by other leading players. As a result, Margaret never received the recognition she deserved for a training initiative that was well ahead of its time. To add strength to her tall, scrawny figure, she worked out with Stan Nicholes, an Olympic trainer hired by Australia's Lawn Tennis Association. Margaret was truly fortunate to have that opportunity. She and the other Australian players enjoyed terrific support from their tennis association, which gave them everything they needed to be successful. Regarding her arduous training, Margaret said, "I loved it. I enjoyed that side of it more than the tennis. I always found it very easy, where for some people it was such hard work."

Despite her historic feats, Margaret never completely conquered her nerves. "She would not serve double-faults at 5–0, 40–love, but it was quite possible that she would at 5–all, deuce," said Ann Haydon Jones. Years later, Margaret said she felt pressure from the British press during her early years and admitted that she never did as well as she should have at Wimbledon. "I think insecurities come from your background and whether you were born a positive person. I think a lot of it has to do with your surroundings, how you're brought up in those areas to have confidence in yourself." She acknowledged that unlike the American athletes, "who were always tremendously confident," she was among the Australians who at that time "hadn't had that built within us."

Margaret faced a subtle form of prejudice that we did not appreciate at the time. The day after she won her Grand Slam in 1970, the *New York Times* wrote, in a column without a byline, "Green-eyed with frosted brown hair, Mrs. Court stands 5 foot 9 and weighs 145 pounds, a size that has aided her as a player but draws second glances from conservative spectators. She bristles at such references as the 'Amazing Amazon' or 'Big Maggi.'" The same article quoted her husband, Barry Court, who raved about her cooking.

Margaret's two main rivals were Maria Bueno and me. Margaret held herself apart and later said, "I couldn't let myself get close to too many people, particularly when I was playing at the top." She described her relationship

with Maria Bueno as a "long, bitter rivalry." As for Margaret and me, we were competing too hard for the same prizes to feel warmly toward each other. Margaret was only a year older than I was, but she had a big head start. She had won the Australian Championship five years in a row before I even saw Australia. She led the first part of our rivalry, 14–1; I led the second part, 12–8. For thirteen straight years, from 1962 through 1974, either Margaret or I finished the year ranked No. 1 in the world.

Both Margaret and I were fortunate to have early access to tennis courts, free coaching, and financial support. I learned the game from Clyde Walker, a kind man in his early sixties who was giving free tennis instruction at five different municipal parks in Long Beach, California. My mother drove me to whichever park Clyde was teaching at on any given day. The Long Beach Tennis Patrons paid most of my entry fees for junior tournaments, which were two or three dollars, but they were not able to help me much with travel expenses. I remember the time Perry Jones, who ran the Southern California Tennis Association, insisted that I travel with a chaperone to Middletown, Ohio, for a girls' national championship. Because I did not have enough money to fly with a chaperone, my mother and I rode the train and slept—sitting up—for three nights. After the tournament, the other girls boarded flights to Philadelphia for the next event, while my mother and I took the train back to California.

When I was sixteen, I also had a chance to work with one of the all-time greats—Alice Marble—who had generously offered to help me. Just listening to a champion like Alice helped me think like a champion. She was tough,

Above: Margaret Smith at Wimbledon in 1962. She won her first singles title there the following year. She remembered Centre Court as electrifying and explosive, "a battle of fitness and a battle of nerves."

Opposite page: Darlene Hard, left, offers an enthusiastic handshake to fellow American Dorothy Knode after winning their Wimbledon semifinal in 1957.

DARLENE HARD

Everyone's favorite doubles partner

•

The best American player in the early 1960s was Darlene Hard. She retired in 1964, four years before tennis opened its tournaments to professionals, with a total of eighteen Grand Slam titles in doubles, three in singles, and only $400 in her bank account. "But I didn't do it for money," Darlene said. "We toured for country and flag and to play better and to be No. 1 or whatever we were working for. I was the last of the amateurs. In our day, I won Forest Hills and I got my airfare from New York to Los Angeles. I won Wimbledon doubles championships seven times, and I got £10 each time, which was like $18. But we still went for the titles. We went for the glory. It kept us out there year after year. I was happy. I loved it. I loved tennis." Darlene won the U.S. singles championship twice and the French once, but doubles was where she shone. A superb volleyer and good-natured soul who made friends easily, she could team up with any partner and win. She proved it by winning major doubles titles with seven different women: Beverly Baker Fleitz, Althea Gibson, Shirley Bloomer, Maria Bueno, Jeanne Arth, Lesley Turner, and Françoise Dürr.

KAREN HANTZE AND BILLIE JEAN

In 1961, Karen Hantze and I became the youngest winners of the Ladies' Doubles at Wimbledon and the first unseeded pair to win that title in thirty years. I was seventeen-year-old Billie Jean Moffitt – or, as the press affectionately called me, "Little Miss Moffitt." Karen, of San Diego, was eighteen. It was our first Wimbledon. Karen and I won again in 1962, and Karen – now Karen Susman – stunned the field by winning the Ladies' Singles without dropping a set. Two years later, at the age of twenty-one, Karen left the international circuit for the traditional role of wife and mother. Karen has had a few nostalgic moments looking back on what she missed, but she knows she made the choice that was right for her.

demanding; she put me through challenging drills and taught me to play every point as if it were match point. She also sent my confidence soaring when—in a stunning and unexpected moment—she told me that my backhand volley was much better than hers. Although I had only three months of weekends with her, my national women's ranking rose from nineteenth in 1959 to fourth in 1960.

The turning point in my career came in late 1964. I was in my third year as a history major at Los Angeles State College, and I was engaged to Larry King, a prelaw student there. I still had my dream of being No. 1 in tennis, but I had yet to win a major singles title. I finally realized that I would never know whether I could make it unless I made a commitment to play full-time. I was able to make that commitment when Robert Mitchell, the same businessman who had helped Margaret Smith, offered to pay my way to Australia so that I could train under the great Australian coach Mervyn Rose. Over a period of four months, Merv made radical alterations in my game, changing my swooping wristy forehand and backhand into the crisp, efficient strokes of a champion. Two years later, in 1966, I won Wimbledon, my first of twelve Grand Slam singles titles.

In 1967, while Margaret Smith was taking a sabbatical from tennis and falling in love with yachtsman and wool broker Barry Court, I won Wimbledon and the U.S. Championships while playing with Wilson's revolutionary T-2000 racket, the forerunner of the sophisticated composite rackets in use today. Rosie Casals and I were the first women to bring the T-2000 to the public. The radically new racket, designed by former French star René Lacoste, featured a circular frame made of steel and was lighter and more maneuverable than the wooden rackets. It worked like a trampoline: if I hit a shot perfectly, the ball streaked over the net; if my timing was off, the ball flew into the fence. The racket had some flaws in it, to be sure, but it was the start of something new—the use of modern technology to generate unheard-of power.

There were no guards to separate players from the fans in the 1960s, so you could find yourself enveloped by well-wishers while walking from point A to point B. When that happened, I stopped to talk and visit with them. Here I am, at Wimbledon, graciously accepting a compliment while Carole Ann Loop, a college teammate who was also competing at Wimbledon, looks on with some amusement.

BILLIE JEAN KING

An ambitious early goal, achieved

•

I grew up in Long Beach, California, about three miles from the ocean. My father, Bill, worked for the Long Beach fire department, and my mother, Betty, was a homemaker. My younger brother, Randy Moffitt, was a natural athlete and became a major-league baseball pitcher. Randy and I both loved performing under pressure. As a child, I never dreamed that I would one day win twenty Wimbledon singles and doubles titles—a record I share with Martina Navratilova—or that I would help change the game of tennis, but I always knew I was going to do something special with my life. I loved signing out books from the library. At school, I never tired of pulling down the giant scrolled map of the world so that I could easily see all the countries. Even as a young girl, I knew I wanted to travel.

When I was about ten, a friend of mine, Susan Williams, invited me to play tennis at the Virginia Country Club. I had never played before. "You'll have to wear white," Susan told me, and of course I had nothing to wear. My mother, who had sewn all of my clothes from the time I was a baby, made me some white shorts, and Susan, who was the best player in Long Beach, lent me a racket. I had a great time, and I started saving up for a racket, plunking nickels and dimes into a mason jar. When I had accumulated eight dollars, I took the jar and went over to Brown's Sporting Goods on Atlantic Avenue, where I was shown a racket with a purple-and-white throat and a purple grip. "This is probably what you're looking for," the man said. It was fine with me. I was entranced from the moment I began hitting the ball with my new racket. By the end of my first session with Clyde Walker at Houghton Park, I knew what I was going to do with my life. When my mother picked me up, I told her I wanted to be No. 1 in the world.

- **12 Grand Slam singles titles**
  - **1 Australian (1968)**
  - **1 French (1972)**
  - **6 Wimbledon (1966–1968, 1972, 1973, 1975)**
  - **4 U.S. (1967, 1971, 1972, 1974)**
- **16 Grand Slam women's doubles titles**
- **11 Grand Slam mixed doubles titles**
- **Year-end No. 1 in the world (1966–1968, 1971, 1972, 1974)**
- **Federation Cup: 26–3 in singles, 26–1 in doubles, 7 team titles**
- **Wightman Cup: 14–2 in singles, 7–3 in doubles**
- **International Tennis Hall of Fame inductee, 1987**

NOTEWORTHY STATISTIC

- **20 Wimbledon titles (6 singles, 10 doubles, and 4 mixed doubles), a record shared with Martina Navratilova**

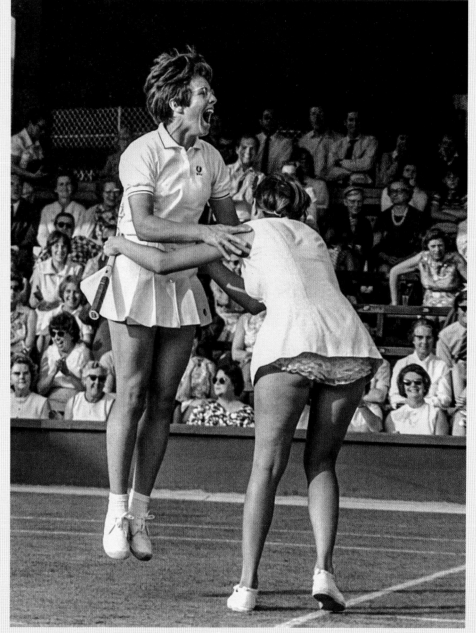

At left: I'm with Ann Haydon Jones before our 1969 Wimbledon final, which she won.

Below: Peaches Bartkowicz and I have just defeated Great Britain's Winnie Shaw and Virginia Wade in three sets in Wightman Cup competition at Wimbledon in 1970. Our strategy was an unconventional one. I covered the entire net, and Peaches, who hated playing the net, covered the entire baseline. It was a miracle that we won.

WHEN I WAS TEN YEARS OLD, I TOLD MY MOTHER I WANTED TO BE NO. 1 IN THE WORLD.

Above, left: I'm holding the stunning Daphne Akhurst trophy after winning the Australian women's singles title in 1968.

Above, right: Margaret Smith, after winning her first of eleven Australian titles eight years earlier, in 1960. She wrote in her memoir that her prize was an umbrella. She also appears to have been given two candlesticks to take home. Fast-forward to 2022, and the women's singles champion won more than $2 million.

I earned my personal record of under-the-table money in 1967—a whopping $7,000—but huge changes in our sport were imminent. The final blows to "shamateurism" were delivered when several of the leading male players, including Wimbledon champion John Newcombe, turned pro. Lamar Hunt of Dallas, an oil tycoon and sports entrepreneur who had founded the American Football League in 1959, had formed a professional tour, World Championship Tennis (WCT), for men.

In Britain, LTA officials, fearful that amateur tennis could soon become a sport without stars, decided to open Britain's tournaments to men and women professionals, whether the rest of the world was ready or not. At their general meeting on December 14, they officially abolished the distinction between professionals and amateurs by a nearly unanimous vote. Britain's tournaments would be open to all, beginning with the British Hard Court Championships at Bournemouth in April 1968. A few months later, representatives from forty-seven member federations of the ILTF voted unanimously to open tennis to professionals in twelve major tournaments in eight countries. Major tournaments throughout the world began offering legitimate prize money, and one had only to look at other professional sports, including golf, to realize that the prize money would escalate steadily.

For women tennis players, however, a new kind of struggle was beginning. When Wimbledon announced the prize money breakdown, every woman in the draw was destined to be a loser. While the men's champion was slated to earn £2,000, the women's winner—one Billie Jean King—would have to settle for £750. The men's total purse would be £14,800, the women's £5,680. The ratio was 2½ to 1.

During the first two years of the new professional era, confusion reigned. No one knew how many tournaments would be open to pros. The major international tournaments were going to offer prize money, but officials of many of the smaller tournaments were not sure what to do. Eventually, those who did not want to get into the business of professional tennis simply vanished from the calendar. The grass-court circuit in the eastern United States, with its traditional stops at the Merion Cricket Club in Haverford, Pennsylvania, and the Essex County Club in Manchester, Massachusetts, faded into oblivion.

I coped with the uncertainty by joining a traveling troupe of men and women players as a contract professional. I was hired by George MacCall's National Tennis League, a commercial organization that kept us playing week in and week out. Within the league, we played in established tournaments like Wimbledon and the U.S. Open, and we also staged tournaments of our own. The men in our troupe were Ken Rosewall, Roy Emerson, Fred Stolle, Pancho Gonzales, Rod Laver, and Andrés Gimeno. The other women were Ann Haydon Jones, my doubles partner Rose Casals, and Françoise (Frankie) Dürr of France, who in 1967 had become the last amateur to win the women's singles at Roland Garros. I was guaranteed $40,000 a year, Ann was guaranteed $25,000, and Rosie and Frankie were guaranteed $20,000 each. The men were paid more. I know that at least one of them made $70,000.

We had a difficult life, traveling during the day and playing at night. Fortunately, we were friends; we had dinner together every night, went dancing together, and always kept our sense of humor. We also sat around and philosophized about the future of the game.

Shamateurism had ended, but tennis was faced with an urgent new question: what were women worth? The rulers of tennis apparently were not impressed by the ballet of Maria Bueno, the athleticism of Margaret Smith Court, or the crowd-pleasing Wimbledon finals played by Britain's Angela Mortimer, Christine Truman, and Ann Haydon Jones. The precedent of grossly unequal prize money, established at the first Wimbledon open to professionals in 1968, had been accepted as gospel by the men who controlled the game. The women had accepted it, too, but they were not going to accept it for long.

CHAPTER SIX

BIRTH
OF A PRO
TOUR

1970

TO

1973

WOMEN tennis players made huge and _historic_ gains in the three years between 1970 and 1973. For the first time ever, we stood up and fought for _respect_ and decent pay. We knew that to accomplish what we wanted, we had to start a tour for women only. The idea of having our _own tour_ was a reflection of the times. The age of _rebellion_ and more liberal thinking that began in the 1960s reached a fever pitch in the early 1970s.

The issues of the previous decade—the Vietnam War, civil rights, women's rights, and environmental pollution—were more a part of our consciousness than ever. It was a heady time for women in general and for women tennis players in particular. We were being seen—and heard—as never before. As a 1972 cover of *Newsweek* magazine trumpeted, "Tennis: The Women Take Over."

The women's liberation movement made us keenly aware of the inequities in our sport, but not everyone on our tour saw herself as a feminist or a radical, even though our actions suggested otherwise. Gladys Heldman, the shrewd and well-connected editor and publisher of *World Tennis* magazine who helped found our tour, never claimed we were a part of the women's movement. We were walking a tightrope in those days, striving for equity without alienating people who thought that feminists were women who hated men. Gladys presented our quest in unthreatening language that stressed our role as entertainers. When people asked her about "women's lib"—the term was a political lightning rod for many—she would smile and say, "It's Women's Lob."

We were fighting for our own cause—for recognition and the right to control our destinies—not some greater principle of women's rights within society. Nor were we actually fighting for strict equality in tennis; those who said we did were not listening. Only at major tournaments like the U.S. Open, where men and women still competed together, did we demand equal pay. At smaller events on the tennis circuit we wanted wages that were fair, that reflected our value as entertainers, and that enabled women tennis players to compete without going broke.

A team of individuals made it happen: Gladys, of course; the powerful Joseph F. Cullman III, chief executive officer of Philip Morris, the tobacco company; the adventurous promoters who stood to lose money on an unproven product; and a small group of women tennis players—the Original 9—who were willing to risk everything in an effort to achieve greater status for women in their sport.

When the decade opened, new sponsors were coming into the game, and prize money was rising. Tournaments, promotors, and male tennis players were making more money than ever. But women were not. In fact, the disparity in prize money was widening at an alarming rate. Ratios of 5 to 1 had been common at your average tournament in 1969; by 1970 they were growing even wider.

The women were being squeezed financially because they had no control in a male-dominated sport. Men owned, ran, and promoted the tournaments. And because many of them were former players themselves, their sympathies lay with

Margaret Court was dominating at the net. Her reach was so expansive that I called her "The Arm." She is shown here competing in a Virginia Slims tournament at the International Amphitheatre in Chicago in 1977, shortly before her retirement. In 1991, she became an ordained minister and founded Margaret Court Ministries.

the male players, who argued that most of the money—if not all of it—should be theirs. The male players said we deserved less for several reasons. First, because they assumed that few people came to watch us play. "They sincerely believed that if you put on a tournament with men and women playing in it, the people came primarily to see the men," said Bob Kelleher, the USLTA's president in 1967 and 1968. "And the only way to get the men to enter was to give them most of the prize money."

The men further maintained that because they could beat us, they deserved far greater pay. This argument completely ignored the fact that we were skilled competitors who provided great entertainment. As Bud Collins, the longtime tennis writer for the *Boston Globe* and commentator for the NBC television network, observed, "I know women don't run as fast or hit as hard, but it's the drama that you're looking for."

Finally—and it's an argument you still hear today—they said that men played best-of-five sets in the Australian, French, Wimbledon, and U.S. Championships, while women played only best-of-three. In truth, the women have always been willing to play best-of-five at the major tournaments. In 1984, the women's tour adopted a best-of-five format for the singles final at its season-ending championships. That format was in place for sixteen years and then abandoned; it added length to the matches, but not always drama.

If we women were seemingly powerless in the first years of professional tennis, we were blessed with an important ally in Gladys Heldman, a forward-thinking, fiercely determined woman who had always believed that women could work and have careers if they wanted them. Gladys, originally from New York City, was an intellectual who earned her bachelor's degree and Phi Beta Kappa key from Stanford University in only three years.

Gladys became interested in tennis after marrying Julius Heldman, a scientist and superb tennis player who captained the UCLA men's tennis team and later worked on the Manhattan Project (which developed the atomic bomb) during World War II. Gladys began playing tennis after her second child was born and became proficient enough to earn the No. 1 ranking in Texas in the early 1950s and a berth in the Wimbledon draw in 1954. Her Wimbledon debut ended in a first-round defeat on a back court, 6–0, 6–0. "It's all right; I still love you," Julius shouted, as Gladys wept. "Only not as much."

Gladys's real achievements, including her founding of *World Tennis* magazine in 1953, came off the court. The magazine, which she molded into "the international literary voice of tennis," in the words of Bud Collins, served as a bullhorn for change. Every month, Gladys and her staff blasted the governing officials of tennis for their archaic and self-serving rules. Gladys advocated opening tennis to professionals for many years before

THE MEN FURTHER MAINTAINED THAT BECAUSE THEY COULD BEAT US, THEY DESERVED FAR GREATER PAY.

Rosie Casals won twelve Grand Slam doubles titles and was the story of "almost" in singles. She made four Wimbledon singles semifinals, two U.S. finals, and two U.S. semifinals.

it happened. Then she focused on documenting the unbalanced prize money ratios between women and men at important tournaments.

As discrimination mounted against women tennis players in 1970, Margaret Court was going about the business of winning all four majors in a calendar year—the Grand Slam. She began her quest by winning the Australian Open on the grass courts of White City Stadium in Sydney with the loss of only twelve games. On the clay courts at Stade Roland Garros, home of the French Open, she twice came within a game of losing to Olga Morozova, a twenty-one-year-old Russian, in the second round. But she persevered and went on to defeat Helga Niessen Masthoff of Germany in straight sets in the final. At Wimbledon, the third leg of the Slam, Margaret sprained her left ankle in the quarterfinals. She withdrew from the doubles events and required pain injections before her semifinal match and again before playing the final against me.

Margaret later said the match was one of the best she ever played at Wimbledon. My recollection is that neither of us was in top form. By the end, Margaret's pain injection had worn off, and I was playing with an injured knee that caused my leg to cramp. Toward the end of the match,

I could no longer follow my serve into the net because of the cramp. Finally, after two hours and twenty-seven minutes, Margaret prevailed, 14–12, 11–9. I underwent knee surgery three days later. Rex Bellamy, writing in the *Times* of London, said it would be remembered as "one of the greatest women's matches played anywhere."

I was not at the U.S. Open later that year to challenge Margaret, as I was recovering from knee surgery. Margaret, still nursing her ankle, was fierce, focused, and determined to end points as quickly as possible. She dispatched Nancy Richey in the semifinal, 6–1, 6–3, and then beat twenty-one-year-old Rosie Casals in the final, 6–2, 2–6, 6–1, to become only the second woman ever to win the Grand Slam.

Margaret's $7,500 paycheck for winning the 1970 U.S. Open was the largest ever paid to a woman tennis player until that time, though far short of the $20,000 and new Ford Pinto that the men's winner, Ken Rosewall, received. In fact, Margaret earned only about $15,000 in prize money for winning all four majors in 1970. Counting the prize money in all the other tournaments she played, she earned only some $50,000 for the year. She was vastly underpaid—as were all of the women pros—and some of us decided to revolt.

ROSIE CASALS

Standing tall in talent and tenacity

•

Rosemary "Rosie" Casals was an exciting, gifted athlete and the best player of her era not to win a major singles title. She ranked in the top ten in the world from 1966 through 1977 and reached a career high of No. 3 in 1970. Only 5 foot 2¼, Rosie was quick, acrobatic, and creative in her shot selection. Her catlike reflexes at the net made her a sensational doubles partner. She won twelve Grand Slam doubles titles, nine in women's (seven of them with me), and three in mixed. In Federation Cup play, Rosie had an outstanding 26–1 record in doubles. (She and I won all eleven of our Federation Cup doubles matches.) Rosie was born in San Francisco to parents who had immigrated from El Salvador, but she was raised by her great-uncle and great-aunt, Manuel and Maria Casals. She learned to play tennis on the public courts at Golden Gate Park. "Everything came easily to me," Rosie said. "I was a good athlete; I moved quickly. Tennis was not work because I had a lot of talent."

TITLE IX OPENS A LONG-CLOSED DOOR

At the grassroots level, opportunities increased exponentially for American girls, first with individual lawsuits and then with the sweeping mandate of Title IX of the 1972 Federal Education Amendments. In the spring of 1972, U.S. District Court Judge Damon Keith, an iconic champion of civil rights, promptly ruled that Cynthia Morris and her doubles partner, Emily Barrett, of Ann Arbor, Michigan, could play on the boys' tennis team at their high school, which had no tennis team for girls. And in a federal court in New Jersey, Ruth Bader Ginsburg, a future Supreme Court Justice who was then a Rutgers University law professor and volunteer with the American Civil Liberties Union, helped Abbe Seldin of Teaneck, New Jersey, earn the right to try out for her high school's boys' team. Ginsburg argued that, in a sport like tennis, gender is "as irrelevant a factor as is race, religion, national origin, political beliefs, or hair color." The district court judge in this case – Judge Leonard Garth – took a different approach from Judge Keith in Michigan: he offered to oversee challenge matches between Abbe and the top boys on the high school team and even suggested he would play Abbe himself! That battle of the sexes never went to trial, as the case was settled out of court in Abbe's favor. Title IX became law on June 23, 1972. In November 1973, my testimony before a U.S. Senate subcommittee helped secure support for an adjunct to Title IX – the Women's Education Equity Act – which created a funding mechanism that ensured that thousands of girls would have teams to play on and scholarships to win.

The catalyst was news that Jack Kramer, promoter of the Pacific Southwest Championships in Los Angeles, which came a few weeks after the U.S. Open, was offering prize money slanted in favor of the men by nearly 7 to 1. The men's purse would be $51,500, the women's only $7,500.

Then Gladys had a brainstorm. If the women were not going to be treated decently at Kramer's tournament, they would have their own tournament. Gladys picked Houston as the site because she and her family were about to move there. She also knew people within the state and local tennis circles who would support us, including Delores Hornberger, who was president of the Women's Association at the Houston Racquet Club, and Jim Hight, who was president-elect of the Texas Lawn Tennis Association. Within days a tournament for eight women was arranged. Prize money would be supported by ticket sales to members of the women's groups associated with tennis in Houston.

When Gladys told Jack Kramer that eight women would compete in Houston from September 23 to 26, 1970, the same week as the Pacific Southwest, the male establishment began fighting back. Stan Malless, chairman of the USLTA's Sanction and Schedule Committee, said the USLTA could not sanction the Houston prize money tournament because it conflicted with another USLTA prize money event, the Pacific Southwest. And the USLTA warned the players that we could be reprimanded or even suspended if we played for prize money at a USLTA-member club whose tournament the USLTA had not sanctioned. The risks were these: We players could lose our rankings, our ability to compete in USLTA tournaments, and the chance to play on the Wightman Cup or Federation Cup teams. The Houston Racquet Club could lose its ability to hold future USLTA tournaments.

But while the USLTA was trying to intimidate us, we were piloting a ship that could not be turned around. Bleachers had been ordered, tickets were being sold, and

Françoise "Frankie" Dürr won the French Championship at Roland Garros in 1967 and won eleven Grand Slam doubles titles (seven women's, four mixed) between 1967 and 1976. She was inducted into the International Tennis Hall of Fame in 2003.

Delores Hornberger and Jim Hight—I praise their courage to this day—were holding firm, determined to hold the tournament. Equally important, Gladys was working on another coup. She was negotiating with her friend Joe Cullman, the CEO of Philip Morris.

Joe was already deeply involved in tennis, as both a player and a sponsor. He had served as chairman of the U.S. Open in 1969 and 1970, and under his direction, Marlboro, a Philip Morris product, had become the Open's first sponsor. Joe also was known as a champion of women and minorities. He was an early activist in the National Urban League, and in 1970 he thought "the women's liberation movement was long overdue."

In Gladys's request, Joe Cullman saw the possibility of merging a cause he believed in with a successful business venture. He viewed the renegade tournament as a perfect vehicle for marketing Virginia Slims, a new cigarette designed primarily for women and identified with the slogan "You've Come a Long Way, Baby." He gave Gladys the use of the Virginia Slims name, and his company contributed $2,500. The $7,500 tournament would be named the Virginia Slims Invitational. We would attempt to sidestep the risks to ourselves and the Houston Racquet Club by signing one-week contracts with Gladys. Past precedent suggested—but did not guarantee—that as contract professionals, the players (as well as the club and the tournament) would be operating outside the USLTA's purview.

Twenty-four hours before the historic event, the contestants arrived. Joining me were Rosie Casals, Valerie Ziegenfuss, Judy Tegart Dalton, Nancy Richey, Jane "Peaches" Bartkowicz, Kerry Melville, and Kristy Pigeon. Julie Heldman, Gladys's daughter, attended but could not compete because of an injury. We called ourselves the "Original 9." I will never forget any of them:

- **ROSIE,** a showstopping shotmaker, was one of the best doubles players in the world and ranked as high as No. 3 in singles in 1970.

- **VALERIE,** a Californian, was ranked in America's top ten on four different occasions.

- **JUDY,** an Australian, ultimately won seven Grand Slam doubles titles and ranked in the world's top ten three times while working six months each year as an accountant.

- **KERRY,** another Australian and world top-tenner, had won the 1968 Australian doubles with Karen Krantzcke; she would go on to win the Australian Open singles in 1977 and the Wimbledon doubles with Wendy Turnbull in 1978.

- **PEACHES,** a native of Hamtramck, Michigan, had never lost a match as a junior tennis player in her age group and had won the national girls' eighteen-and-under title three straight times, equaling Sarah Palfrey's record.

- **NANCY** had won the Australian singles championship in 1967 and the French Open singles in 1968; she ranked among the world's top five from 1966 through 1970.

- **KRISTY,** the national U.S. junior champion in 1968, was ranked among the top ten women in the United States from 1968 through 1970.

- **JULIE** was ranked No. 5 in the world in 1969 and would equal that ranking once again in 1974.

Less than an hour before our tournament's first match, the players voted unanimously to compete in the Virginia Slims Invitational, in defiance of the USLTA. We then took turns signing a one-sentence agreement to become contract professionals with Gladys's *World Tennis* magazine for $1.

I immediately headed to the club's pay phone and called USLTA President Alastair Martin. By now, we were just minutes from the start of our tournament, but I wanted to give him one last chance. He wanted us to play for the USLTA and for the love of the game and offered no assurances that the prize money distribution would be more balanced in the future. Furthermore, the USLTA had scheduled only two women's tournaments over the next six months. That was nowhere near enough. We needed a tour, and he was not going to do that. We were at an impasse. I told him, "We do not want to do this, but you have given us no choice."

My heart pounding, I hung up the phone and raced over to join the other women. We knew we were gambling. We had no proof that we would be able to establish a series of tournaments beyond the initial tournament in Houston. We faced humiliation if we failed. Several of the men players said we were fools and would never succeed. Our timing, however, turned out to be excellent. Society was ready for us, as was the press. As we held up our dollar bills for the *Houston Post* photographer, Béla Ugrin, we marked the beginning of women's professional tennis as we know it today. Any woman who has earned a paycheck on the professional tour can trace her good fortune to this moment.

In retrospect, the USLTA's threat of suspension proved to be more bark than bite. Alastair Martin neither suspended nor disciplined us. We were simply no longer under their jurisdiction. The USLTA awarded six of the top year-end ranking positions for 1970 to members of the Original 9, with myself, Rosie Casals, and Nancy Richey assuming the top three spots. Members of the Original 9 continued to play for the U.S. Wightman Cup and Federation Cup teams. The USLTA fined the Houston Racquet Club $250 for holding an unsanctioned tournament, then sanctioned our event retroactively in February 1971 and even included it in the 1971 USLTA yearbook.

During the Houston tournament, we held a meeting and talked honestly about money. I told everyone that if we were going to make a tour work, we had to find out how much money we needed to survive. That meant we all had to admit how much money we made under the table, because if we had our own tour, we would be playing for prize money supplied by sponsors and gate receipts, not secret guarantees. Although I was one of the few who benefited from the secret-guarantee system, I thought it was grossly unfair. A star with a guarantee could lose in the first round and still make more money than the woman who won the tournament.

I told how much I made under the table—$1,500 to $2,000 during a tournament week. Nancy Richey said what she made. Val Ziegenfuss said she was lucky if she got enough to pay her expenses. After adding up the secret guarantees plus expenses incurred by women who earned no guarantees, we figured that a total purse of $10,000 would be enough to support a tournament of sixteen women, and we established that as the minimum standard for our tournaments of the future. For tournaments with a thirty-two draw, $18,000 would be the minimum. In every case we wanted to make sure that first-round losers earned enough to cover their expenses.

The winner of the 1970 Virginia Slims Invitational was Rosie Casals, who defeated Judy Tegart Dalton to win the $1,600 first prize. But in another sense, we had all won that week. Women's tennis would never be the same. We were committed to having a circuit of our own within a few months, by January 1971, and we wanted Gladys to run it. She had money and power, and she had Joe Cullman, whose $2,500 contribution to the tournament was probably the best advertising investment his company had ever made. Gladys repeatedly said she was too busy to run a new tour. To get her to change her mind, we crafted a sly plan that tapped into her eccentricity and ego. We had her daughter, Julie, let her know that two men, my husband,

Above, left: Australian Kerry Melville (later Kerry Melville Reid) could beat anyone on her best days. She won twenty-seven singles tournaments during her career, including the 1977 Australian Open.

Above, right: Australian Judy Tegart Dalton reached the Wimbledon singles final in 1968. In doubles, she won seven Grand Slam titles.

Opposite page:
Virginia Slims hired
Ted Tinling to help
keep players on the
women's tour in style.
Here we are with Ted
in 1973. From left,
Virginia Wade, Evonne
Goolagong, Rosie
Casals, and me.

Larry, whom I had married in 1965, and Dennis Van der Meer, the prominent tennis coach, had agreed to run the women's tour. Informed of that alternative, Gladys capitulated. From then on, progress came quickly. Virginia Slims agreed to pay $40,000 to sponsor eight sixteen-women tournaments. The tour was born.

The number of women under contract to Gladys Heldman quickly grew beyond the Original 9. Ann Haydon Jones of England and Françoise Dürr of France became two of our biggest stars. Another mainstay was Betty Stöve of the Netherlands.

Margaret Court and Great Britain's Virginia Wade did not sign with Gladys. They played in some of our events during the first few years, but they were never a part of our effort to build up the women's game. While we played mostly in the United States, they split their time between tours overseen by the national associations in the United States, Europe, Australia, and South Africa. They were fearful of breaking away from the national governing bodies of their sport. They didn't want to take the risk.

By 1971, Virginia Slims had broadened and extended its sponsorship, giving us a $309,000 tour with nineteen tournaments. Other sponsors also helped: British Motor Cars, Kmart, and Ford Motor Company were among the first to come forward. Bio-Strath sponsored the London Hard Court Open in Hurlingham, England, our first tournament outside the United States. Gladys herself was a sponsor, adding funds to tournaments when sponsorships fell short, working without compensation, and providing us with free advertising in her magazine.

Virginia Slims spent thousands of additional dollars polishing the tour's image. They purchased scoreboards, produced a program, and even dressed us. In 1972, Joe Cullman hired designer Ted Tinling, who supplied us with all the clothes we needed for several years. (In those days, manufacturers provided us with free outfits that displayed their logo but did not pay us to wear them.) Ted took the time and effort to design clothes that matched the taste and personality of each player. He made us look good.

Val Ziegenfuss recalled in 1987 that she still had about 100 of Tinling's dresses hanging in her closet. "Those dresses are special," she said. "I have a dress in which the whole skirt is white sequins. Talk about heavy! But when it picked up the light, it was like the color of the rainbow. I also have a beautiful halter dress. The top was black velvet, and the skirt was silver lamé. Can you imagine sweating and playing tennis in velvet? But we were putting on a show. We were trying to put people in the stands."

Pam Teeguarden, another tour regular, reminisced about her self-described "Star Wars dress." It was made of silver lamé and had a silver belt around the waist. "When I took off my sweater," she said, "I'd get standing ovations."

A primary goal of the Original 9 was for woman athletes to be appreciated for their accomplishments, not just their looks. But that goal didn't change the

fact that we were entertainers. We understood that we were in the entertainment business. Fashion didn't make us less credible. You can be both a feminist and a fan of entertainment and fashion.

We celebrated our first birthday in 1971 with the $40,000 Virginia Slims International at the glamorous Hofheinz Pavilion at the University of Houston. I came away with the $10,000 first prize, the largest ever awarded to a woman tennis player up until that time. Our advance ticket sales of $25,000 set another record for women.

We were winning, but we still had many battles ahead. Two new superstars had emerged—Evonne Goolagong and Chrissie Evert—and they did not join our tour. Evonne was nineteen years old, Chrissie seventeen. Their careers were guided by the adults around them.

Evonne Fay Goolagong, of New South Wales, Australia, was graceful and effortless, in the manner of Maria Bueno and Suzanne Lenglen. She seemed to float rather than run over the court. Her backhand was sensational. She could hit it flat, with slice, or with topspin. She could do anything with it. Her only weaknesses were her second serve and her concentration. She could be vulnerable if she grew bored. "My success," she wrote in her memoir, *Evonne! On the Move,* "seems to depend on the skill of my opponent, and I like it when she makes me run because that keeps my interest up. For me the most fun is catching up with and hitting a ball that looks impossible to reach. If there's not enough prodding from my opponent, if she's not challenging, the Goolagong fog descends and I vanish in a haze of inattention."

Above: Winning never consumed Evonne Goolagong, shown here during the 1972 French Open. She played tennis as though simply being on the court was the greatest joy in the world.

EVONNE GOOLAGONG

Inner strength behind the outward calm

●

Evonne Goolagong grew up in the Australian outback, in the tiny town of Barellan, a wheat-farming community with nine hundred residents in New South Wales. Evonne lived with her parents and siblings in a rundown tin shack on the edge of town. Her father was a sheep shearer. Evonne's first baby toys included some old tennis balls her father found in a used Chevrolet he had bought. Later, her father borrowed a racket belonging to his employer's wife, and Evonne was soon playing on the clay courts at the War Memorial Tennis Club next door to her home. She became part of a junior program run by Bill Kurtzman, who thought Evonne was one of the best tennis prospects he had ever seen. He telephoned Vic Edwards, a renowned teaching professional from Sydney, and Edwards came to see her play. Evonne was only nine. At age thirteen, she moved to Sydney to train full-time with Edwards, who became her legal guardian. Evonne's ability to leave her family and cope with the attention focused on her race—some in the media called her "Aborigine Yvonne"—were the first examples of the reservoir of strength and self-assurance that lay hidden behind her calm exterior. "I got very homesick and cried every night," Evonne remembered. "But I never told anyone. I knew that if I told somebody that I was homesick, I'd be back in Barellan. If I was able to handle that, I must have been tough in other ways, too." Evonne had already accepted tennis stardom as her destiny. "It was drummed into my head that one day I would go to Sydney," she explained. "Then when I went to Sydney, it was drummed into my head that one day I would go overseas and play. It was something I knew from a very early age."

- **7 Grand Slam singles titles**
    - **1 French Open (1971)**
    - **2 Wimbledon (1971, 1980)**
    - **4 Australian Open (1974–1977)**
- **6 Grand Slam women's doubles titles**
- **2 WTA Finals titles (1974, 1976)**
- **Federation Cup: 22–3 in singles, 13–2 in doubles**
- **International Tennis Hall of Fame inductee, 1988**

Evonne's coach, Vic Edwards, called her lapses "walkabouts," borrowing a word for the nomadic lifestyles of Evonne's indigenous ancestors. Evonne once mentioned the word "walkabout" in a press conference. "I'm sorry I did," she said later. "I was getting tired of interviews and people asking, 'And *why* did you lose your concentration at this stage?' and I said, 'I just went walkabout.' Everybody laughed." It might have been funny at the time, but it became a label that Evonne could never shake.

In 1971, Evonne became the first woman since Althea Gibson to win at Roland Garros on her first try. She then won at Wimbledon, beating me in the semifinals and Margaret Court in the final. Walter Bingham, writing for *Sports Illustrated,* said that while playing Margaret, Evonne "gave a vivid demonstration of how wide and how long a tennis court can be" with her explosive passing shots, which traveled "an inch over the net and maybe an inch inside the line."

Evonne Goolagong returned home to Sydney to a ticker-tape parade. "It was a big thrill for everyone, but at the time I did not appreciate it as much as I really should have," she said later. "I didn't realize how important winning Wimbledon was. I was just having a good time; I had nothing to lose against these players. I was ready to go for everything, and everything seemed to come off."

It would be nine long years before Evonne won Wimbledon again. By then, more popular than ever, she was Evonne Goolagong Cawley and the mother of a three-year-old daughter, Kelly. She was the first mother to win Wimbledon since Dorothea Lambert Chambers in 1914.

Two months after Evonne Goolagong first won at Wimbledon in 1971, an even bigger star surfaced in women's tennis: Chrissie Evert, a precocious sixteen-year-old from Fort Lauderdale, Florida. (She is Chris Evert in the record books but prefers Chrissie, the name I am using here.) Winning meant everything to Chrissie, the most competitive person I have known and one of the toughest competitors ever. She was likened to Helen Wills Moody because of her steely, unsmiling expression on the court. And like Helen and Maureen Connolly, Chrissie had the ability to concentrate at all times.

Her unwavering focus, combined with her great, natural coordination and her father's marvelous training, made Chrissie Evert one of the giants of the game. She was the ultimate professional, always a model sportswoman. She rarely questioned a call, and she never did anything that interfered with her opponent's ability to concentrate or perform. Crowds admired her all-American looks, and she cultivated her image as America's sweetheart, right down to her hair ribbons and brightly polished fingernails.

Chrissie was a 5-foot-3, ninety-eight-pound high school sophomore in 1970 when she routed Françoise Dürr, who was ranked No. 4 in the world, in a small tournament in Charlotte, North Carolina. She then upended Margaret Court, who had just won the Grand Slam a few weeks before. Chrissie's name was incorrectly spelled "Everet" on the scoreboard, but within a couple of hours, everyone in Charlotte knew her name. Chrissie, who beat Margaret in two

Opposite page, top: Evonne was feted with a parade in Sydney, Australia, after winning her first Wimbledon in 1971.

Opposite page, bottom: Seven years later, she reminded the world that women could be champion tennis players and mothers, too. Here she is, with her daughter, Kelly, after beating Tracy Austin to win the Maureen Connolly Brinker International in Dallas in 1978.

tie-break sets, has called that victory the most exciting of her life. "I was there alone, and I rushed to the phone and called my dad," she recalled. "He couldn't believe it. It's unbelievable for a fifteen-year-old to beat the No. 1 player in the world."

Chrissie lost to Nancy Richey in the final, but she had helped women's tennis make an impression. The two women received a standing ovation from the 3,500 spectators after the match. The *Charlotte Observer* noted, "A bigger crowd turned out Sunday to see Chrissie than watched the [men's] Davis Cup match between the United States and Ecuador in the Charlotte Coliseum two years ago."

In August 1971, having won both of her matches as the youngest woman ever to play for the American Wightman Cup team against Great Britain, Chrissie was ready for Forest Hills. And Forest Hills, in turn, was ready for her. In 1971, the U.S. Open was desperately in need of a star. Three of the top men who were contract professionals under Lamar Hunt—Rod Laver, defending champion Ken Rosewall, and Roy Emerson—bypassed the tournament in order to rest up for one of Hunt's more lucrative events, and defending champion John Newcombe lost in the first round. Missing among the women were Margaret Court, who was pregnant; Evonne Goolagong, who had stayed home in Sydney; and Virginia Wade, who was injured. Tournament chairman Bill Talbert, sensing that Chrissie Evert was among the most appealing in the draw, scheduled her first-round match for the stadium court. "Tennis is show business, and you have to create excitement," he said years later. "Chrissie *was* excitement. She was cute and attractive and everything you wanted a tennis player to be."

Chrissie said she was petrified at the thought of walking out onto the stadium court in front of fourteen thousand people. Once she started winning, however, she loved it. Her second-round match against Mary Ann Eisel, a good grass-court player who had been ranked as high as eighth in the world, launched Chrissie toward stardom. Mary Ann won the first set, 6–4, and served for the match at 6–5, 40–love. Chrissie saved the first two match points by lashing out with the boldness and spontaneity of a champion, hitting two clean winners off Mary Ann's serve. Mary Ann, shaken, then double-faulted to bring the score to deuce. Mary Ann had three more match points in that game but won none of them. Chrissie went on to win the set, the match, and the hearts of America.

"Miss Evert left the court to a roaring ovation," wrote Herbert Warren Wind, the distinguished tennis writer for the *New Yorker* magazine. "She had captured

CHRISSIE SAID SHE WAS PETRIFIED AT THE THOUGHT OF WALKING OUT ONTO THE STADIUM COURT IN FRONT OF FOURTEEN THOUSAND PEOPLE.

Sixteen-year-old Chrissie Evert enchanted tennis fans throughout the world during her extraordinary run to the semifinals of the 1971 U.S. Open.

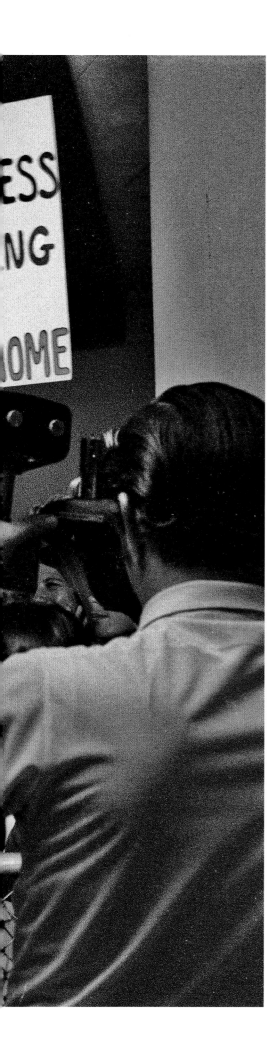

the imagination of the spectators—and the millions watching over national television—as no other young American player had in years. From that moment on, she was the tournament. I cannot remember attending a major tennis event where there was so little conversation about the men players."

After the match, the press asked Chrissie what she was thinking when she faced triple match point. "I was trying to decide how I should walk off the court," she answered. "Would I smile at the crowd or would I look dignified and serious? But each time Mary Ann served I seemed to see the ball bigger and bigger. I decided to hit for certain spots on her side to make winners, and they just went in each time." Chrissie kept winning, and her victories brought her to the semifinals, where she met me.

I knew I had to beat Chrissie for the sake of our fledgling tour. Chrissie was still an amateur, and if she beat me, the Slims' top player, people would think the amateurs were better than the pros. The crowd of 13,647 nearly filled the stadium, most of them pulling for Chrissie and another upset. But I was primed, and I beat her soundly, 6–3, 6–2. I then beat Rosie Casals in the final to win my second U.S. singles title.

At the end of 1970, I had told Larry that I wanted to win $100,000 in 1971. I was daydreaming, but I also thought we could spark more interest in the women's pro tour and attract more spectators if we had a $100,000 winner. Because everyone understands money. I thought, If I play as many tournaments as possible and play well, I could do it.

And I did. I finished 1971 by becoming the first woman athlete in any sport to win $100,000 in prize money in a single year. After I passed the historic mark with a victory over Rosie Casals in the Virginia Slims Thunderbird in Phoenix, the fans cheered for ten minutes. Rosie and I doused each other with champagne, in the tradition of World Series champions. I actually finished 1971 with $117,000 in total prize money earnings! It sounds like nothing today, but it was huge at the time. For context, it was more than Major League Baseball stars Willie McCovey, Brooks Robinson, and Johnny Bench made that year!

In 1972, the USLTA announced that it would stage its own women's tour, starring Evonne and Chrissie. A longtime USLTA official, Edy McGoldrick, was named to administer it. At the same time, the USLTA renewed its threats of suspension for anyone who played on our tour. By then, however, the USLTA could not hope to control us on its terms. We had come too far, and our backing from our sponsors was too strong. The Original 9 had grown to sixty, and our

CHRISSIE EVERT

A "controversial" backhand weapon arrives

•

Christine Marie Evert, born in 1954, was five years old when her father, Jimmy Evert, put a racket in her hands at Holiday Park, the Fort Lauderdale, Florida, tennis club where he worked as a teaching professional. Chrissie was too small and weak to hit her backhand with one hand, so Jimmy Evert taught her to hit it with two. In later years, he tried to transition Chrissie to a one-handed stroke. He'd hit with her for half an hour, all one-handed, and then he'd see her the next day hitting with both hands. "It was a controversial stroke at the time," Jimmy Evert recalled, "and some people said Chris would never be a good player with the two-handed backhand." History proved otherwise. Chrissie's two-hander became a weapon that toppled champions. With her hands close together on the handle of the racket, Chrissie could hit the ball well out in front of her body, with both arms extended for maximum power. She could hit the ball flat, with topspin, or with slice. Because a last-minute flick of her wrists was all she needed to direct the ball, her opponents never knew where she was going to hit it. Simultaneously, Jimmy Connors was developing his own two-handed backhand, which made him a champion on the men's tour. Chrissie and Jimmy, who both won Wimbledon singles titles in 1974, ushered in a new era. Young players copied the two-handed stroke, and the teaching pros started teaching it. Adopted by thousands of tennis players, it changed the game forever.

- **18 Grand Slam singles titles**
  - **7 French Open, a record (1974, 1975, 1979, 1980, 1983, 1985, 1986)**
  - **3 Wimbledon (1974, 1976, 1981)**
  - **6 U.S. Open (1975–1978, 1980, 1982)**
  - **2 Australian Open (1982, 1984)**
- **3 Grand Slam women's doubles titles**
- **4 WTA Finals titles (1972, 1973, 1975, 1977)**
- **Federation Cup: 40–2 in singles, 17–2 in doubles; 29-match winning streak, a record**
- **Wightman Cup: 26–0 in singles, 8–4 in doubles**
- **Year-end No. 1 in the world (1975–1977, 1980, 1981)**
- **International Tennis Hall of Fame inductee, 1995**

NOTEWORTHY STATISTICS

- **Won 125 straight matches on clay, the longest winning streak on any single surface**
- **Reached at least the semifinals of a record 34 straight Grand Slam tournaments (1971 U.S. Open through 1983 Wimbledon)**

SHE COULD HIT THE BALL FLAT, WITH TOPSPIN, OR WITH SLICE.

Chrissie Evert and I share a special moment during our rain-interrupted final at Wimbledon in 1973. I won the match, but Chrissie was only a year away from her first Wimbledon singles title.

prize money had swelled to $660,000. The USLTA never suspended us, but they did make life difficult in subtle ways. Peachy Kellmeyer, who worked for Gladys, recalled that the USLTA would not allow its officials to officiate at our tournaments. "One week, we didn't have enough lines people, and when a guy came in to install the Xerox machine, they put him on a line," Peachy recalled. "He had never seen a tennis match. He had never played tennis." More painful was the USLTA's "Evonne and Chrissie show," which deprived our tour of additional star power and fans.

When the women professionals arrived at Forest Hills for the 1972 U.S. Open, we were in the midst of yet another battle. Although a woman—Chrissie Evert—had saved the Open a year earlier, the prize money ratio in 1972 still favored the men by more than 2 to 1. We decided to put Bill Talbert, the tournament chairman, on notice. I met several times with him, and after winning the tournament and accepting my $10,000 prize—which was $15,000 less than what Ilie Năstase earned for winning the men's title—I gave an ultimatum in an interview with the press: "If it isn't equal next year, I won't play, and I don't think the other women will, either."

The year 1973 was a momentous one for every woman in tennis. Serious efforts to unite the two women's tours into a single prize money circuit led to an initial agreement in the spring and, ultimately, a genuine truce in June. The announcement was made by John Granville, head of the Virginia Slims division at Philip Morris, and Edy McGoldrick, director of Women's Professional Tennis for the USLTA. Following the 1973 U.S. Open in September, both tours would merge, with Virginia Slims remaining as the major sponsor of women's tennis.

The sacrificial lamb, if she could ever be thought of as a lamb, was Gladys. The tennis establishment did not want her running the women's tour. "I was out, but the war was over, and that was the most important thing," Gladys recalled. "Instead of having two tours and constant fighting, it ended absolutely wonderfully in that the women players still had the support of Virginia Slims, and for the first time the USLTA was working with them instead of fighting them."

Shortly before the 1973 Wimbledon championships, we achieved another milestone: the founding of the Women's Tennis Association (WTA). I had wanted an organization

Bobby Riggs sizes up Margaret Court in Richmond, Virginia, several weeks before their match in San Diego. If Margaret looks a bit uncertain in this photograph, she had reason to be. Her match against Riggs would become known as the Mother's Day Massacre.

DIVERSIFYING THE
VIRGINIA SLIMS TOUR

I felt it was critical that we diversify the Virginia Slims tour racially. Gladys Heldman, our tour director, agreed, and she recruited Black players from the American Tennis Association (ATA), which had provided opportunities for Black people who were denied entry into white-run clubs and tournaments for more than half a century. Decades later, our first Black players remembered the experience as exciting, interesting, and disappointing.

In 1971, Bonnie Logan became the first to join the tour. Bonnie had won seven straight ATA singles titles from 1964 to 1970 and, as a freshman at Morgan State University, a historically Black university in Baltimore, had won the No. 2 *Men's* Singles title in the Central Intercollegiate Athletic Association Championships. In so doing, she became the first woman ever to win a CIAA men's title and the first to win a championship in an NCAA-affiliated men's conference. In 1972, she would become the first Black woman to compete in the South African Open in Johannesburg. After playing the tour, she worked for thirty-two years as a physical education teacher and coach in the Baltimore City Public Schools.

Two additional Black players joined the tour in 1973: Ann Koger and Sylvia Hooks. Ann had perfected her game on "the old colored tennis courts" in Baltimore and had competed in ATA tournaments as well as USTA events, both of which were racially integrated. She competed on the men's team at Morgan State along with Bonnie and would later coach the women's tennis team at Haverford College in Philadelphia for thirty-five years.

Sylvia, who grew up in Hamtramck, Michigan, had competed at Central State University, another historically Black university, in Wilberforce, Ohio. She would later earn a master's degree at Stanford University and enjoy a thirty-year teaching career at De Anza College in Cupertino, California.

A special Slims fund helped our first Black players with some expenses, but the tour was still a financial struggle. Sylvia, who left the tour after one year, said she was unprepared for the financial demands. Without a high ranking, she inevitably met a top player in the first or second round. "It felt like you were a draw-filler and not really a professional tennis player," she said. "There's no way you could continue if you weren't rich or had a sponsor. And if you were a person of color, it was hard to get a sponsor. You never felt comfortable. You were always wondering where the next dollar was coming from."

Racial insults left deeper wounds. When a tournament in Miami, Florida, refused to provide housing for our Black players, I delivered an ultimatum. I said, "If you don't give them housing, we're not going to have a tournament." Ultimately, the tournament put them up at a Holiday Inn, but the hurt remained. Said Sylvia: "It was a shame that a Julie Heldman or Billie Jean King always had to be protecting you, always had to step up for you, get you housing, decent housing."

Ann recalled the time she and the other Black tour players were told to use the servants' entrance to reach the courts at a country club that was hosting one of our events. "They got upset when we came in the front gate," she said. "They said, 'No, you're not allowed.' The next time we came to the gate, they said the same thing. The third time – I was the big mouth – I said, 'We're coming through this gate.' When they said, 'You can't do that,' I said, 'You'll have to stop me.'"

Nevertheless, there were many good moments. Bonnie recalled one of her favorites as her match with me in Arizona. "The score was 6–2, 6–2," Bonnie said. "I'd like to think I won those games, not a gift."

Said Sylvia: "I will forever respect Billie Jean King for never giving up in her undying belief that things should be fair. We must keep trying to make the world a better place. Because those of you who think it's so much better for people of color today, you are so wrong. It is still a struggle."

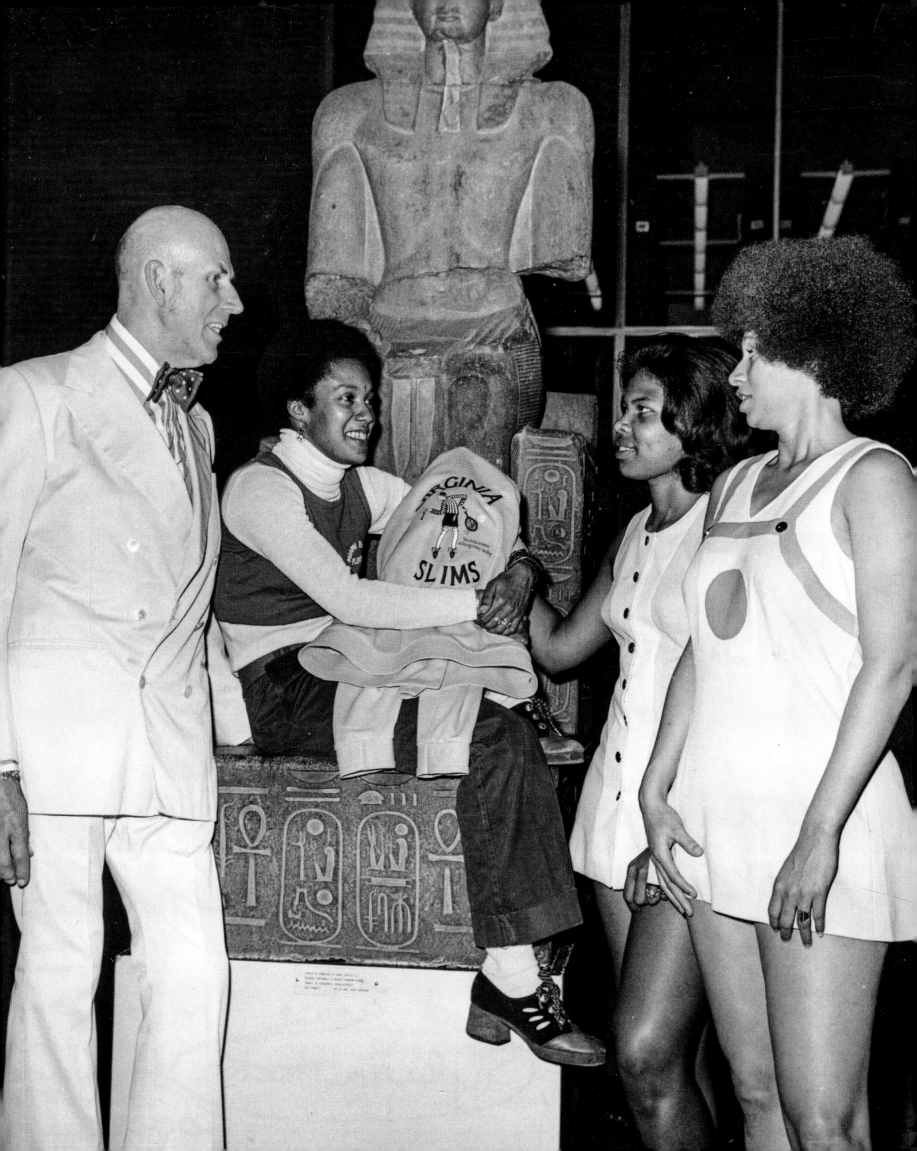

like it since the mid-1960s and had begun selling the idea to the players in 1968, with the help of Rosie Casals, Ann Jones, and Frankie Dürr. It is hard to believe, but in 1973 many women professionals still did not think we needed a union; they thought that because the women were going to be together on one tour, all the issues facing us had been settled. That unity, however, did not guarantee us a voice in our future. I did not want the USLTA and the International Lawn Tennis Federation making decisions about women's tennis without our input.

I decided to hold one last meeting to try to convince the women that we needed our own organization. I was exhausted, having been up half the previous night with a stomach ailment. When sixty-three women had gathered in the Gloucester Hotel in London, I told Betty Stöve to stand in front of the door and not allow anyone to leave. "Either we're going to have the association or we're not," I told the women. "I'm totally burned out. I'm not going to waste one more breath of air." Hours later, we had our association, with bylaws already prepared by my husband, Larry. I was elected president, Virginia Wade vice president, Frankie Dürr secretary, and Betty Stöve treasurer. Martin Carmichael, a New York attorney, would become our first executive director. Virginia quit her post after two weeks.

The 1973 U.S. Open was the first major tournament where women played for a purse equal to the men's. I had made it easy for Tournament Chairman Bill Talbert to accomplish this by recruiting Bristol-Myers to make up the $55,000 prize money difference. Margaret Court won this historic U.S. Open and the $25,000 first prize, a 150 percent increase over the $10,000 I had won the previous year. Runner-up Evonne Goolagong received $12,000.

Bobby Riggs, an egotistical, chauvinistic man of fifty-five, played an important role in women's tennis in 1973. Riggs had won the triple crown at Wimbledon in 1939, the same year as Alice Marble, more than a quarter of a century earlier. With Bobby's help, we took women's tennis to the masses. The man on the street, the woman in the office, the sports fan in the bar—all had heard of women's tennis by the end of 1973. As Rosie Casals declared: "I've always said that Bobby Riggs did more for women's tennis than anybody."

It was in late February of 1973 that Riggs challenged me to a $5,000 match, winner take all. He wanted to play me—and beat me, presumably—to prove a point. Bobby had been arguing that because women tennis players were not as good as men, they did not deserve to get as much prize money. He was also upset that the women professionals were making more money than older men, like himself, who played on the men's senior tour.

I knew a match with Riggs would have appeal,

THE 1973 U.S. OPEN WAS THE FIRST MAJOR TOURNAMENT WHERE WOMEN PLAYED FOR A PURSE EQUAL TO THE MEN'S.

Bobby Riggs and I had a terrific time promoting our showdown. Here I am checking out his bicep, above, and entertaining the press, below.

because Bobby was a showman and a con artist—the ultimate hustler. He had become well known in tennis circles for his ability to defeat lesser opponents while subjecting himself to great handicaps. He would offer to play some unsuspecting club member while holding a suitcase in one hand or a dog on a leash, make a huge bet, and then win and collect. I turned Bobby down, however, because at that moment I did not want to deal with a sideshow. I wanted to protect women's tennis, not jeopardize it, and, although I thought I could beat Bobby, I was not sure.

Riggs then challenged Margaret Court, and she accepted. I think she was enticed by the money, a guaranteed $10,000. Margaret said at the time that playing Riggs would be like taking a stroll in the park. She was dead wrong, of course. The match, played during the height of the women's movement and promoted by Riggs's endless chauvinistic blather, took on political overtones that made it bigger than any women's match had ever been. Margaret, who hated women's liberation and embraced everything traditional in tennis, had unwittingly walked into a circus carrying the banner of women's rights. To make matters worse, Margaret, who did not relish undue pressure, had everything to lose. As one columnist put it, "Can a woman beat even a very old man? It's not a very promising argument for the women."

Margaret was at the top of her game. She had won the 1973 Australian Open without losing a set; she would finish the year having won eighteen of twenty-five tournaments, including the French and U.S. Opens; and she would become the first woman athlete to win $200,000 in one year. Nevertheless, she was unprepared psychologically for what she faced on Mother's Day, in a secluded resort complex near San Diego. Journalists had come from thousands of miles away, and CBS was going to televise the

match nationally. Australians would rise at 6:00 a.m. to see the match live. In the midst of the commotion, Bobby Riggs talked endlessly about his fitness program and the 415 vitamin pills he took each day.

When Margaret walked onto the court, Riggs tried to rattle her by giving her a Mother's Day bouquet. Margaret curtsied and from that moment was in the palm of Riggs's hand. Riggs destroyed her, 6–2, 6–1, not with speed and power but with junk shots—dinks, lobs, and spins. "I didn't expect so many soft shots," Margaret said afterward. "We girls don't play like that."

Years later, Margaret remembered the match as a nightmare. "It was a mistake that I ever did it," she said. "I'd never been in anything like that before. It was showbiz. I thought, What in heaven's name am I doing out here?"

I did not see the match, because I was boarding a plane from Japan, where a group of Virginia Slims players had just played in that country's first professional tournament ever. When I turned on my radio, there was static, but I could make out the words "Bobby Riggs has just annihilated Margaret Court . . ." Walking down the aisle to my seat, teeth clenched, I could not imagine what had happened to Margaret. Now I would have to play him. When Bobby called to challenge me a few days later, I accepted. I had no choice.

During the next few months, the showdown was arranged by Jerry Perenchio, a big-time promoter whose résumé included a $5 million fight between Muhammad Ali and Joe Frazier. Bobby and I were to play September 20 at the Houston Astrodome, not for $10,000 in prize money but for $100,000, winner take all. I was also paid another $50,000 for doing one or two commercials.

Two hours before the match, I was so nervous that I felt sick. My mouth was dry, and I was nauseated. A hundred thoughts flashed through my mind. I thought about my career and my dreams as a child. I thought about women and low self-esteem, and I thought about the acceptance of women as skilled and striving athletes. I thought about Title IX, which had just passed the year before. My brain was going a mile a minute. I was at top throttle as I awaited the biggest match of my life.

Then, when I finally went out onto the court—I was carried out like a royal princess on an Egyptian litter, Bobby in a Chinese rickshaw—I felt exhilarated. This was what I had always wanted: arenas, razzle-dazzle, and nighttime tennis.

Opposite page, top: I loved this moment! The promoter, Jerry Perenchio, had me ride into the stadium on a litter carried by four bare-chested men in togas. Pam Austin, a tour player and sister of future champion Tracy Austin, is holding the sign that says "Bye." The extravaganza would be retold decades later in the 2017 movie *Battle of the Sexes,* starring Emma Stone, Steve Carell, and Andrea Riseborough.

Opposite page, bottom: I'm showing off my paycheck while boxing champion George Foreman holds my trophy.

Opposite page: I did not hit as hard as I could have against Bobby. I kept the ball in play and let him run, run, run. Five decades later, people still tell me where they were on this day. The dress I wore resides in the collections of the Smithsonian Institution's National Museum of American History.

I was wearing one of Ted Tinling's creations: a mint-green dress with a dark-blue bodice covered with little mirrors, a blue sweatband, and bright-blue tennis shoes. Bobby, wearing a warm-up jacket with the Sugar Daddy logo, gave me an enormous caramel sucker in a gesture of goodwill; I gave him a pig wearing a pink bow. A crowd of 30,472 watched from the stands. Away from the dome, a worldwide audience of 90 million was watching on television. Many were seeing tennis for the first time. Thankfully, I was unaware until years later that when Howard Cosell, the most famous sports commentator at that time, introduced Bobby and me, he listed Bobby's major tennis accomplishments but none of mine. He only talked about how I looked.

When I led, 2–1, in the first set, I knew I could win. I could see that Bobby was sweating profusely and hyperventilating, and I could tell that he had underestimated me. I played him just as I had planned: I did not hit my hardest, I did not rush the net at every opportunity, and I did not always end the point when I had the chance. I moved him from side to side, played his backhand, and gave him plenty of junk, which forced him to generate the pace. When I did put the ball away, I smashed away his lobs and angled away volleys he could only watch and admire. Bobby had been insistent about playing three out of five sets, and I had trained hard for this. I could have gone ten sets if necessary. I won the match, 6–4, 6–3, 6–3.

What did I prove? I knew that my victory over a man twenty-six years my senior was no great feat. Yet if I had done nothing sensational in beating Riggs, I had shown thousands of people who had never taken an interest in women's sports that women were skillful, entertaining, and capable of coming through in the clutch. The match legitimized women's tennis and elevated women athletes. It was the culmination of an era, the noisy conclusion to the noisiest three years in the history of the women's game.

The symmetry of those years was impossible to escape. We began our quest in Houston in 1970, rebels with a cause and an uncertain future. And we came back to Houston in 1973 after proving that we could make it on our own. We began our quest in Houston in 1970 because a man, Jack Kramer, underestimated our value as athletes and entertainers. And we came back to Houston in 1973 because another man, Bobby Riggs, dared to make the same mistake. "You've come a long way, baby," was our slogan in 1970. Three years later, when I shook hands with a defeated former champion, we had come a very long way, indeed.

CHAPTER SEVEN

GROWING PLEASURES, GROWING PAINS

1974 TO 1981

BY THE mid-1970s, our one-hundred-year-old sport was looking very new. The professionalism of tennis, our burgeoning tour, my triumph over Bobby Riggs, and the arrival of two compelling new stars—Chrissie Evert and Evonne Goolagong—had helped spark the "tennis boom," a surge in the sport's popularity that brought a tidal wave of money, fans, and new ideas to the game.

Page 180: Hana Mandlíková of Czechoslovakia serves at the U.S. Open.

Page 183: Chrissie Evert in winning form at the French Open at Roland Garros.

Opposite page: Happy faces after our successful negotiations with the All England Club in 1975: From left, Air Chief Marshal Sir Brian Burnett, chairman of the All England Lawn Tennis Club; myself; Ann Haydon Jones, of Wimbledon's Committee of Management; and Jerry Diamond, executive director of the Women's Tennis Association. I knew that if we could get Wimbledon to move in the right direction, we would be on our way to achieving equal prize money.

At the same time, endorsement opportunities mushroomed as corporations scrambled to link their products to the increasingly popular sport. A new wave of gifted teenagers grabbed the spotlight. We saw the first oversized rackets. The Women's Tennis Association (WTA) hired its first certified athletic trainers; Connie Spooner came aboard first in 1974 and was followed by Sandy Treadwell and Donna Pallulat. World rankings, once determined by consensus, became computerized in 1975. Women sports writers and television commentators were now covering our sport. They would include Mary Carillo, a former tour player who became an insightful TV analyst. In 1976, the WTA added a Futures Tour, a secondary tour where lower-ranked players could earn some prize money and gain the experience they needed to transition to the primary tour. And with immense pride, we saw our game's stature and celebrity advance the public's evolving acceptance of LGBTQ persons.

A key figure in our evolution was Jerry Diamond, a native New Yorker and public relations executive who had served as tournament director of a women's event in San Francisco. Jerry was working at a major car dealership in that city when I asked him to take over the helm of the WTA in 1974. We were $35,000 in debt, and I knew our organization could not survive unless it was financially sound. Hiring Jerry Diamond was one of my last big achievements during this phase of my career. He will be remembered as the best negotiator in tennis.

Jerry came aboard with one employee, a secretary, Grenn Nemhauser, and worked for six months without pay. He knew he would get paid eventually, but he did not take home a check until after he had sold a couple of endorsements and a television package to CBS. Under Jerry's leadership, both the WTA and the tour prospered. The players continued to devote 10 percent of their prize money to developing the WTA, which added more than two dozen employees, including tour referees, public relations directors, and athletic trainers. Prize money soared from $1 million in 1974 to more than $7 million in 1980, and our schedule boasted a tournament somewhere in the world virtually every week of the year. A good portion of our prize money came from two new sponsors: Colgate-Palmolive, which joined Virginia Slims as a major sponsor in 1977, and Avon Products, which replaced Virginia Slims in 1979 with the most expensive corporate sponsorship yet. The weeklong 1979 Avon Championships at Madison Square Garden drew a record 59,225 spectators overall; the final drew 13,752, the largest crowd to watch a match at a women's tournament until that time.

With Jerry's help—and a brilliant legal strategy (some might have called it a power play)—we took a huge step toward equal pay in early 1975 when we aced

Chrissie Evert remains the greatest woman clay court player ever. She won all three U.S. Open Championships contested on the surface, including this one in 1975.

our negotiations with the All England Club, which had been awarding the women only 60 percent of what it gave the men.

"I remember going to England with Billie to argue with the All England Club for equal prize money," Jerry recalled. "The attorney for the WTA, Larry Aufmuth, helped put together in legal form the strategy I had figured might win us a decision at the meeting. We had prepared a contract for the women to sign that stated they would play in another tournament during Wimbledon the following year if the women's prize money at Wimbledon was not comparable to the men's.

"About 80 or 90 percent of the women signed it," he continued. "Almost every major player in the world agreed to play in another tournament during Wimbledon of 1976, on grass. Our goal was to go to the Hall of Fame at Newport, Rhode Island, and establish a grass-court tournament there. I had a sponsor lined up that was prepared to put up some pretty big money. I knew that Wimbledon, like the U.S. Open, would never throw the women out because they would lose their lucrative television contract.

"We met with about twenty members of the All England Club Committee, right in the Directors Room, and basically told them in nice language that either they raised the prize money or the women would not play the event. They snickered and said let's wait and see what happens when the time comes. And I said, 'No, you don't seem to understand: It's not an emotional issue anymore. The women have signed a contract to play in another tournament, and if they decide they want to play in your tournament, we'll legally prevent them from doing so. They have no choice, and you have no choice.' We eventually settled for 80 percent of the men's total purse, with the women's champion to receive 90 percent of what the men's champion received."

The large influx of money during the 1970s caused radical changes. More and more athletes pursued the game, and competition became fiercer. Equipment improved, and the players' technique—everything from footwork to service motions—improved.

Chrissie won the French Open on the slow red clay at Stade Roland Garros a record seven times. Here, she is holding the beautiful Coupe Suzanne Lenglen in 1980.

Above: Chrissie Evert signs autographs for her adoring fans at the U.S. Open.

Below: Chrissie Evert accepts the symbolic $40,000 paycheck after winning the 1975 Virigina Slims Championship at Los Angeles Memorial Sports Arena.

Below: Leslie Allen upon her arrival in Sydney to play the 1977 Australian summer circuit. Four years later, she defeated Hana Mandlíková in the final of the 1981 Avon Championships of Detroit to become the first Black woman to win a title on the primary tour of the Women's Tennis Association. Leslie, who grew up in Ohio and didn't become serious about tennis until she was in high school, polished her game at the University of Southern California and became known for her big serve and aggressive net play.

These changes led in 1975 to clay replacing the historic grass courts at the West Side Tennis Club in Forest Hills, where the U.S. Open was played. In previous eras, the grass had remained relatively green and lush through the tournament finals. But the newly revamped tennis shoes, with soles designed to grip and avoid skidding, and the harder, more powerful play chewed up the courts more quickly than ever. The result was an uneven surface, bad bounces, and endless player complaints. The USLTA, keenly aware of the problem, plowed under the famous courts and replaced them with a clay surface of crushed natural green stone manufactured by Har-Tru. The surface, which produces relatively true bounces, is far slower than grass and significantly slower than hard courts.

Although Wimbledon and the Australian Open also suffered chewed-up grass, no changes were made at the time. The Australians finally switched to hard courts in 1988, but I think the lawns at Wimbledon, the home of true lawn tennis, will always remain.

The U.S. Open's switch to clay helped change the balance of power in tennis. Whereas grass had favored players like Margaret Court who served and ended the point quickly at the net, the slower clay promoted longer points and favored consistency. The dominance of Chrissie Evert—she won 55 of the 76 tournaments she played between 1974 and 1977—was enhanced by the switch. Chrissie, who learned to play on clay in Florida and who remains the greatest clay-court player in the history of women's tennis, won all three U.S. Open singles titles played on Har-Tru. Her consistency, concentration, and endurance made her virtually unbeatable on the slow surface. Chrissie said that, on clay, "I can do whatever I want with the tennis ball. I can handle any situation and don't feel threatened by anyone."

Of course, Chrissie was superb on faster surfaces, as well: She won three more Open titles on hard courts, after the tournament moved to the new National Tennis Center in Flushing Meadow, New York, in 1978. In one of her enduring records, she won at least one Grand Slam singles title every year for thirteen straight years, from 1974 to 1986.

Above: Chrissie
Evert and Martina
Navratilova won two
Grand Slam doubles
titles together,
including the 1976
Ladies' Doubles title
at Wimbledon.

Thousands of miles from Florida, behind the Iron Curtain, another champion also learned to play tennis on clay, but quite differently. Martina Navratilova was an attacking, net-rushing player whose left-handed serve and backhand volley would become legendary. Martina came from Czechoslovakia, a nation of fifteen million people with a 100 percent literacy rate and a proud history in tennis. Czechoslovakia, which in 1993 was split into the Czech Republic and Slovakia, celebrated its first Wimbledon champion in 1954, when the bespectacled thirty-four-year-old Jaroslav Drobný beat nineteen-year-old Ken Rosewall in the men's singles final. Jan Kodeš, another Czech, won the French men's championships in 1970 and 1971 and captured the Wimbledon title in 1973. Věra Suková, the first female star from Czechoslovakia, reached the Wimbledon final in 1962.

Martina did little of note when she made her debut on the USLTA tour in 1972 at age seventeen. But she became extremely popular with the players and the crowds. She learned English quickly and developed a taste for American freedoms and a passion for American foods. As a result of her love affair with American junk food, Martina gained twenty-five pounds in two months. On one occasion, when players kidded her about being the tour's "pancake champ," she paused between bites of a hamburger, grinned, and rattled off the theme of a popular television commercial: "I can't believe I ate the whole thing."

MARTINA NAVRATILOVA

- **18 Grand Slam singles titles**
    - **3 Australian (1981, 1983, 1985)**
    - **2 French (1982, 1984)**
    - **9 Wimbledon: a record (1978, 1979, 1982–1987, 1990)**
    - **4 U.S. (1983, 1984, 1986, 1987)**
- **31 Grand Slam women's doubles titles**
- **10 Grand Slam mixed doubles titles**
- **8 WTA Finals titles (1978, 1979, 1981, 1983–1985, 1986 [March], 1986 [Nov.])**
- **Federation Cup: 20–0 in singles, 20–1 in doubles**
- **Year-end No. 1 in the world (1978, 1979, 1982–1986)**
- **International Tennis Hall of Fame inductee, 2000**

NOTEWORTHY STATISTICS

- **20 Wimbledon titles, a record shared with Billie Jean King (9 singles, 7 doubles, 4 mixed doubles)**
- **Achieved the longest winning streak in professional tennis (74 matches in 1984)**

Martina Navratilova was born in 1956 into a sports-minded family. Her mother, Jana, was an avid tennis player and a fine skier; her grandmother had ranked as high as No. 2 among Czechoslovak women tennis players before World War II. Martina's parents were divorced when she was three, and her mother subsequently moved to Revnice, a village of five thousand near Prague. There Jana met and married Mirek Navratil, who was also an accomplished tennis player. (Navratilova is the feminine form of Navratil.) When Martina was six, her stepfather, whom she always referred to as her father, began teaching her to play tennis. At age eleven, on August 20, 1968, Martina and her doubles partner awoke to the sight of Soviet tanks in the street. Some six hundred thousand Soviet troops had swept into Czechoslovakia to subdue the political reform movement known as the Prague Spring. A year or two later, when a Soviet player tapped Martina's hand instead of shaking it after losing, Martina blurted, "You need a tank to beat me." In her memoir, *Martina,* she described her disillusionment and that of her people. "When I was twelve or thirteen, I saw my country lose its verve, lose its productivity, lose its soul. For someone with a skill, a career, an aspiration, there was only one thing to do: get out." Despite worries that she might not see her family again, Martina defected to the United States in 1975. To fulfill her goal of becoming No. 1, she knew she had to compete consistently where "the big tennis" was. Six years later, she became a U.S. citizen.

Eleven years after her defection, in August 1986, Martina went home again. In one of the most moving events of her career, she returned to Prague as a member of the U.S. Federation Cup team to compete in the final against her native country, Czechoslovakia. The Czechoslovak government was forced to issue a visa to Martina in order to hold the event in their beautiful new Štvanice Tennis Stadium. The crowd cheered Martina, and during her first match, which was played outside the stadium court, trains slowed down as they passed so that passengers and crew could look out the widows and savor a few moments of history. In a dramatic finish to a Federation Cup tournament in which forty-one nations had competed, Chrissie Evert won the first match against Helena Suková (the daughter of Věra Suková),

Opposite page: Martina Navratilova with *Tonight Show* host Johnny Carson and, below, with her mother, Jana.

"YOU NEED A TANK TO BEAT ME."

and Martina clinched the victory when she beat her former countrywoman Hana Mandlíková. During the closing ceremonies, Martina cried and told the crowd she hoped she would not have to wait eleven years to return. "The countryside was more beautiful than I remembered it," Martina later said. "Prague was more beautiful than I remembered it. Everyone was so friendly. It exceeded all my expectations."

Officials within the Czechoslovak Federation were less amused by her rapid Americanization and threatened to restrict her travel. When the federation nearly prevented her from playing in the 1975 U.S. Open, Martina decided she would not return to Czechoslovakia. During the Open, a few hours after losing in the semifinals, she requested political asylum in the United States. Months of turmoil awaited, but so did the accomplishments she craved.

Amid our sport's rapid evolution into a major entertainment business, we enjoyed two storybook Wimbledons—one modern, the other steeped in tradition. In 1974, Chrissie Evert and her then-fiancé Jimmy Connors captured the singles titles in what could only be called a "Love Double." Chrissie and Jimmy, not wanting to disrupt their blossoming careers, later called off the engagement, and both eventually married other people. But their love match made headlines worldwide and added another spark to the public's growing passion for tennis.

Three years later, in 1977, the year of Wimbledon's one hundredth birthday and Queen Elizabeth's silver anniversary as monarch, Englishwoman Virginia Wade—less than two weeks shy of her thirty-second birthday—finally won the Ladies' Singles on her sixteenth attempt. As I watched Virginia close out the match, I told Marjorie Fraser, the women's locker room attendant, "This script was written in heaven."

Virginia had ranked in the world's top ten since 1967 and had won two Grand Slam titles, but until 1977 she had never reached a Wimbledon final. She had reached the semifinals only twice. Frequently, she had lost in an early round to a lower-ranked opponent. "Our Ginny," as the British media often referred to her, was an emotional player to begin with, and the majesty and tradition of her country's championship added to the pressure she must have felt.

Because Virginia carried herself with a regal air, many members of the British press found her easy prey when she failed. Not all of the London newspapers lambasted her, of course; traditional papers like the *Times* and the *Daily Telegraph* were invariably fair to all of the athletes. The tabloids, on the other hand, produced some of the most tasteless headlines I have ever read anywhere in the world. "Ginny Fizz" was one of their favorites.

Either Virginia finally learned how to endure Britain's expectations or she simply outlasted them. Her triumph occurred under circumstances remarkably like those of Angela Mortimer in 1961 and Ann Jones in 1969. Angela and Ann triumphed at Wimbledon late in their careers and only after shedding the burden of being Britain's greatest hope. Similarly, Virginia was considered past her

> BECAUSE VIRGINIA CARRIED HERSELF WITH A REGAL AIR, MANY MEMBERS OF THE BRITISH PRESS FOUND HER EASY PREY WHEN SHE FAILED.

prime when she made her successful run for the title in 1977. By then, the Brits were touting a new star, Sue Barker, whose photograph appeared on the cover of the BBC's Wimbledon program guide.

Virginia, like many of the women professionals, benefited from World TeamTennis (WTT), a professional team tennis league first proposed in 1973 by Dennis Murphy, Fred Barman, Jordan Kaiser, Frank Fuhrer, and my husband, Larry King. WTT, which launched in 1974, was the first professional league in which men and women competed as teammates and equal participants, with each interteam match featuring men's and women's singles, men's and women's doubles, and mixed doubles. It comprised sixteen American-based teams, including the Boston Lobsters, the Detroit Loves, and the Phoenix Racquets. Spawned by the tennis boom—which saw the number of tennis-playing Americans spike from ten million in 1970 to thirty-four million in 1974—WTT gave men and women players a lucrative salary in addition to the prize money they earned by competing in tournaments. The league disbanded after the 1978 season but returned as TeamTennis in 1981 and continues to this day.

Virginia and I played on the same team, the New York Sets, which later became the New York Apples. During the season, which ran from May through August, we women practiced with our male teammates daily, received constructive coaching, and improved our games technically. We also became

VIRGINIA WADE

•

Virginia Wade, the daughter of an Anglican vicar, was born in Bournemouth, England, in 1945 but spent most of her childhood in Durban, South Africa. She and her family moved back to England when she was sixteen. She was a Renaissance woman in the mold of Helen Wills Moody. She played the piano, enjoyed the ballet and theater, and studied mathematics and physics at the University of Sussex. She is the last college graduate to win a Wimbledon singles title. Virginia was an intense player with a beautiful serve and a classic net game. She was rarely dominating, but she was gutsy and determined. As I once said, "It didn't matter what the score was: she'd never pack it in, never stop going for it." Queen Elizabeth II honored her twice: in 1969 as a Member of the Most Excellent Order of the British Empire and in 1986 as an Officer of the Order of the British Empire. In 1982, Virginia became the first woman ever elected to the Wimbledon Committee.

- 3 Grand Slam singles titles
    - 1 Wimbledon (1977)
    - 1 U.S. (1968)
    - 1 Australian (1972)
- 4 Grand Slam women's doubles titles
- Federation Cup: 36–20 in singles, 30–13 in doubles
- Wightman Cup: 12–23 in singles, 7–14 in doubles
- Best year-end world ranking: No. 2, 1975
- International Tennis Hall of Fame inductee, 1989

stronger mentally because of World TeamTennis's innovative format, which was designed to create excitement for the spectators and pressure for the players. Our matches consisted of one five-game set (not six), with no-ad scoring: When the score reached deuce, it was sudden death, and the winner of the next point won the game. Furthermore, because the matches were played in an arena, players had the sensation of being on center court every night.

Virginia came into Wimbledon more fit than ever and with an improved net game, a strengthened serve, and a new attitude. She was seeded third and, for the first time in her life, she believed she could win. She did, upsetting Chrissie Evert, the No. 1 seed, in the semifinals and beating Betty Stöve of the Netherlands in the final. Virginia accepted the gilded salver from Queen Elizabeth II, and as she held the trophy high, the crowd spontaneously began to sing "For She's a Jolly Good Fellow."

"The result means everything to me," Virginia said afterward. "Everyone thought I was past it and couldn't do it. I wanted to prove I deserved to be out there among the champions. I felt I belonged—that I was the best player who hadn't won Wimbledon so far."

Above: She's on top of the world—or close to it. On her sixteenth attempt, a fit and confident Virginia Wade finally won Wimbledon.

The *Sports Illustrated* headline that followed could not have been more fitting: "GINNY FIZZ BECOMES GINNY TONIC."

The 1977 Wimbledon was also memorable for the arrival of the first of a new wave of prodigies. Tracy Austin, a fourteen-year-old from Rolling Hills Estates, California, weighed ninety-five pounds, had braces on her teeth, wore her hair in pigtails, and dressed in pinafores trimmed in gingham. There was nothing else childlike about her. She played with a fearlessness and tenacity seldom seen in tennis. Martina Navratilova once noted: "One cannot think of Tracy as a child. If you do, she will beat you." Tracy won her first match; she lost her second decisively to Chrissie Evert but still managed to win 38 percent of the points.

The sixteen-year minimum age requirement for contestants, previously imposed by the International Tennis Federation (ITF), was waived for Tracy's international debut. The age limit, which had never been tested in court, probably could not have sustained a legal challenge, and ITF officials technically did the right thing in abolishing it. In retrospect, however, the ITF had reason to be concerned about the age of the players, and Tracy herself was among the first to make them realize it. Sensible age limitations throughout the sport might have prevented a great deal of heartache, not to mention injuries to shoulders, backs, and legs, along with scars to mental health. Several years after the ban had been lifted, the governing bodies of men's and women's tennis set limits on the number of professional tournaments youngsters could play in order to protect them from the physical grind and emotional trauma of a highly competitive adult world. The rules would help the next generation of players, but they would come too late to help Tracy.

Above: Sixteen-year-old Tracy Austin is on her way to winning the 1979 U.S. Open.

Opposite page: Fourteen-year-old Tracy lost to Chrissie Evert in the second round of Wimbledon in 1977.

The Big Three in the late 1970s and early 1980s were, from left, Tracy Austin, Chrissie Evert, and Martina Navratilova.

TRACY AUSTIN

Tracy Austin, born in 1962, grew up in Rolling Hills Estates, California. She was the youngest of five children in a family of excellent tennis players. Her mother, Jeanne, was once a ranked player in Southern California. Her sister, Pam, played on the women's circuit for a few years, and her brother John played on the men's circuit. (In 1980, John and Tracy became the first brother and sister to win the Wimbledon mixed doubles title.) Another brother, Jeff, played for UCLA. Tracy was given her first tennis racket at age two and a half. By age four, she was enrolled in a special kiddies' program run by Vic Braden, a teaching professional and entrepreneur, at the Jack Kramer Tennis Club. In 1967, holding a racket that was two-thirds as long as she was, she appeared on the cover of *World Tennis* magazine. From that time forward, Tracy lived for tennis. She later came under the tutelage of teaching professional Robert Landsdorp. Her early achievements included twenty-five national junior titles. She transitioned to the professional tour almost instantaneously, but she experienced challenges nevertheless. Shy in public, she struggled when sports writers asked her questions she had never thought about. "The press kept harping on how little I was in my pinafores and my pigtails," she said many years later. "They said my mom tried to make me look like a little girl. But I was a little girl. I didn't mature quickly, physically or emotionally. Some girls at fourteen wear makeup, are 5 foot 8, and have developed physically. That didn't happen to me." Nevertheless, she had the preternatural assets of a champion: discipline, an unwavering work ethic, and mental fortitude. As Pam Shriver observed, Tracy "didn't break down under pressure."

- **2 Grand Slam singles titles**
  2 U.S. Open (1979, 1981)
- **1 Grand Slam mixed doubles title**
- **1 WTA Finals title (1980)**
- **Federation Cup: 13–1 in singles**
- **Best year-end world ranking: No. 2 (1980, 1981)**
- **International Tennis Hall of Fame inductee, 1992**

NOTEWORTHY STATISTIC

- **Logged 22 victories against Chrissie Evert and Martina Navratilova between 1978 and 1981.**

Above: From left, Chrissie Evert, Martina Navratilova, Olga Morozova of Russia, and Julie Anthony of the United States, before their women's doubles final in the 1975 French Open at Roland Garros. Chrissie and Martina won.

Martina Navratilova suffered from homesickness and loneliness during the months that followed her defection. On the tennis court, she agonized over every failure, no matter how small. One bad line call could snap her concentration and send her to defeat. "I was eighteen years old, like a kid leaving home to go to college," she recalled. "But all of a sudden I was alone, four or five thousand miles from my family. I couldn't go back there, and they couldn't come see me. And I was doing it in front of the whole world. I think it would have been less turbulent had my life been more private, but that was impossible. Going through adolescence is a pretty scary trick for anybody, but this made it even more difficult for me to grow up."

Martina's career was at a low ebb at the 1976 U.S. Open, where she was the No. 3 seed. She entered the tournament with little preparation, and her weight had ballooned to an all-time high. She lost in the first round to American Janet Newberry and then sobbed uncontrollably as the cameras zoomed in on her. It was a portrait of desolation seen in living rooms throughout the world.

Help soon came from a new friend and mentor: Sandra Haynie, an American women's golf champion known for her calm and businesslike approach to the game. Sandra knew little about the technicalities of tennis, but she understood the psychology of sports. With Sandra's help, Martina took a giant step toward maturity. She won six tournaments in 1977, and in 1978 she

won her first Wimbledon. The Czech newspapers, which had steadfastly referred to her as "another woman player" since her defection, did not report it. A year later, in 1979, when Martina again strode onto Wimbledon's Centre Court, her mother, Jana, watched from the stands and cried tears of happiness and pride. The Czech government had issued her a two-week visa after she received a formal invitation from the All England Club. When Martina won the final point against Chrissie Evert, Jana jumped up and danced around her seat with joy. In another departure from normal procedure, Czechoslovakia's national television station showed a tape of the final.

The next day, Martina and I teamed up against Betty Stöve and Wendy Turnbull in a historic women's doubles final. A victory would give me my twentieth Wimbledon title and break the record I shared with Elizabeth Ryan, who won nineteen Wimbledon doubles championships between 1914 and 1934. Martina and I won the doubles match in three sets, but it was not a grand occasion for me, because I could not stop thinking about Elizabeth. She had suffered a stroke the day before the doubles final and had died en route to the hospital. She was eighty-eight years old. Elizabeth left us with a poignant reminder: Our records can be as impermanent as our lives. New generations inevitably come along to grace the courts that we cherished. New names become etched upon our great trophies, pushing older names deeper and deeper into the past.

At right: Martina Navratilova in 1975, the year she defected from Czechoslovakia to the United States.

Above: Eleven years later, she returned home to Prague for the Federation Cup. In this photo, a passing train slows down so that passengers can view their former countrywoman (in the blue skirt, serving), one of the greatest champions of all time.

Opposite page: Pam Shriver and Martina Navratilova won twenty Grand Slam doubles titles together, including this one at Wimbledon in 1982.

Indeed, women's tennis in the late 1970s had never looked more youthful. Pam Shriver, Tracy Austin's rival on the junior circuit, turned professional at fifteen and the following year became the darling of the 1978 U.S. Open. Pam said her "most glamorous moments" came in the biggest arena in tennis: the United States Tennis Association's new National Tennis Center in New York City. The USTA (the word "Lawn" was dropped in 1976) had left the impossibly cramped West Side Tennis Club and moved to the grounds of the 1964–1965 New York World's Fair. The highlight of the National Tennis Center—a converted stadium named after Louis Armstrong, the famous jazz musician— could seat eighteen thousand.

Pam, curly haired and 6 feet tall, was a serve-and-volley stylist from Baltimore, Maryland, who blanketed the net with an unusual and significant new weapon: the oversize Prince racket. The aluminum racket, designed by Howard Head, a retired engineer and the inventor of metal skis, featured a circular face that was 60 percent larger than that of a conventional racket. It had a sweet spot—the hitting area in the center of the racket face—three times larger than normal and allowed players more room for error.

Some players ridiculed the Prince racket in the beginning because of its cumbersome appearance. Some of Pam's friends called it a snowshoe, a trampoline, or an old duffer's racket. Nevertheless, midsize and oversize rackets proliferated in the late 1970s and early 1980s and revolutionized the game, evolving into powerful tools made with newer materials like graphite and boron. With these weapons, players were able to hit harder than ever, and one by one they abandoned their standard-size rackets. Pam's wise decision to embrace the Prince before others did may have contributed to her fast start at the 1978 Open, which saw her upend Martina Navratilova in the semifinals before losing to Chrissie Evert in the final.

The youth movement gained momentum the next year when Tracy Austin, now sixteen, snapped Chrissie's historic clay-court winning streak at 125 matches at the 1979 Italian Open. It was a stunning feat and a harbinger of things to come. At the U.S. Open a few months later, Tracy defeated Martina in the semifinals and then toppled Chrissie in the final to become the youngest female to win the U.S. title. (Maureen Connolly was three months older than Tracy when she triumphed in 1951.) In setting that record, Tracy prevented another. She stopped Chrissie's winning streak at four U.S. Championships, a string matched only by Helen Jacobs and Molla Bjurstedt Mallory decades earlier.

Equally significant, Tracy's victory was a trumpet call to parents, coaches, and agents that stardom and riches were within a teenager's reach. Regrettably, few could foresee the toll that the professional circuit would take on young competitors. "I think many young players have learned and benefited from

PAM SHRIVER

Pam Shriver, born in 1962 in Baltimore, Maryland, is remembered for a magnificent doubles record. She won 111 doubles titles during her career, the third most in the tour's history. But Pam was also a superb singles player who won twenty-one singles titles. From 1980 to 1988, she ranked among the world's top ten, three times finishing the year as high as No. 4. She and Martina Navratilova won seventy-nine doubles titles, twenty of them in Grand Slam events. They also achieved the longest winning streak in women's doubles history: 109 matches from June 1983 through July 1985. Kathy Jordan, a Californian, and Elizabeth Smylie of Australia snapped the streak in the 1985 Wimbledon final. Intellectually agile, Pam was never at a loss for memorable comment. After her playing career, she became a highly successful television commentator for networks in the United States, Great Britain, and Australia.

- **21 Grand Slam doubles titles, 20 with Martina Navratilova**
- **Doubles Grand Slam, with Martina Navratilova, in 1984**
- **Olympics: 1988 Seoul (gold medal, women's doubles, with Zina Garrison)**
- **Federation Cup: 5–0 in singles, 14–1 in doubles**

- **Best year-end world ranking: No. 4 (1983–1985)**
- **International Tennis Hall of Fame inductee, 2002**

NOTEWORTHY STATISTIC

- **Her 20 Grand Slam doubles titles with Martina Navratilova is a team record shared with Margaret Osborne duPont and Louise Brough**

INTELLECTUALLY AGILE, PAM WAS NEVER AT A LOSS FOR A MEMORABLE COMMENT.

what happened to me, but they have also been hurt by the fact that I won the U.S. Open at sixteen," Tracy said years later. "I think I started a belief that one could win the U.S. Open at sixteen, and therefore people started to put a lot of pressure on young players. And I think the young girls put pressure on themselves. They expected much more. And I never expected to win the U.S. Open at sixteen. It wasn't something that had crossed my mind before that. There wasn't any pressure. It just happened. Whereas now, it's possible."

For a period in 1979 and 1980, Tracy's future looked bright. Indeed, she appeared ready to eclipse Chrissie altogether, beating her at her own immaculate baseline game five straight times. (Her career advantage over Chrissie would be 9–7.) "We had the same type of game, but she was younger, she was a little faster, she was more eager, she had a little less pressure," Chrissie reflected in 2017. Chrissie took three months off from the tour to reassess her future. She returned newly determined and with a new fearlessness. In the semifinals of the 1980 U.S. Open, she snapped her losing streak against Tracy by going for winners, approaching the net, and smashing overheads off Tracy's lobs. Following what she called her "most emotional victory," Chrissie defeated another teenage star, eighteen-year-old Hana Mandlíková of Czechoslovakia, to win her fifth U.S. Open title.

The teenage contenders of the early 1980s also included Andrea Jaeger, of Lincolnshire, Illinois. Andrea was coached by her father, Roland Jaeger, a former amateur boxer in Europe who started to play tennis after moving to

Above: Virginia Ruzici of Romania won the women's singles title at the 1978 French Open and the women's doubles with Mima Jaušovec of Yugoslavia. Years later, Virginia would occupy a unique place in tennis history as the inspiration behind the birth and development of two future superstars: Venus and Serena Williams.

HANA MANDLÍKOVÁ

- 4 Grand Slam singles titles
    - 2 Australian Open (1980, 1987)
    - 1 French Open (1981)
    - 1 U.S. Open (1985)
- 1 Grand Slam doubles title
- Federation Cup: 13–1 in singles
- Best year-end world ranking: No. 3 (1984, 1985)
- International Tennis Hall of Fame inductee, 1994

Hana Mandlíková was born in 1962 in Prague, Czechoslovakia. She played with a ballerina's grace that echoed the legacies of Maria Bueno and Evonne Goolagong. Not merely enchanting, she was spectacular—an all-court player who could hit any shot from any position. Like many players who grew up in Eastern Europe, Hana had to clear financial hurdles in order to launch her professional tennis career. Although the Czech Tennis Federation helped, Hana said that the system did not provide her with everything she needed as a child. Her father, Vilem, a sportswriter and a former Olympic sprinter, spent a good deal of his own money on her training. In 1977, at age fifteen, Hana came to the United States for the first time and won the girls' sixteen-and-under title at the Orange Bowl in Florida. A year later, she was runner-up to Tracy Austin in the Wimbledon Junior Championships. In 1979, accompanied by her father, Hana came to the United States to try the professional tour. Money continued to be a day-to-day challenge. Betty Stöve, who became Hana's coach in 1980, said that Hana had to win money in her first tournament in order to go on to the next one. Hana withstood the pressure: she won five tournaments in 1979. In 1980, under Betty's guidance, her career took off. She won the 1980 Australian Open and, in winning the 1981 French Open, became the first player since Margaret Court to beat Chrissie Evert on the red clay at Roland Garros. After losing, Chrissie concluded: "Hana has it all." Hana retired at age twenty-eight. Although she won fewer majors than we might have expected, her unbridled athleticism made her one of the most exciting players of her era. Later, she captained the Czech Republic's Federation Cup team and for nine years coached Jana Novotná, a future star who would occupy a special place in tennis history.

Opposite page: Hana Mandlíková serves with a flourish.

Above: Andrea Jaeger competed with an adult's skill and tenacity, but she was a young teenager with the interests and vulnerabilities of most young teenagers.

the Chicago area. Andrea was a prodigy who at thirteen won the eighteen-and-under title at the prestigious Orange Bowl in Florida. She turned professional at fourteen and, a few days before her fifteenth birthday, reached the quarterfinals at Wimbledon. Andrea played backcourt tennis, hit a wicked two-handed backhand, and had no prejudice against using the powerful new rackets. Andrea won ten tour events between 1980 and 1983 and ranked as high as No. 3 in the world. But a shoulder injury would force her into retirement when she was just nineteen.

Not long after losing to Chrissie at the 1980 U.S. Open, Tracy Austin developed a serious case of sciatica, an inflammation of the sciatic nerve in her lower back. What followed was an eight-month ordeal consisting of rest and painstaking rehabilitation. Her comeback began with sessions in which someone hit a tennis ball directly to her for a period of seven minutes. Tracy's persistence paid off. She returned to the tour and—still only eighteen years old—won her second U.S. Open in 1981.

The awards ceremony was a joyous occasion not only for Tracy but also for her vanquished opponent, Martina Navratilova, who received a thunderous ovation from the fans. In a transformative moment, an American crowd embraced a muscular woman athlete who did not fit the traditional feminine stereotype and who, years later, would come out as gay.

The crowd's embrace of Martina represented a milestone for women athletes—and for all people who do not identify as heterosexual—and it echoed my own experience several months earlier.

In April 1981, a woman with whom I had had an affair filed a lawsuit suit against me, putting an unwelcome spotlight on my personal life, which, until then, had remained private. The lawsuit, which I won later that year, nevertheless caused me to lose nearly $1.5 million in endorsements, television commercials, corporate appearances, and coaching opportunities. But just weeks after the unwelcome publicity occurred, when I was introduced at a TeamTennis match in San Diego—at that time a Republican stronghold—I was thrilled to receive a long standing ovation.

FOR BLACK PLAYERS, MORE HISTORIC FIRSTS

In this photo, legendary champion Arthur Ashe poses with up-and-coming players in a studio replica of the 1877 Wimbledon Room. From left, Ashe, Leslie Allen, Lawrence Hooper, Renee Blount, Lloyd Bourne, and Kim Sands. In 1979, Renee Blount, a former All-American in singles and doubles at UCLA, became the first Black woman to win a professional tour event when she captured the Avon Futures of Columbus (Ohio). Leslie Allen, who had played on the University of Southern California's national championship team in 1977, went a step further. In 1981, she became the first Black woman to win a title on the WTA's primary tour when she triumphed at the Avon Championships of Detroit. Leslie reached a career-high ranking of No. 17 in the world that same year and qualified for the season-ending Avon Championships. In 1974, Kim Sands became the first Black woman to receive a women's tennis scholarship at the University of Miami. Years later, she would return to her alma mater to coach the women's tennis team.

Here, in 1975, I am holding the Wimbledon salver for the sixth and final time. I was in top form that year and beat Evonne Goolagong in the final, 6–0, 6–1.

Martina Navratilova lost the 1981 U.S. Open final to Tracy Austin and then cried tears of happiness when the crowd thundered its approval of her effort—and of her.

When the crowd celebrated me for who I was, and when another crowd, a few months later, celebrated Martina for who she was, I knew something big was happening. My reaction in San Diego was surprise, then awe, then sheer joy. In the U.S. Open stadium, with millions around the world watching, Martina cupped her hands over her eyes and burst into tears.

The closing scene of the Open—Tracy smiling, Martina crying—was momentous in so many ways. Tracy's back problems would flare up again, bringing the prime of her professional tennis career to an end; Martina's best days were just beginning; and a new era of tolerance and gender equity was starting to unfold. Women's tennis was going to get tougher and more powerful in the 1980s, and Martina was going to lead the way.

CHAPTER EIGHT

NEW
MONEY
BEGETS
NEW
ATHLETES

1982
TO
2000

BY THE TIME we reached the 1980s, our battle for financial equity had largely been won. In 1982, Martina Navratilova became the first woman to win <u>$1 million</u> in prize money in one season. Ten years later, Monica Seles won $1.6 million in prize money—more than the men's leading money winner, Stefan Edberg, who won $1.4 million! And prize money was only part of the picture. <u>Endorsements</u> were where the big money was being made.

Page 218: The German Tennis Federation fueled Stefanie Graf's rise with financial support and access to premier coaching.

Page 221: Martina Navratilova invested her own money in her career, and the payoff arrived in dollars and titles, including a historic nine singles championships at Wimbledon.

Opposite page: Martina achieved a new level of fitness and heightened everyone's awareness of its importance.

This era began with leading players earning endorsement income worth double or even triple their prize money earnings; it ended with exciting new stars being offered million-dollar endorsement contracts before they had played a professional match. With so much at stake, players' approach to the game became increasingly focused and scientific. Advanced levels of training once scoffed at became de rigueur as women embraced weight training and nutritional regimens along with regular on-court practice.

There was also an increased focus on players' physical and mental health. In 1989, the Women's Tennis Association (WTA) hired Kathleen Stroia, a certified athletic trainer and physical therapist, and by 1995, Kathleen had established a critically important program called Athletes Assistance (later known as Mental Health & Wellness). Quietly and with little fanfare, this multilingual WTA service came to the aid of women tennis professionals who were coping with any number of emotional and mental health challenges, including abuse from intimate partners, parents, and coaches.

In 1999, the United States Tennis Association (USTA) named a woman as its president for the first time. She was Judy Levering of Lancaster County, Pennsylvania. Two years earlier, in her role as first vice president, Judy had helped persuade the USTA to name its glorious new stadium after Arthur Ashe, who in 1968 became the first African American man to win the U.S. Open.

Martina Navratilova epitomized the new chiseled athlete who was shaped and supported by the soaring incomes in our sport. From 1982 through 1986, the years that will be remembered as her prime, Martina compiled a stunning won-lost match record of 427–14. In a regimen new to women's tennis, she practiced and trained seven hours a day, lifting weights, running sprints, and performing agility exercises. Equally important, she used her growing wealth to create her own team of supporters. She hired a coach, an athletic trainer, and a nutritionist. The money in tennis was creating new opportunities for players, and others would soon follow Martina's example by investing in their careers. In the decades to come, every touring pro would have an entourage, one that might even include a psychologist.

Incredible as it sounds, Martina had not had a coach since her defection to the United States in 1975. That changed late in the summer of 1981, when she hired Renée Richards, a New York ophthalmologist with a unique history in men's *and* women's tennis. Renée was the former

MARTINA NAVRATILOVA EPITOMIZED THE NEW CHISELED ATHLETE WHO WAS SHAPED AND SUPPORTED BY THE SOARING INCOMES IN OUR SPORT.

Richard Raskind, who had played for Yale University and had earned a high ranking in the East. Dr. Raskind was competing in men's thirty-five-and-over tournaments when, in the early 1970s, he underwent sex reassignment surgery and became Renée Richards. Renée was allowed to join our tour in 1976, despite protests from some of the women. Her success as a competitor was limited, but she became a splendid coach. Under Renée's guidance, Martina changed her backhand grip, which gave her an improved flat backhand drive along with her bread-and-butter slice. She also developed a ruthless infallibility at the net and rock-solid consistency at the baseline.

In a society that viewed slender, lithe women as the ideal, Martina had to have enormous faith in herself to further build up her already muscular body. "She looks like a man" was the frequently heard pejorative. But Martina had her own definition of femininity. "I never found myself particularly attractive," she said in 1982. "I wasn't bad looking, but I had a strong face. My body was more like a boy's than a girl's. But I've been growing into it, and the last few years I've felt more like a woman than ever before."

Martina's dominance became complete in 1983 when—on her eleventh try— she won the only major title that had eluded her, the U.S. Open, with the loss of only nineteen games. In the year and a half that followed, no one could touch her. I remember thinking that her play bordered on the unreal, in part because of her unbelievable speed and power. She moved and placed her shots so quickly that her opponents had little time to prepare and were consistently rushed.

Above: If you combine singles, doubles, and mixed doubles into one all-around category, Martina Navratilova was the best all-around women's tennis player in history.

At left: Martina Navratilova thanks her racket for an especially fine shot during her victory over Chrissie Evert in the 1984 U.S. Open final.

Below: Martina won an unprecedented ninth Wimbledon singles title in 1990. She shared the previous women's record of eight with Helen Wills Moody. Among the men, Roger Federer has also won eight Wimbledon singles titles.

CHRISSIE & MARTINA

A rivalry for the ages

•

The seesawing nature of the Chrissie Evert–Martina Navratilova rivalry made it the longest and greatest in women's tennis. They played each other eighty times from 1973 through 1988, with Martina winning forty-three of them. The rivalry worked because both women were ambitious and flexible, because they were nearly the same age (Chrissie was a year and a half older than Martina), and because their contrasting styles—baseliner versus net-rusher—produced terrific entertainment. They made each other better. Martina strengthened her baseline game in order to compete with Chrissie; Chrissie began working with weights, switched to a more powerful graphite racket, and began attacking more at the net to compete with Martina. "I made Martina more disciplined," Chrissie said. "She made me more physically fit." Chrissie said she probably would have retired earlier had Martina not presented her with a new challenge. Chrissie and Martina, forever linked in tennis history, had become friends soon after Martina arrived in the United States in 1973, and Chrissie was one of the few people who knew that Martina planned to defect. They played doubles together for a while and won two Grand Slam titles, the 1975 French Open and the 1976 Wimbledon. The doubles partnership ended, however, once Martina began to threaten Chrissie's supremacy in singles. Later, when their careers neared an end, they shared a friendship—and status—that is unique to all-time greats.

No matter who won, their respect for each other never wavered. Chrissie won their 1985 French Open final, above, and Martina won their 1985 Wimbledon final, at right.

Martina won six straight majors—a record shared with Margaret Court—from the 1983 Wimbledon through the 1984 U.S. Open. In doing so, she captured a $1 million prize offered by the International Tennis Federation (ITF) for anyone who could win four straight majors, whether in a calendar year or over a period of two years. The feat became known as a "Cash Slam" (we could also call it a "Martina Slam"), and it was criticized by traditionalists and some members of the media. By 2012, the ITF had backed away from this more liberal definition, stating in its constitution that a player achieved a Grand Slam by winning the four major titles in one calendar year.

Heading into the 1984 Australian Open, which was held in December, Martina had a chance to win the traditional Grand Slam. But it was not to be. As Frank Deford observed in *Sports Illustrated*, "Although Navratilova had lost but once in the past 18 months . . . there was a growing feeling on the tour that she was ripe for the taking, that the sheer weight of numbers pressed on her." Playing too cautiously and without her usual spontaneity, Martina lost in the semifinals to a fearless Helena Suková, a nineteen-year-old from Czechoslovakia. Helena then lost in the final to Chrissie Evert.

This period marked the turning point in the careers of Tracy Austin and Andrea Jaeger. Tracy, winner of the U.S. Open at age sixteen and again at eighteen, made several attempts to compete after injuring her back a second

Above: Russia's Anna Kournikova, with a blend of talent and beauty, inspired a new wave of young tennis players.

THE MORE THINGS CHANGE,
THE MORE GLAMOUR REMAINS

While women's tennis evolved toward a more rugged and physical plateau, another strong movement began. The "feminization of women's tennis," as I called it, was endorsed by the Women's Tennis Association, which in 1985 began producing a calendar featuring female tennis players wearing slinky gowns, bathing suits, heavy makeup, and jewelry. I was not as opposed to the feminization of women's tennis as some might suspect. Even though I have always wanted women to be appreciated for their accomplishments, I think every beautiful woman has the right to promote her assets. I also think tennis's female stars were not trying to apologize for their muscles (as some claimed) as much as they were marketing themselves commercially. Although male sports stars were marketable primarily on the basis of skill, some female tennis players still thought they had to show a glamorous side. The agents who made the endorsement deals helped fuel the trend by distributing photographs of their clients dressed not as tennis players but as fashion models. They had learned that a player did not need to be No. 1 to become rich. Nevertheless, a player *did* have to be accomplished. Anna Kournikova, of Russia, is a perfect example. She appeared on the cover of *Sports Illustrated* and was one of the most frequently searched personalities on Google – not only because she was extremely beautiful but also because she ranked as high as No. 8 in the world. She teamed with Martina Hingis to win two Australian Open doubles titles (1999 and 2002) and two WTA Finals titles (1999 and 2000). In her best singles performance at a Grand Slam tournament, she reached the Wimbledon semifinals in 1997. She was a huge inspiration for a new generation of girls, not only in Russia but throughout the world.

time but complained of nagging pain. During her rehabilitation in 1982, she began to enjoy life away from the circuit, and her incredible single-mindedness began to wane. She competed intermittently during the 1980s and attempted a comeback as late as 1994 before permanently retiring. After leaving the tour, she went on to enjoy a long and successful career as a television commentator.

In 1983, Andrea Jaeger beat me decisively in the Wimbledon semifinals to reach her second and last major final. She was eighteen; I was thirty-nine, and it was my last match ever at Wimbledon. It was Andrea's last, as well. Andrea had been happy enough when she was a little sprite of fifteen, but as she matured, her outlook changed. For reasons that were never clear to me, Andrea apparently played on despite painful injuries to her feet, neck, shoulder, and pelvis. She finally faced reality at the 1984 Los Angeles Olympics, where tennis—absent from the Games since 1924—was being featured as a demonstration sport. Andrea struggled through her first match but afterward could not lift her arm above her head. After leaving the tour in 1985, she obtained a degree in theology and devoted her life to charitable causes.

When Andrea left the game, Jerry Diamond, the WTA's executive director, voiced his concern over our sport's loss of some of its most promising young women. "There are a ton of players who are running into physical, emotional, and mental problems," Diamond said then. "The pro game is ruining a heck of a lot of good talent. The whole area requires review. Many of the young girls, because they're not emotionally or intellectually mature, find themselves unable to cope. There are tremendous pressures caused by agents, parents, and others."

In 1985, the Women's International Professional Tennis Council—a board that included members of the WTA and the ITF—barred players fourteen and under from competing in professional events and limited fifteen-year-olds to a reasonable schedule.

Above, top: Zina Garrison, shown here at the 1993 U.S. Open, in 1990 became the first Black woman since Althea Gibson to reach the Wimbledon final. Zina lost to Martina Navratilova.

Above, bottom: Zina Garrison and Pam Shriver were golden at the 1988 Olympics in Seoul, South Korea.

Opposite page: Lori McNeil holds the Maud Watson trophy after winning the 1993 DFS Classic in Birmingham, England. Maud Watson, the first woman to win Wimbledon, won the very same trophy in the 1880s.

Zina Garrison and Lori McNeil distinguished themselves not only as athletes but also as the first Black women to rank near the top of the game since Althea Gibson in the 1950s. Zina and Lori were born one month apart in 1963 and grew up playing against each other at MacGregor Park, a public park in Houston. Both developed their games under the guidance of John Wilkerson, the MacGregor Park coach. And both won the all-Black American Tennis Association's national championship, the same championship Althea had won four times before she was allowed to compete in tournaments sanctioned by what was then the all-white United States Lawn Tennis Association.

In September 1986, at a tour stop in Tampa, Florida, Lori and Zina made history when they played each other in the first all-Black women's final. Lori recalled the match as "emotional and difficult." Zina remembered it differently. "We were so relaxed it didn't bother either of us. We practiced that morning together, got in the car, and went to the tournament." Lori won in three sets.

In 1990, Zina became the second Black woman to reach the Wimbledon final. During her career, she won 14 total tour events and nearly $4.6 million in prize money. Lori won 10 tour events and $3.4 million in prize money.

Zina and Lori, like all Black players, continued to face discrimination. Some had trouble finding private housing while competing in junior tournaments. When Zina was a junior player, she was staying in a private home in New Jersey when a commotion awakened her. In the front yard, outside her window, some angry neighbors were burning a cross.

The 1998 Swiss Fed Cup team celebrates after beating France and qualifying for the final against Spain. From left, Patty Schnyder, Emmanuelle Gagliardi, and Martina Hingis. Spain prevailed in the final, 3–2.

Above: Conchita Martínez, left, and Arantxa Sánchez Vicario won the bronze medal at the 1996 Olympics in Atlanta. In Federation Cup play, they led Spain to five championships in the 1990s.

I admire Zina and Lori because, more than other rising players of their era, they were fighting battles off the court and on, just as we fought for women in the 1960s and 1970s. The racism they faced, whether overt or unintentional, might have chipped away at their confidence, but they persisted and won. In so doing they continued the decades-long process of smoothing the path for Black women who came after them. Those women included Chanda Rubin, of Lafayette, Louisiana, who in 1996 won a Grand Slam doubles title, the Australian Open, with Arantxa Sánchez Vicario.

Meanwhile, new stars from Europe and South America sparked a rise in popularity of women's tennis worldwide. The new contenders included Gabriela Sabatini of Argentina, Helena Suková of Czechoslovakia, Arantxa Sánchez Vicario of Spain, Manuela Maleeva of Bulgaria, and—most famously—Stefanie Graf of Germany and Monica Seles of Yugoslavia. For the first time since the days of Suzanne Lenglen, women's matches in the French Championships at Roland Garros now drew as much interest as the men's. The women's Italian Open, disassociated from the men's championship in 1979, returned to Rome's Foro Italico in 1987 and was a huge success.

GABRIELA SABATINI

Argentina's Gabriela "Gaby" Sabatini, who grew up in Buenos Aires, dazzled audiences with her beauty, grace, and style. She was a goddess in Argentina, where people approached her on the street and kissed her hand. A poll revealed that she was second in popularity only to the president. She took a big circular windup on both her forehand and one-handed backhand, sweeping up the back of the ball, generating heavy topspin, and finishing with a triumphant follow-through. Her backhand down the line was an exceptional weapon that enabled her to beat Stefanie Graf in the final of the 1990 U.S. Open. The only Argentine woman to win a Grand Slam singles title, she ranked in the world's top five from 1988 to 1993. In 1988, she carried the Argentine flag in the opening ceremony at the Olympics in Seoul, where she won the silver medal in singles. She was inducted into the International Tennis Hall of Fame in 2006.

The inclusion of tennis as a medal sport in the 1988 Olympics—for the first time since 1924—further globalized the game, and the inclusion of wheelchair tennis as a medal sport in the 1992 Paralympic Games expanded access to people with physical disabilities.

The Soviet Union began putting more effort and money into its players and by 1987 had a top-twenty star in Natasha Zvereva of Belarus, its first since Olga Morozova. Natasha, asked whether she would prefer to win Wimbledon or the Olympics someday, replied, "The Olympics." She later won the bronze medal in doubles with Leila Meskhi at the 1992 Summer Olympics in Barcelona. Not incidentally, she also won eighteen Grand Slam women's doubles titles, fourteen of them with Gigi Fernández of Puerto Rico.

National support for tennis continued to grow in Japan, which had held its first professional tournament in 1973 and by the mid-1990s had a top ten player in Kimiko Date. Kimiko reached the singles semifinals of all four Grand Slam events, won the Japan Open a record four times, and enjoyed a year-end, career-high ranking of No. 4 in 1995.

And in China, tennis mushroomed as an exploding middle class embraced the game as a family-friendly activity that also conveyed social status. Within a generation China would become one of the sport's greatest supporters, sponsoring a major tournament, showcasing tennis in the Olympics, and producing a champion in Li Na.

A very different story unfolded in South Africa, a tennis-loving nation that had sent its top women players abroad as early as the 1920s and had won the Federation Cup in 1972. By the early 1970s, the world was less and less willing to accommodate a nation that harbored an apartheid system of institutionalized racial segregation, and South Africa's sports teams faced protests and boycotts. The International Olympic Committee expelled South Africa in 1970. Poland withdrew from the Federation

Cup in 1973 in protest of South Africa's participation, and men's Davis Cup teams from India, Mexico, and Colombia refused to compete in South Africa in the mid-1970s. The ITF expelled South Africa from international competition in 1978, then readmitted the nation in October 1991 following the overturning of apartheid.

The depth of international talent sparked growth in the Federation Cup team championships, our world cup of women's tennis. We had thirty-two nations competing in 1980; we had forty-seven in 1990; and in 2000, we hit one hundred nations for the very first time. Spain, led by Arantxa Sánchez Vicario and Conchita Martínez, won the Cup five times in the 1990s. Arantxa and Conchita, the winningest Federation Cup players in history, won a combined 97 singles matches and, playing together, 18 doubles matches.

The rise of the Federation Cup coincided with the quiet conclusion of the Wightman Cup in 1989. The annual competition between Great Britain and the United States had suffered from declining interest and years of American domination. The United States won the final matchup, its eleventh in a row, 7–0, at the College of William & Mary in Williamsburg, Virginia. In all, Britain won only ten of the sixty-one competitions held since 1923.

Gabriela Sabatini became one of the most financially successful tennis players ever. She partnered with the German perfume company Muelhens in the late 1980s to create fragrances graced with her beautiful name. Their popularity continues unabated.

ARANTXA SÁNCHEZ VICARIO

Arantxa Sánchez Vicario of Spain enjoyed one of the strongest all-around records in women's tennis. She ranked among the world's top five eight times between 1989 and 2000 and finished the year No. 2 in 1993, 1994, and 1996. She won four Grand Slam singles titles – three at Roland Garros and one at the U.S. Open – and ten Grand Slam doubles titles (six in women's, four in mixed). She won four Olympic medals (two silver, two bronze). In Federation Cup play, she and Conchita Martínez, the 1994 Wimbledon champion, amassed 115 victories in singles and doubles combined.

The emergence of so many talented young Europeans could be traced in part to their national tennis federations. The German Federation, for example, charted the progress of its potential champions by computer, paid their traveling expenses, and provided them with superior coaching. Czechoslovakia by this time was also highly committed to its future stars, funneling its top prospects into regional training centers and, ultimately, into a national center in Prague. Czech coaches, headed by former men's Wimbledon champion Jan Kodeš, were among the best in the world. Those with the highest coaching certificates had studied physiology and psychology and had earned their master's degrees in the theory of sport. As in Germany, the Czech Federation offered free coaching to players and underwrote their expenses.

In America, by comparison, the burden of producing champions was largely carried by individual families. Elite juniors might receive some help from local patrons, their regional USTA sections, or agents who contracted for a percentage of future earnings when the junior turned pro. But it was mostly parents who had to pay for instruction, court time, and travel, all of which could exceed $20,000 a year, with no guarantee that their children were receiving the best possible coaching. Children whose families could not afford the enormous costs rarely had a chance to succeed in tennis.

In 1987, the USTA established a junior development committee, of which I was a member, and, in 1988, it began investing heavily in junior tennis in an effort to increase America's chances of producing a new champion. The USTA introduced grade-school children to the game, provided regional training facilities for promising juniors, and helped finance members of a national junior team. It established its first National Training Center in 1991 and today supports two, one in Orlando, Florida, and one in Carson, California.

It was Germany that nurtured our next great female tennis champion—Stefanie Graf—along with her male counterpart, Boris Becker. Germany might have done so sooner, if the world wars had not decimated its once thriving tennis scene. After World War I, Germany was not invited back into the International Lawn Tennis Federation for ten years. By the 1930s, Germany had renewed its tennis tradition and had female stars in Cecilia "Cilly" Aussem and Hilde Krahwinkel Sperling and a men's champion in Gottfried von Cramm. That renaissance was dashed by World War II, which left Germany once again defeated and in ruins. The first Germans with no recollection of the war era were children born in the 1960s, and a series of fine German players came from that generation, joining the tour in the late 1970s and early 1980s. Bettina Bunge, Sylvia Hanika, and Claudia Kohde-Kilsch came first and were followed by Germany's most successful woman of all, Stefanie Graf.

Stefanie—who was known as Steffi throughout her playing career—was only thirteen when she began playing the tour full-time in 1983, two years before age restrictions went into effect. Over the next few years, she developed from a skinny little girl with an excellent forehand into a tall, sinewy athlete with a terrific serve and one of the most dangerous forehands ever seen in tennis.

Above: Stefanie Graf, with her killer forehand, was in top form at the 1999 French Open at Roland Garros.

Above: In 1988, Stefanie Graf became the third woman—after Maureen Connolly and Margaret Court—to win a Grand Slam. Stefanie's Slam is the only one completed on three different surfaces: grass, clay, and hard courts. It is also the only Slam that required 28 individual match victories. Not until 1986 did the draws of all four majors comprise 128 competitors and require the champion to win a total of seven matches. In Stefanie's 28 victories, she lost only two sets. The Olympic gold medal that followed made it a "Golden Slam."

STEFANIE GRAF

She chose winning over smiling

•

Stefanie Maria Graf, born in 1969, grew up in the village of Brühl, near Heidelberg, West Germany. Her father, Peter, a car and insurance salesman, gave her a sawed-off racket before her fourth birthday and created a makeshift court inside the house by fastening a string between two chairs. Peter and Stefanie batted the ball back and forth, and Peter, sensing talent, offered rewards: a breadstick for ten successive hits, ice cream and hot strawberries for twenty-five. Peter frequently slammed the ball away from Stefanie on the twenty-fourth exchange, "because you can't have ice cream every time." At age five and a half, Stefanie played in the seven-and-under division of the annual "Bambino Tournament" in Munich. Conny Konzack, a West German freelance journalist specializing in tennis, said that even then "you could see this girl would be something in tennis."

At age thirteen, Stefanie won the national German eighteen-and-under championship and also began her first full year on the women's professional tour. The sportswriters nicknamed her "Gräfin" (German for countess) and praised her for her "German attitude," which embodied toughness, ambition, and a streak of stubbornness. Stefanie also acquired a reputation as the girl who never smiled. Some thought her father pushed her too hard. Her mother once said to her, "Steffi, I would love to see one picture of you in the papers in which you are smiling." Stefanie replied, "What do you want me to do, Mother, smile or win?"

- 22 Grand Slam singles titles
    - 4 Australian Open (1988–1990, 1994)
    - 6 French Open (1987, 1988, 1993, 1995, 1996, 1999)
    - 7 Wimbledon (1988, 1989, 1991–1993, 1995, 1996)
    - 5 U.S. Open (1988, 1989, 1993, 1995, 1996)
- Won the Grand Slam, 1988
- 1 Grand Slam women's doubles title
- Olympics
    - 1988 Seoul (gold medal, singles; bronze medal, doubles)
    - 1992 Barcelona (silver medal, singles)
- 5 WTA Finals singles titles (1987, 1989, 1993, 1995, 1996)
- Federation Cup: 20–2 singles, 8–2 doubles
- Year-end No. 1 in the world (1987–1990, 1993, 1994, 1995 [tied with Monica Seles], 1996)
- International Tennis Hall of Fame inductee, 2004

NOTEWORTHY STATISTIC

- No. 1 on WTA tour for a career total of 377 weeks, a record

"WHAT DO YOU WANT ME TO DO, MOTHER, SMILE OR WIN?"

Clockwise from top: Stefanie en route to her Grand Slam in 1988; with the late Princess Diana; soaking in the history etched on the Wimbledon salver with finalist Arantxa Sánchez Vicario in 1996.

THE HEART OF STEFANIE'S GAME WAS HER FOREHAND, A PRODUCT OF QUICKNESS, TIMING, AND STRENGTH.

Stefanie's father and coach, Peter Graf, was keenly aware of the risks posed by too much competition too soon, and he limited her schedule to fifteen or fewer tournaments a year. During prolonged breaks from the tour, Stefanie would return to Brühl, her home village, where she worked to improve her game, particularly her backhand, which she almost always sliced, and her serve. Players who sniped that she was protecting her ranking by not playing more should have known better. Women's tennis could not afford to lose another star.

The heart of Stefanie's game was her forehand, a product of quickness, timing, and strength. She was so fast that she could hit the forehand from any position on the court. I was announcing her first-round match on a back court at Wimbledon when she was still relatively new, and I exclaimed, "Feet! Just look at her feet!" It was unbelievable. Her footwork was fabulous.

She was the first player to hit that big forehand while standing in the backhand corner. She took a circular windup and then unleashed herself into the ball, hitting it flat, without topspin, and striking it at its highest point. Without spin to slow it down, the ball streaked over the net like a bullet—faster than the shots of some men—and landed deep in her opponent's court. "It is a special stroke," said Pavel Složil, who helped coach her. "You must have very good footwork, and your timing must be excellent. It is not so easy to learn something like this. This is the future of the game of tennis: to go for it and not play the ball a hundred times over the net."

Indeed, the stroke came to symbolize Stefanie's fearlessness. "I always take the risk," she said, "no matter what stage of the match."

Stefanie won eight tournaments in 1986 and rose to No. 3 in the world. In 1987, a week shy of her eighteenth birthday, she defeated Martina Navratilova, 6–4, 4–6, 8–6, to become the youngest champion in the history of Roland Garros up until that time.

In 1988, Stefanie won the first three major tournaments of the year—the Australian, French, and Wimbledon—to come within one leg of winning the first Grand Slam since Margaret Court's eighteen years before. Stefanie beat Chrissie Evert in the final of the Australian Open, which was played on hard courts at Melbourne Park instead of Kooyong's grass courts for the first time. At Paris, she crushed Natasha Zvereva, 6–0, 6–0, in the first shutout in a singles final ever at the French Championships. At Wimbledon, she demolished her first six opponents, conceding only seventeen games, and then defeated six-time defending champion Martina Navratilova with a breathtaking show of youth, speed, and power. American Mary Joe Fernández, who lost decisively to Stefanie in the fourth round, described what it was like to play her: "She had the best

A month shy of her fourteenth birthday, Jennifer Capriati signed endorsements totaling a reported $6 million over five years and reached the final of her first professional Women's Tennis Association tour event.

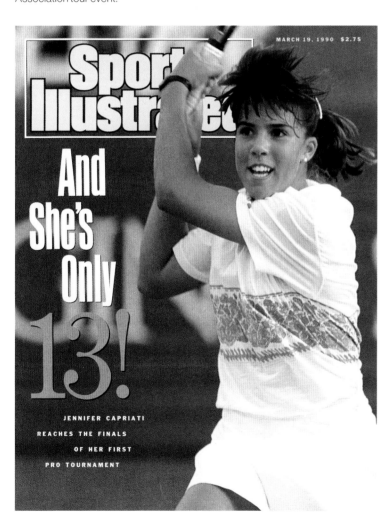

MARCH 19, 1990 $2.75

Sports Illustrated

And She's Only 13!

JENNIFER CAPRIATI
REACHES THE FINALS
OF HER FIRST
PRO TOURNAMENT

serve in the game and a huge forehand, and she played with such a quick tempo. You would be off the court before you knew what happened."

Two months later, at the U.S. Open, nineteen-year-old Stefanie wrapped up the Slam with a three-set victory over Gabriela Sabatini. Then, with barely enough time to savor her victory, she traveled to Seoul, South Korea, where she won the Olympic gold medal in singles and helped invent a new term: the "Golden Slam."

During her seventeen-year professional career, Stefanie Graf won 107 tournaments, including twenty-two Grand Slam titles, and ranked No. 1 in the world eight different times. Her accomplishments are astounding—even more so considering that she retired at age thirty, when she was still ranked No. 3 in the world.

Women's tennis rocked anew in 1990 at Roland Garros, where fourteen-year-old Floridian Jennifer Capriati, having just completed eighth grade, reached the semifinals, and sixteen-year-old Monica Seles became the youngest French Open champion ever. A year later, Jennifer became the youngest Wimbledon semifinalist ever at fifteen years, ninety-six days. When she and Monica met in the semifinals of the 1991 U.S. Open, their showdown, which Monica won, 7–6 in the third, was called "the best 18-and-under match ever played."

Trained for stardom from the age of four, Jennifer Capriati was viewed as a can't-miss prodigy. She was powerful and relentless, pounding the ball from anywhere on the court. Happy and unpretentious, she also captivated the media. Under pressure from the Capriati camp, the WTA had relaxed its rules that limited the number of events young players could enter. With the help of International Management Group (IMG), the powerful player-management firm, she became a millionaire when she was only thirteen.

JANA NOVOTNÁ

After losing a 4–1 lead in the third set against Stefanie Graf in the 1993 Wimbledon final, Jana Novotná of the Czech Republic cried on the shoulder of the Duchess of Kent. All of us who have seen a near-certain victory slip away cried a little with her. But Jana never stopped trying. She lost in the 1997 Wimbledon final, this time to Martina Hingis. But, in 1998, Jana put memories and nerves behind her and defeated Nathalie Tauziat of France to win the Ladies' Singles at Wimbledon. We lost Jana to cancer in 2017. She was only forty-nine years old.

But there would be an ominous side to Jennifer's story. As S.L. Price wrote years later in *Sports Illustrated*: "Endorsements, magazine covers: All the treasures of the modern age were laid at Capriati's feet. No one bothered to ask if any of it was good for her."

Jennifer's schedule became packed with adult responsibilities: tournaments, exhibitions, and sponsor obligations. Equally important, she lost her coach, Tom Gullikson. As *Tennis* magazine reported, the USTA Player Development program felt it could no longer justify subsidizing Gullikson, and he and the Capriati camp could not reach a financial agreement that would have allowed him to continue coaching Jennifer. John Evert, an IMG agent (and brother of Chrissie), observed in *Tennis* that without Gullikson's steadying influence and have-fun-and-give-it-100-percent approach, something seminal was lost. "And the team started to break down."

Jennifer enjoyed a reprieve at the 1992 Summer Olympics in Barcelona, Spain. Free from the spotlight and sheltered with her peers in the Olympic Village, she upset Stefanie Graf to win the gold medal. But the joy was short-lived. She left the tour after losing in the first round of the 1993 U.S. Open. She would begin a slow comeback in 1996, but five more years would pass before the can't-miss prodigy etched her name in the record books.

Monica Seles, two years older than Jennifer, ushered in a new kind of power, one that was a level above that of previous generations. She was a ferocious baseline attacker, a left-hander who hit both forehand and backhand strokes with two hands and exceptional force. She also brought a new sound to women's tennis. The grunts, shrieks, and screeches that she emitted every time she struck the ball were a new factor for her opponents to reckon with.

In an echo of fashionistas of the past, Monica gave us a bolus of glamour with her fashion savvy and dramatic flair. Her idols included Madonna and the 1920s superstar Suzanne Lenglen. "Wouldn't it be neat to be a

Monica Seles, a left-hander, struck the ball with two hands off both sides.

mystery woman and bring high fashion back to the sport?" she said, in a 1991 interview with Curry Kirkpatrick of *Sports Illustrated*. "To be like Suzanne, like Madonna—out there but untouchable? Like, unreachable!"

Monica dominated the tour in 1991, winning the Australian Open, French Open, and U.S. Open. Along the way she snapped Stefanie Graf's hold on the WTA's No. 1 ranking. A Grand Slam might well have been within Monica's reach, but she withdrew unexpectedly from Wimbledon, citing a case of severe shin splints.

Monica closed out the year by beating twenty-year-old Gabriela Sabatini in the Virginia Slims Championship final at Madison Square Garden in the first five-set match among women since 1901. Monica won, 6–4, 5–7, 3–6, 6–4, 6–2, in three hours and forty-seven minutes to claim the $250,000 first prize.

Monica won eight Grand Slam tournaments during the three-year period from 1990 to early 1993. Then, in April 1993, nineteen-year-old Monica became the victim of a shocking crime. While sitting down during a changeover during a tournament in Hamburg, Germany, she was stabbed between the shoulder blades with a nine-inch boning knife. The perpetrator was Günther Parche, an unemployed lathe operator and fan of Stefanie Graf. Parche, who had stalked Monica during the tournament, told police that he stabbed Monica so that Stefanie could pass her in the rankings. The sudden, unprovoked attack, in full view of ten thousand people, forever changed how tennis tournaments managed the security of their most valuable asset—the players.

Above: Monica Seles brought fresh glamour and a new level of power to tennis. We will never know all that she might have accomplished had she not been attacked by a mentally unstable fan.

MONICA SELES

Monica Seles, an ethnic Hungarian, was born in 1973 and raised in Novi Sad, Yugoslavia, which is now Serbia. Her father, Karolj, a former triple jump specialist who worked as a political cartoonist and documentary filmmaker, began teaching her to play tennis when she was five. Although Karolj was a tennis novice, he had studied biomechanics at university. He allowed Monica's novel groundstrokes—two-handed on both the backhand and forehand side—to evolve naturally, and he taught her to attack the ball as it bounced up from the court rather than wait for it to come to her. Equally important, he made the game fun. He drew cartoons on tennis balls for her when she was a child and, throughout his life, sent her cartoon-embellished coaching tips and encouragement. Monica won Yugoslavia's national tournament at age nine and was Yugoslavia's Sportswoman of the Year at age ten. At age thirteen, accompanied by her older brother, Zoltan, she moved to the United States to train at the Nick Bollettieri Tennis Academy in Bradenton, Florida. Her parents followed several months later. At fifteen, she won her first WTA singles title; at sixteen, her first Grand Slam title.

- **9 Grand Slam singles titles**
    - **4 Australian Open (1991–1993, 1996)**
    - **3 French Open (1990–1992)**
    - **2 U.S. Open (1991, 1992)**
- **3 WTA Finals singles titles (1990–1992)**
- **Olympics: 2000 Sydney (bronze medal, singles)**
- **Federation Cup: 15–2 singles, 2–0 doubles**
- **Year-end No. 1 in the world (1991, 1992, 1995 [tied with Stefanie Graf])**
- **International Tennis Hall of Fame inductee, 2009**

LINDSAY DAVENPORT

The height of precision and power

•

Lindsay Davenport, a 6-foot-2½ Californian born in 1976 into a family of volleyball stars, was the best striker of the ball of her era. Playing with power, consistency, and deftness with the racket, she won six Grand Slam titles: three in singles (the 2000 Australian Open, 1999 Wimbledon, and 1998 U.S. Open) and three in women's doubles. She won the gold medal at the 1996 Summer Olympics in Atlanta and the 1999 WTA Championships. She won 55 tour titles altogether, was a Fed Cup stalwart with a 33–3 overall record (26–3 in singles, 7–0 in doubles), and earned more than $22 million in prize money. She was inducted into the International Tennis Hall of Fame in 2014.

And it left us with two unanswerable questions: What more would an unharmed Monica have achieved? And how many fewer titles might Stefanie have won? While recovering from the stabbing at a clinic in Colorado, Monica watched Stefanie beat Mary Joe Fernández in the 1993 French Open final. When Stefanie held up the Suzanne Lenglen trophy, Monica wrote in her memoir, "I couldn't stop myself from thinking, *That should've been me*." A month later, when Stefanie won Wimbledon, Monica could still barely lift her arm above her shoulder.

Monica spent twenty-seven months away from the tour. Her physical wound healed, but her emotional wounds remained wide open. She struggled with depression and found solace in food, which caused her to gain as much as forty pounds. She described her battle with "unconscious eating" in her memoir, *Getting a Grip: On My Body, My Mind, My Self*.

Her troubles were magnified when her beloved father and coach, Karolj, was diagnosed with cancer in 1993. And she was shocked and outraged by the mild punishment—two years of probation—imposed on her attacker, whose knife had come within millimeters of her spine.

When Monica finally returned to the tour in 1995, fans cheered her. She appeared to pick up where she left off, reaching the final of the U.S. Open and then capturing the 1996 Australian Open. She finished 1996 ranked No. 2 in the world. In 1999, Monica, by then a U.S. citizen, played on the championship Fed Cup team that I coached. (Perhaps the strongest Fed Cup team ever, it included four world No. 1 players: Monica, Venus and Serena Williams, and Lindsay Davenport.) I talked to Monica before the week started and acknowledged the challenges she still faced. She told me she still got scared when she walked on the court. I wanted her to feel safe, so we had two security guards standing protectively behind her wherever she went.

I loved coaching Monica in Fed Cup and will never forget how she warmed up for a match. She would drill those double-fisted strokes against a wall while standing only about three feet away. *Forehand! Backhand! Forehand! Backhand!* The ball never bounced. It just shot off her racket like bullets out of a machine gun. When I served as Olympic captain in Sydney, Australia, in 2000, I'd ask her to execute this warm-up just so I could watch. I still don't know how she did it.

But inside, Monica was never the same. Her father's death in 1998 affected her deeply, and her extra weight was causing

I LOVED COACHING MONICA IN FED CUP AND WILL NEVER FORGET HOW SHE WARMED UP FOR A MATCH.

her body to begin to break down. "I love to go out and practice," she said in an interview with *Tennis* magazine in 1999. "But I could put the racquet down today and never pick it up again in my life. It's very strange." She played her last professional match in 2003, when she was not yet thirty.

The power tennis introduced by Monica Seles reverberated throughout the sport. It arrived in its most triumphant form with Venus and Serena Williams. Between them, the two sisters won thirty-one Grand Slam singles titles—twenty-three for Serena, seven for Venus through July 2022—and teamed together to win fourteen Grand Slam doubles championships and three Olympic gold medals. They triggered a tidal wave of interest in women's tennis and stood as role models for women of color throughout the world.

Venus and Serena were destined for stardom before they were born. Their parents, Oracene Price and Richard Williams, were raising three daughters from Oracene's first marriage when they decided to have additional children after being awakened to the tremendous opportunities in tennis. Serena recalled in her memoir that "at some point my dad was watching a match on television, and he couldn't believe how much money these women were making, just for hitting a tennis ball." Richard was awestruck that the tournament winner—Romania's Virginia Ruzici, the 1978 French Open champion—made nearly as much during the tournament as he made in a year as the owner of a small security business. He and Oracene were both good athletes, and with books and videos, they taught themselves the game. Richard also wrote a seventy-eight-page strategic plan that would become part of the Williams family history.

Above: Venus Williams strikes her forehand with an open stance. Oracene Price, Venus's mother, introduced the open stance to her husband, Richard Williams, who taught it to Venus and Serena.

Venus Williams, left, and Serena were famous before they were out of grade school.

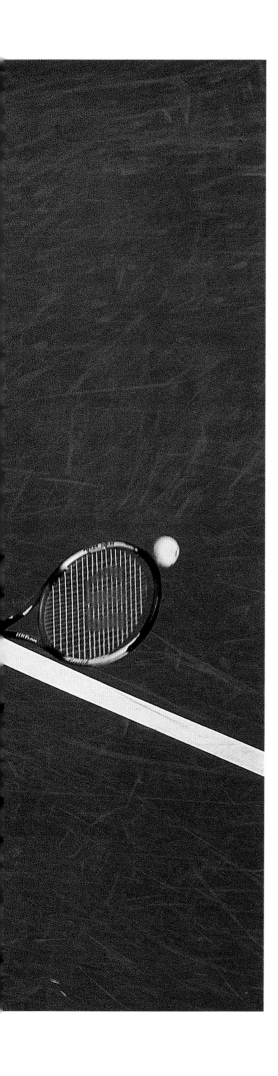

Venus was born in June 1980, Serena fifteen months later, in September 1981. The family lived in Compton, California, a working-class city with a high poverty rate in Los Angeles County. Richard began teaching Venus on the public courts in Compton and Watts when she was four. Serena had a full-size racket in her hand by the time she was three. More than tennis, Richard and Oracene taught them discipline. Richard posted motivational signs around the court—*If you fail to plan, you plan to fail.* He also instilled in his daughters an unwavering belief that they could become the best tennis players in the world. Richard achieved the status of legend with the 2021 movie *King Richard*, which depicts these early years of Venus's and Serena's development.

The girls were terrific athletes, prodigies. I first saw Venus and Serena when they were eight and seven, respectively, at a Domino's Pizza World TeamTennis clinic. It was clear they had huge potential. Serena's serve was almost impossible to believe. Even as a very young child, she had a beautiful rhythm.

At age ten, Venus was ranked No. 1 in the pressure cooker of Southern California's twelve-and-under girls' tennis and was already famous. She was featured in *Sports Illustrated* and appeared on the front page of the *New York Times*. She was signing autographs, playing in exhibition tournaments with celebrities, and being pursued by multiple agents. Richard Williams anointed her "a ghetto Cinderella." She was slightly built, only eighty pounds, but she was tall for her age—5 foot 4—and still growing. She was fast; she had run a 5:29 mile at age eight. And she hit the ball hard. Every time. Serena was still in the background, but barely. She, too, was winning junior titles.

When Venus was still ten, the family moved to Florida, where the girls trained at Rick Macci's elite academy, which provided housing and unlimited coaching in return for future reimbursement. Richard continued coaching his daughters (along with Macci) and, spurning conventional wisdom, removed them from the USTA's junior circuit. He thought the fiercely competitive junior tournament schedule conflicted with the girls' academic studies while also exposing them to what he perceived as degrading comments from other players and parents.

In 1994, Venus was fourteen years old, stood 6 foot 1, and was eager to compete professionally. She and another fourteen-year-old, Martina Hingis of Switzerland, turned pro that year under the relaxed age guidelines known as the "Capriati rules," which allowed fourteen-year-olds to play a dozen tour events. Beginning in 1995—in a measure I strongly supported—young teens could join the tour in phases but could not play an unlimited schedule until they were eighteen.

Despite not having played a junior tournament in three and a half years, Venus made a seamless transition to the women's professional tour. Steeled by world-class competition within the tennis academy and in exhibitions held in center-court arenas, she won her first professional match in 1994 at the WTA's Bank of the West Classic in Oakland, California. She defeated Shaun Stafford, a former NCAA singles champion who ranked No. 59 in the world. "I was a little surprised how I wasn't nervous at all, or excited or jumpy, or, you know, yelling and screaming," Venus said afterward. "But I wasn't surprised, because I know I can play and that no one's going to stop me."

In the second round of the tournament, Venus took a set from the reigning French and U.S. Open champion, Arantxa Sánchez Vicario.

Serena turned professional in 1995, a year after Venus. The two sisters were soon knocking off top players with their athleticism, intensity, and mental toughness. In the trend set by Monica Seles, they pounded the ball from the baseline and exhaled loudly on impact. They played with an open stance—perfected it—which gave them more power while reducing the steps they needed to take to reach the ball during groundstroke rallies. In the words of Georges Goven, a former French player and coach, the sisters had "in some fashion invented a tennis that was more economical in terms of the footwork, while being more effective."

MARTINA HINGIS

•

Martina Hingis was born in 1980 in Kosice, Slovakia, to two ranked tennis players, Melanie Molitorová and Karol Hingis. She was named after Martina Navratilova, whose career overlapped with her mother's, and was handed a racket at age two. In 1988, determined to see her daughter realize a championship future, Melanie took Martina to Switzerland, where they defected just before Martina's eighth birthday. Martina told David Jones of the *Guardian* that her mother "moved just for me. She put everything she knew into me. Tried to get us a better living."

Martina matured quickly and was soon setting "youngest-ever" records. At fifteen years, nine months, she became the youngest Grand Slam champion in history when she and Helena Suková won the 1996 women's doubles at Wimbledon. At sixteen years, three months, she won the 1997 Australian Open to become the youngest Grand Slam singles champion. She was the smartest player I've ever seen. She couldn't hit as hard as many of her peers, but she was an all-around player with a brilliant mind. She could mix up her shots and go to net when appropriate. If she got a short ball, she went in and finished off the point. Martina retired three times, first at age twenty-two, when she was struggling with injuries; then again in 2007; and finally in 2017, after establishing herself as the preeminent doubles player on the women's tour. She won the doubles Grand Slam in 1998 with Mirjana Lučić of Croatia at the Australian Open and with Jana Novotná of the Czech Republic at the French Open, Wimbledon, and U.S. Open.

- **5 Grand Slam singles titles**
    - **3 Australian Open (1997–1999)**
    - **1 Wimbledon (1997)**
    - **1 U.S. Open (1997)**
- **13 Grand Slam women's doubles titles**
- **7 Grand Slam mixed doubles titles**
- **Olympics: 2016 Rio de Janeiro (silver medal, women's doubles)**
- **2 WTA Finals singles titles (1998, 2000)**
- **Federation Cup: 18–4 in singles, 11–3 in doubles**
- **Year-end No. 1 in the world (1997, 1999, 2000)**
- **International Tennis Hall of Fame inductee, 2013**

In other ways, the Williams sisters differed. At 6 foot 1, Venus was the twenty-first-century Althea Gibson, with long arms and a long reach. Serena was shorter, at 5 foot 9, and had a sturdier build. Venus was more fluid on the court, Serena more explosive.

Playing a smart, reasonable schedule, Venus and Serena rose steadily over the next few years and soon took their place in history. Venus reached the final of the 1997 U.S. Open at age seventeen, the first unseeded player to do so since the professional era had begun nearly thirty years earlier. But it was Serena who upset the natural order when, at seventeen, she became the first Williams sister to win a major title, the 1999 U.S. Open. Venus then made her big breakthrough in 2000, capturing the Wimbledon and U.S. Open singles titles and gold medals in singles and doubles (with Serena) at the Summer Olympics in Sydney, Australia.

The sisters would share much of the sport's spotlight for the next seventeen years. In so doing, they helped lift women's tennis toward an apex of athleticism, power, and wealth. Their skills and unshakable confidence made them two of the toughest players to beat. At the same time, they inspired their successors. With Venus and Serena came a tidal wave of diversity that just a decade earlier would have been unimaginable.

Above: In 1999, I captained what was probably the most powerful Fed Cup team ever assembled: From left, Venus Williams, Monica Seles, Serena Williams, and Lindsay Davenport. We beat Russia in the finals.

BEHIND THESE WOMEN, A SINGULAR WOMAN

The historic barriers to greatness in tennis were not only financial and racial; they were also political. Youlia Berberian won the Bulgarian singles championship nine times beginning in 1962, but Soviet restrictions prevented her from playing many events outside her country. "I never played any of the majors," Youlia said. "I was in my twenties when I actually heard the word Wimbledon for the first time. The Iron Curtain was no joke and was standing very strong until it was brought down in 1989."

Youlia's daughters — Manuela, Katerina, and Magdalena Maleeva — also faced travel challenges but fared better. With their mother serving as coach and political intermediary, they were able to enjoy long, lucrative professional careers. Manuela, the most successful, had a year-end ranking among the world's top ten from 1984 through 1992. All three sisters ranked among the world's top six on the WTA computer at some point during their careers, and in 1993, all were ranked among the world's top twenty at the same time. Collectively, the Maleevas won 40 WTA titles and nearly $10 million in prize money. Bulgaria's Fed Cup team was essentially Team Maleeva, with three sisters competing and their mother as captain. Martina Navratilova, after losing to Magdalena in the quarterfinals of the 1992 U.S. Open, remarked: "I will be remembered as the player who lost to all three sisters. At least I have beaten their mother. Thank God there are no more Maleevas."

At a time when so many top women were coached by men, Youlia was among the first great female coaches. Moreover, her influence extended far beyond the tennis court. She was a humanitarian who advocated for disabled children and refugees. She served as a member of the Bulgarian Parliament from 1997 to 2001, representing the anticommunist United Democratic Forces. Her accomplishments included leading the passage of Bulgaria's Child Protection Bill. The title of her memoir aptly captures her life's quest: *I Want, I Believe, I Can.*

Fabulous fortunes, as reported by *Forbes*

Forbes magazine began tracking the top-earning athletes in 1990, and female tennis players have always been among the very wealthiest women. In August 1991, Monica Seles (No. 1 among women, with $7.6 million in prize money and endorsement earnings) and Jennifer Capriati (No. 26, with $5.1 million) graced the magazine's cover. Stefanie Graf (No. 16, with $7.3 million) and Gabriela Sabatini (No. 22, with $6.3 million) joined them that year in ranking among the world's thirty highest-paid athletes, male or female.

CHAPTER NINE

VENUS, SERENA, AND THE WORLD

2001
2022

TO

IT WAS a new century, and women's tennis was nearing peak form—the incredible sport we know and love. Never before had women's tennis been so internationally and racially diverse, so financially healthy, or so popular. The six-year, $88 million title sponsorship agreement with Sony Ericsson in 2005 was the largest sponsorship in women's sports and professional tennis at that time.

Page 258: Serena Williams's serve was the most feared stroke in women's tennis.

Page 261: Teenagers Emma Raducanu, foreground, and Leylah Fernandez played a U.S. Open final to remember.

At left: Serena Williams's serve was sheer poetry. Flow, acceleration, timing, and power fused into one of the greatest weapons in tennis history.

By 2020, prize money had reached $180 million, and the Women's Tennis Association (WTA) estimated a record-breaking global audience of seven hundred million total viewers for its combined events. Not even the global Covid-19 pandemic, which interrupted tournament play for five months in 2020, could prevent the continued expansion of the depth of talent on our tour.

In 2020, the United States Tennis Association (USTA) named Stacey Allaster, formerly head of the WTA, as the first woman tournament director of the U.S. Open. In 2021, the French Federation named Amélie Mauresmo, who won Australian Open and Wimbledon singles titles in 2006, as the first woman tournament director of the French Open. And in 2022, WTA President Micky Lawler announced a new multiyear tour sponsorship with Hologic, a medical device and diagnostics company focused on women's health.

This era belonged to Venus and Serena Williams. Perhaps no statistics illustrate the sisters' dominance more than these: They met nine times in Grand Slam finals from 2001 to 2017, and together they won fourteen Grand Slam titles in doubles. But while inseparable in history, the Williams sisters also stand apart. Through July 2022, Venus had won seven Grand Slam singles titles, Serena twenty-three, just one short of Margaret Court's all-time record of twenty-four.

The Williams sisters' first duel in a Grand Slam final—at the 2001 U.S. Open—was as significant as it was memorable. The women's singles final had long been sandwiched between the two men's semifinals on Saturday. For the first time, our final was moved to its own prime-time slot—4 p.m. Saturday—with the men's semifinals moved to Friday. Venus and Serena more than lived up to the honor in what was also the first Grand Slam final ever to feature two Black players. The match drew a larger television audience than a major college football game that followed. Venus, seeded fourth, defeated tenth-seeded Serena, 6–2, 6–4.

THIS ERA BELONGED TO VENUS AND SERENA WILLIAMS. THEY MET NINE TIMES IN GRAND SLAM FINALS FROM 2001 TO 2017, AND TOGETHER THEY WON FOURTEEN GRAND SLAM TITLES IN DOUBLES.

VENUS VS. SERENA

Venus and Serena Williams played each other thirty-one times from 1998 through 2021, and it was never easy for either of them. "It's like playing a mirror," Serena once said. They were evenly matched at ten wins apiece as late as 2009 before Serena pulled away and built a 19–12 advantage. Their rivalry ranks second in the number of matches played to the eighty-match rivalry shared by Chrissie Evert and Martina Navratilova. Friends throughout, Venus and Serena teamed up to win twenty-two doubles titles, including fourteen in Grand Slam events, and three Olympic gold medals.

Despite their dominance, Venus and Serena faced a battalion of challengers, as thirty different women representing nineteen different countries won one or more of the majors between 2001 and 2021. Maria Sharapova became the first Russian to win all four Grand Slam titles. Naomi Osaka, a woman of Japanese and Haitian heritage, won four majors while carving a path outside of tennis as an influential civil rights activist. Ashleigh "Ash" Barty reawakened Australia's storied tradition of champions with stunning, pressure-packed victories. And Emma Raducanu of Great Britain became the first qualifier ever to win a Grand Slam title. In a stunning feat at the 2021 U.S. Open, Emma won three matches in the qualifying tournament and then seven more in the main draw—all without dropping a set.

Our international lineup of stars also included Kim Clijsters of Belgium, Victoria Azarenka of Belarus, Garbiñe Muguruza of Spain, Petra Kvitová of the Czech Republic, Angelique Kerber of Germany, Jelena Ostapenko of Latvia, Simona Halep of Romania, and Bianca Andreescu of Canada. From the United States, we saw Lindsay Davenport and Sloane Stephens. Nineteen-year-old Iga Świątek became the first Polish player, male or female, to win a major singles title, and Tunisia's Ons Jabeur became the first Arab player to reach the top ten in the WTA rankings and reach a Grand Slam final.

We saw women from China become the first from their country to win major championships. Li Ting and Sun Tian won the gold medal in women's doubles at the 2004 Athens Olympics; Zheng Jie and Yan Zi won Grand Slam doubles titles at the 2006 Australian Open and Wimbledon; and Li Na won Grand Slam singles titles at the 2011 French Open and 2014 Australian Open.

China's Li Ting, left, and Sun Tian Tian captured the gold medal in doubles at the 2004 Olympic Games in Athens.

LI NA

*She lifted tennis in China
to new heights*

●

- **2 Grand Slam singles titles**
  - **1 Australian Open (2014)**
  - **1 French Open (2011)**
- **Fed Cup: 27–4 in singles, 8–6 in doubles**
- **Best year-end ranking: No. 3 (2013)**
- **International Tennis Hall of Fame inductee, 2019**

In 2011, Li Na of Wuhan, China, became the first Asian player to win a Grand Slam singles event with her French Open victory over Francesca Schiavone of Italy. She won her second major title at the 2014 Australian Open with a victory over Dominika Cibulková of Slovakia. Li Na was far more than just a champion. She was also a major driver of the escalating interest in tennis in China, home to some 15 million tennis players. More than 116 million television viewers in China watched her French Open final in 2011, and more than 21 million followed her on Weibo, one of the biggest social media platforms in China. In 2013, *Time* magazine included her in its annual list of the 100 most influential people in the world. She retired in 2014 with nine career WTA victories and $16.7 million in prize money earnings.

With Li's success and the growing number of Chinese tennis professionals (both women and men), the number of WTA tournaments in Asia swelled from four in 1990 to eleven in China alone in 2019. The China Open, established in 2004, became one of the world's premier tournaments in 2009. It was showcased in the Beijing Olympic Green Tennis Center, which had been constructed for the 2008 Olympic Games.

In 2019, the WTA Finals, the tour's lucrative year-end event, was moved from Singapore, where it had been held for five years, to Shenzhen, China, where it was to be held for the next ten years. However, to everyone's dismay, the 2020 event, with $14 million in prize money, was canceled because of the Covid pandemic. Covid restrictions interfered again in 2021, causing the WTA to move the tournament to Guadalajara, Mexico.

IN 2013, *TIME* MAGAZINE INCLUDED HER IN ITS ANNUAL LIST OF THE 100 MOST INFLUENTIAL PEOPLE IN THE WORLD.

We also saw one of the most remarkable comebacks in the history of our sport. Jennifer Capriati, motivated by her own personal love of tennis, put a period of rebellion behind her and recovered her original promise. She won the French and Australian Opens in 2001 and successfully defended her Australian title in 2002 after saving a record four match points. She retired in 2004 at age twenty-eight and was inducted into the International Tennis Hall of Fame in 2012.

This was also an era that acknowledged our history. In 2006, I learned that the board of the USTA had voted unanimously to rename the U.S. Tennis Center at Flushing Meadows the USTA Billie Jean King National Tennis Center. And in 2020, the International Tennis Federation (ITF) rebranded the Fed Cup the Billie Jean King Cup by BNP Paribas. The ITF also inaugurated an exciting new Cup format, with the top twelve nations competing at one location in a weeklong finale, and established the biggest annual prize in women's team sports. The $1.2 million pot matched that of the men's Davis Cup. Our world cup of women's tennis was now a truly global event: of the 210 national tennis federations, a record 127 of them entered teams in 2022.

Above: With her legendary "splits forehand," Kim Clijsters extended her reach a step beyond the norm and produced a searing return that skimmed the net and bounced low.

KIM CLIJSTERS

Among the many superlatives one could ascribe to Belgium's Kim Clijsters, two are unforgettable: her signature forehand and her sportsmanship. Kim was so flexible (her mother was a gymnast) that she could nearly do the splits when executing her sliced forehand, an open-stance stroke that flipped a would-be defensive retrieval into a sizzling offensive return. It was a one-of-a-kind shot for a one-of-a-kind player whom everyone liked. Kim won the WTA's Karen Krantzcke Sportsmanship Award eight times.

In 2005, Kim won the U.S. Open and ranked No. 2 in the world. But injuries and waning interest caused her to retire two years later, when she was only twenty-three years old. "I was fed up with tennis," she said. "I cried after matches that I'd won and I couldn't apply myself fully. Moreover, after I won the U.S. Open, I felt I'd achieved everything. I longed for a normal life." During a two-year break from tennis, Kim married and, in 2008, became the mother of a daughter, Jada. Newly inspired, she began what she called her "second career" in 2009. Playing in only her third tournament since returning to the tour, Kim defeated Caroline Wozniacki of Denmark to become the first unseeded player and wildcard entrant to win the U.S. Open and the first mother to win a major singles title since Evonne Goolagong Cawley in 1980.

- **4 Grand Slam singles titles**
    - **1 Australian Open (2011)**
    - **3 U.S. Open (2005, 2009, 2010)**
- **2 Grand Slam women's doubles titles**
- **3 WTA Finals singles titles (2002, 2003, 2010)**
- **Fed Cup: 21–3 in singles, 3–1 in doubles**
- **Best year-end world ranking: No. 2 (2003, 2005)**
- **International Tennis Hall of Fame inductee, 2017**

NOTEWORTHY STATISTIC

- **3 Grand Slam singles titles as a mother, a record shared with Margaret Court**

Clockwise from far left: Bianca Andreescu of Canada, the 2019 U.S. Open champion; Caroline Wozniacki of Denmark after her epic victory in the 2018 Australian Open; Coco Gauff of the United States, 2022 French Open finalist; Jelena Janković of Serbia, No. 1 in the world in 2008; Maria Sharapova of Russia, 2004 Wimbledon champion; Iga Świątek of Poland in Doha, Qatar, in 2022; Petra Kvitová of the Czech Republic, Wimbledon champion in 2011 and 2014; Elena Rybakina, born in Moscow but representing Kazakhstan, winning the Ladies' Singles at Wimbledon in 2022; Justine Henin of Belgium, winner of seven Grand Slam singles titles; Jennifer Capriati of the United States after winning the 2001 French Open.

In every respect, our game had grown. The television exposure was greater, the money was bigger, and the women were taller and stronger than ever. Lindsay Davenport was 6 foot 2½, Maria Sharapova 6 foot 2, and Venus Williams 6 foot 1. Garbiñe Muguruza, Victoria Azarenka, and Petra Kvitová were 6 feet tall. Naomi Osaka stood 5 foot 11, Jelena Ostapenko 5 foot 10, Serena Williams 5 foot 9, and Kim Clijsters 5 foot 8½. We saw multiple players with average serving speeds of 108 miles per hour, and the WTA officially recognized the 131-mile-per-hour serve hit by Sabine Lisicki of Germany at the 2014 Stanford Classic as the fastest woman's serve ever. We saw players hug the baseline during rallies, pounding ground strokes milliseconds after the bounce and aimed ever closer to the lines. And in a welcome change of pace, we saw a return of an old, deftly wielded weapon: the drop shot.

Above: Only ten women have won all four major titles. Maria Sharapova is one of them. Her game featured an explosive serve, a stunning crosscourt backhand, and high-risk shotmaking that ended points with a slash of her racket.

ESTHER MARY VERGEER
AND DIEDE DE GROOT

Two Dutch women brought wheelchair tennis into the limelight and changed the world's understanding of what people with a physical disability could accomplish. Esther Mary Vergeer, who ranked No. 1 in the world in wheelchair tennis from 1999 until her retirement in 2013, won forty-eight Grand Slam titles (twenty-one singles, twenty-seven doubles) and four Paralympic gold medals in singles. Equally important, she was relentless in promoting the sport. Diede de Groot, at left, succeeded Esther as the world's dominant player. In 2021, Diede won the calendar year Grand Slam in wheelchair tennis as well as the gold medal in singles at the (postponed) 2020 Tokyo Paralympics. Diede won all four majors in doubles in 2019 with Aniek van Koot, also of the Netherlands.

VENUS WILLIAMS

An unending love affair with tennis

•

Venus Ebony Starr Williams has loved tennis from the time she began playing on the public courts in and around Compton, California. Over the next twenty years, she established herself as one of the all-time greats and won almost everything there was to win. In 2008, after capturing her fifth Wimbledon singles title, she might have retired. She did not. In 2011, when she was diagnosed with Sjögren's syndrome, an autoimmune disorder, she might have retired. And in 2018, when she dropped out of the top twenty in the WTA rankings, she might have retired. But in 2021, at age forty-one, Venus was still competing, still striving, still leaving the court with that graceful twirl and wave to her cheering fans. For Venus, tennis never got old. I think part of her secret could be found in the enviable balance of her life. Venus was never one-dimensional. She earned an associate degree in fashion design, and she launched her own interior design firm, V Starr Interiors, and a clothing line, EleVen. I'll never forget the sensation she caused at Roland Garros in 2010 when she played in one of her own fashion creations—a lacy black dress with skin-tone undershorts that, according to the *New York Times,* had "photographers snapping furiously at every lunging serve." Venus also gave back to her sport by serving as a valuable spokeswoman for equity and mental health. Her father, Richard Williams, wrote a seventy-eight-page strategic playbook before she was born that put Venus on a rapid path to stardom. Venus wrote the chapter on how to stretch that path into an enjoyable, diversified, and long-lasting career.

THROUGH 2021

- **7 Grand Slam singles titles**
    5 Wimbledon (2000, 2001, 2005, 2007, 2008)
    2 U.S. Open (2000, 2001)
- **14 Grand Slam women's doubles titles, all with her sister, Serena**
- **WTA Finals singles title, 2008**
- **Olympics**
    2000 Sydney (gold medals, singles and doubles)
    2008 Beijing (gold medal, doubles)
    2012 London (gold medal, doubles)
    2016 Rio de Janeiro (silver medal, mixed)
- **Fed Cup: 21–2 in singles, 4–3 in doubles**
- **Best year-end world ranking: No. 2 (2002)**

NOTEWORTHY STATISTIC

- **5 Olympic medals (4 gold, 1 silver) is a record shared with Britain's Kitty McKane Godfree (1 gold, 2 silver, 2 bronze)**

FOR VENUS, TENNIS NEVER GOT OLD.

Continuing developments in racket technology—as well as string technology—helped make the power possible. The players in the 2000s served harder than Stefanie Graf and Monica Seles, but their rackets were more powerful, and the strings allowed for more spin. Stefanie used a carbon-fiber racket in winning her Grand Slam in 1988, as did players in the Williams era. "But innovations in graphite technology have evolved to allow lighter-weight products on the market," explained Jason Collins, senior director of global product, racquet, at Wilson Sporting Goods. "Rackets today are lighter, provide a lot of power and stability, and come in a variety of head sizes." Innovations in string technology, he said, enable elite players to get "incredible movement on the ball—both with spin and direction."

I believe the racket and string technologies were great equalizers for the tour's smaller women. So despite the advantages enjoyed by tall players, tennis still had room for the small champion. Everyone thinks you have to be tall to have the best serve in the world. You don't. One of the most successful "small" stars of this era was Justine Henin. Only 5 foot 5½, she captured seven Grand Slam titles and was one of Serena Williams's true rivals. Justine and Serena met fourteen times between 2001 and 2010, with Serena winning eight matches and Justine six. In Grand Slam tournament matchups, Justine led, 4–3.

Along with fame and fortune, I have always said, comes the privilege of pressure. For decades, we have known that international travel, sponsor incentives, and media scrutiny could shake players' emotional equilibrium. And with the arrival of social media, we had a stress multiplier. Social media gave players the power to tell their story independently of traditional media, but it also exposed them to the public's opinions, which could cross the line into bullying. The WTA, which had been providing mental health services to players for more than thirty years, by 2021 supported a department of performance health that offered state-of-the-art preventive health care, treatment, and rehabilitation in sport sciences and medicine. The team, overseen by Kathleen Stroia, senior vice president, Sport Sciences & Medicine and Transitions, included ten primary health care providers and three mental health professionals.

The early 2000s were Venus Williams's prime years as a player, and they were also memorable for her role in our quest for equality. During our negotiations with Wimbledon in 2005, Venus met with the All England Club's leadership the day before she was to play in the Wimbledon final and urged them to equalize prize money for women and men. The following afternoon she went out and proved that women were equal to men as athletes and entertainers. In the longest women's singles final ever at Wimbledon, Venus triumphed over Lindsay Davenport, 4–6, 7–6 (4), 9–7.

ALONG WITH FAME AND FORTUNE, I HAVE ALWAYS SAID, COMES THE PRIVILEGE OF PRESSURE.

Above: Venus Williams adorned her powerful game with her own fashion flare.
Here, she is wearing one of her own festive designs, which was inspired by Tina Turner.

Above: Justine Henin is honored at the Town Hall in the City of Brussels, Belgium, following her victory over Kim Clijsters in the 2003 French Open. Justine won the 2006 and 2007 French Open titles without dropping a set.

JUSTINE HENIN

Her backhand drew crowds

●

Belgium's Justine Henin was a fan favorite because women could identify with her. In an age of tall, powerful players, Justine was comparatively smaller at 5 foot 5½ and 126 pounds. She won with grit, an all-court game, and her one-handed backhand—one of the most beautiful shots in tennis—which she hit with topspin or slice. Spectators headed to her court just so they could see it. When she could no longer summon the determination she needed to compete at the highest level, she left the game. She retired in 2008 at age twenty-five, the first woman to do so while ranked No. 1 in the world. "There are no regrets," Justine said. "I did everything I had to do in tennis." She returned in 2010 but played for only a year before permanently leaving the tour.

- **7 Grand Slam singles titles**
    - **1 Australian Open (2004)**
    - **4 French Open (2003, 2005–2007)**
    - **2 U.S. Open (2003, 2007)**
- **Olympics: 2004 Athens (gold medal, singles)**
- **2 WTA Finals singles titles (2006, 2007)**
- **Fed Cup: 15–2 in singles, 0–2 in doubles**
- **Year-end No. 1 in the world (2003, 2006, 2007)**
- **International Tennis Hall of Fame inductee, 2016**

Wimbledon's leaders weren't convinced at that time, but they would be soon. In 2006, Larry Scott, the WTA's chairman and CEO, masterminded a plan that leveraged support for prize money equity from the British government. The plan combined an op-ed by Venus Williams in the *Times*, calling on Wimbledon not to be on the "wrong side of history," with public support from British Prime Minister Tony Blair and members of Parliament. In 2007, unable to hold out any longer, Wimbledon equalized the purse. Roland Garros followed immediately after. In a fitting coda to this victory, Venus won the 2007 Wimbledon title and—for the first time in 123 years—the woman champion's prize equaled that of the men's. In 2008, Venus won her fifth and final Ladies' Singles title at Wimbledon and her last Grand Slam singles title, just as Serena was entering one of the most dominant phases of her career.

Serena Williams's power game included a weapon like none other: the most beautiful serve in the history of our sport. Everyone talked about it, including all-time great Pete Sampras. Serena's first serve, which routinely traveled at 110 miles per hour and has been clocked at 128.6 miles per hour, was the most feared stroke in the women's game. The rhythm of that serve was perfect. The racket acceleration, multiplied by her height and hard-earned muscle, produced short points—not only aces and service winners but also weak returns from her opponents that were easily slashed away at unreachable angles. That serve helped her survive a lot of tough matches; she would not have won as many titles without it.

Serena's personal style evolved with her. From her black catsuit to dresses that evoked a ballerina's flourish, she was a fashion chameleon who never lost sight of the role of style in entertainment. We saw her in hair beads, then braids, a tint of blond, and, finally, natural Black hair that, with its untamed volume, spoke volumes: *This is who I am*.

Throughout her career, Serena has never backed away from confronting a perceived wrong. Every so often, something ignited a deep-rooted grievance, whether the spark arrived as a racist outburst from a fan, a controversial umpire's ruling, or a critique of her weight or form-fitting clothing. No experience was more seminal than Indian Wells, California, in 2001. Serena was to play Venus in the semifinals, but Venus withdrew because of tendinitis in her knee only minutes before the match was to begin, with fans already in the stands. The next day, some fans—believing that Serena's victory over Venus had been prearranged by their father, Richard—booed Venus and Richard when they arrived to watch the final. Some fans then booed and heckled Serena.

Serena boycotted the tournament for the next thirteen years, Venus for fourteen. In 2015, citing a "new understanding of the true meaning of forgiveness," Serena announced her return to Indian Wells in an op-ed in *Time* magazine. "The false allegations that our matches were fixed hurt, cut and ripped into us deeply," she wrote. "The undercurrent of racism was painful, confusing and unfair. In a game I loved with all my heart, at one of my most cherished tournaments, I suddenly felt unwelcome, alone and afraid." Serena concluded, however, that, "together we have a chance to write a different ending."

The ending was indeed different. As Serena entered the Indian Wells stadium for her first-round match, the crowd welcomed her with a thunderous ovation, and Serena started to cry. After winning her match, she said she felt as though she had already won the tournament. "I feel like I'm already holding up a trophy," she said. "I have never felt that way before." Unfortunately, Serena had to withdraw from the tournament before the semifinals because of a knee injury. She explained her decision to what was this time an understanding crowd, and Simona Halep went on to defeat Serbia's Jelena Janković for the title.

After Serena beat Vera Zvonareva of Russia to win her fourth Wimbledon and thirteenth Grand Slam singles title in 2010—and surpass my career total of twelve—she quipped in an on-court interview, "Hey, Billie, I got you."

Of course, we weren't counting in the 1960s and 1970s. We were trying to grow the game, transforming it from an amateur to a professional sport. We didn't obsess over Grand Slam tournaments, and we skipped them all the time. For years, Australia's rewards didn't match the effort required for most of the world to play there, while World TeamTennis offered a dependable income along with the opportunity to perform in large arenas, gain significant television exposure, and train with one's team—both women and men.

Serena Williams jumps for joy with the Venus Rosewater Dish after winning her fifth Wimbledon singles title in 2012.

SERENA JAMEKA WILLIAMS

The (extra) things that she carried

•

Before she was first, before the world anointed her "the greatest," Serena Williams was second. She was the younger of two prodigies, the one people noticed after their jaws had dropped when noticing her sister, Venus. Envious of Venus and constantly striving to beat her, Serena developed an underdog's persistence and ferocity. As an eight-year-old, frustrated that her parents were entering Venus in tournaments but not her, Serena entered herself in a ten-and-under event in which Venus was going to play. Her parents became aware of this rebellious act only when they discovered Serena playing her first-round match. Serena more than proved her point. She reached the finals before losing to Venus.

Growing up in Compton, California, in Los Angeles County, Serena was also shaped by her experience as an outsider whose parents were self-taught and didn't grow up around the game. In tennis, she wrote in her 2009 autobiography, *Serena: My Life,* "There's a sense of entitlement, of belonging. Like you have to be born to it."

Each generation inherits history, and people of color inherit centuries of systemic disadvantage. That reality was exposed most cruelly in 2003 when Yetunde Price, a half sister Serena had grown up with, was shot and killed while sitting with her boyfriend in an SUV in Compton. The shooter was a gang member; Yetunde was an unintended victim. In 2016, Serena and Venus

Opposite page: In August 2022, forty-year-old Serena Williams announced in a *Vogue* magazine cover story that she would be "evolving away" from her monumental tennis career sometime after the 2022 U.S. Open—the tournament in which she had won her first of twenty-three Grand Slam titles twenty-three years earlier. She would embrace a new life chapter focused on family and her venture capital firm.

opened the Yetunde Price Resource Center in Compton. The center, a mental health leader in underserved communities, offers trauma-informed programs that promote healing.

Hardship and history aside, Serena has become tennis royalty, admired and even worshipped by millions. She is on the guest lists of global celebrities; her résumé includes line after line of honors, awards, and filmography. She has acquired numerous corporate sponsors, has launched her own venture capital firm (Serena Ventures), and has become one of the wealthiest women athletes ever. Her $94 million in career prize money through 2021 was twice as much as the next closest money winner, who happened to be Venus, with $42 million.

Meanwhile, Serena's charm and caring shine through, sometimes in surprising ways. After winning her French Open titles, she made her on-court remarks at Roland Garros *en Français*—a graceful but rarely heard gesture by an American player. Her charitable endeavors benefit causes and children around the world.

"THERE'S A SENSE OF ENTITLEMENT, OF BELONGING. LIKE YOU HAVE TO BE BORN TO IT."

But the world *was* counting as Serena's numbers rose. Her eighteenth Grand Slam title, against Caroline Wozniacki of Denmark in the 2014 U.S. Open final, equaled the total won by both Chrissie Evert and Martina Navratilova. Her nineteenth, against Maria Sharapova of Russia at the 2015 Australian Open, equaled the number won by Helen Wills Moody. Her twenty-first, against Garbiñe Muguruza of Spain at the 2015 Wimbledon Championships, brought her within one of Stefanie Graf's total of twenty-two and to the brink of a rare calendar year Grand Slam, achieved previously only by Maureen Connolly in 1953, Margaret Court in 1970, and Stefanie in 1988.

Serena arrived at the 2015 U.S. Open as the current holder of all four Grand Slam titles, an accomplishment she called the "Serena Slam." But she had never won all four tournaments in a calendar year.

The buildup before the Open was almost unimaginable. I can only liken it to the frenzy before my Battle of the Sexes with Bobby Riggs. Somehow, Serena had to rise above it. We got an early inkling of how hard that would be when Serena started shakily in her second-round match. She struggled through a three-set match in the third round and then faced the always arduous task of playing her sister, Venus, in the quarterfinals.

Serena's three-set victory over Venus put her in the semifinals against unseeded Roberta Vinci, a thirty-two-year-old Italian who ranked forty-third in the world and was appearing in her first Grand Slam semifinal ever. Serena, a twenty-five-to-one favorite, had beaten Roberta in straight sets in all four of their previous singles matches. But Roberta was a patient, versatile player, and she had enjoyed success against Serena in doubles. Roberta and fellow Italian Sara Errani—who together had won all four Grand Slam doubles titles—had beaten Serena and Venus at the 2013 Australian Open.

MARIA SHARAPOVA

From Sochi to Shark Tank, *a unique road traveled*

●

Maria Sharapova was born in 1987 in Sochi, a Russian resort town near the Black Sea, to a family of modest means. At age four, she pulled a racket from her father's sports bag and began hitting against a wall at a public park. "For whatever reason, I had this ability," she wrote in her memoir, *Unstoppable.* "I could hit that ball against that wall for hours. It was not my skill people remarked on. It was my concentration—that I could do it again and again without getting bored. I was a metronome." A successful local tennis coach named Yuri Yudkin encouraged Maria's father, also named Yuri, to take Maria to the United States so that her potential could be realized.

When Martina Navratilova saw six-year-old Maria play at a clinic in Moscow, she echoed Yuri Yudkin's advice. Maria and her father soon traveled to Florida, equipped with only $700 in savings and a three-year visa. Yuri took odd jobs and struggled to make ends meet for a few years while Maria trained, and a generous Florida physician allowed them to live in his home for nearly a year. Ultimately, Maria's talent carried them through. At age nine, she earned a full scholarship to the famed Nick Bollettieri Tennis Academy in Bradenton. By age eleven, she had signed with IMG, the player-management firm, and had a Nike contract worth a minimum of $50,000 a year. It was just the beginning. Powerful, tall, and blessed with supermodel looks, Maria reached the pinnacle of athletic and commercial success. With magazines naming her everything from "most eligible" to "hottest," she became one of the wealthiest women athletes in history. From 2006 through 2016, she ranked first in *Forbes* magazine's listings of the highest-paid women athletes in the world. *Forbes* has estimated her total career earnings at $325 million, with nearly $39 million of that from prize money and the rest from endorsements. Maria appeared on *Shark Tank,* the business reality television series, and was mentored by NBA Commissioner Adam Silver. In 2012, she launched the Florida-based candy company Sugarpova, which sold 1.3 million bags of candy during its first year.

- **5 Grand Slam singles titles**
    - **1 Australian Open (2004)**
    - **2 French Open (2012, 2014)**
    - **1 Wimbledon (2004)**
    - **1 U.S. Open (2006)**
- **WTA Finals singles title, 2004**
- **Fed Cup: 7–1 in singles**
- **Best year-end ranking: No. 2 (2006)**

"I COULD HIT THAT BALL AGAINST THAT WALL FOR HOURS."

AMÉLIE MAURESMO

Amélie Mauresmo of France, who won the Australian Open and Wimbledon in 2006, coached Andy Murray, Britain's top male player, from 2014 to 2016. Men have been coaching women since the days of Suzanne Lenglen in the 1920s, but only rarely have women coached leading men. Conchita Martínez of Spain, who won Wimbledon in 1994, also broke new ground in 2015 when she became the first woman to coach a men's Davis Cup team.

For Serena, the occasion proved too much. I watched as Roberta played as if it was the 1970s. You would have thought she was using a wooden racket! She chipped her backhand, she sliced, she hit drop shot volleys. She mixed in change-of-pace or no pace. Serena loves it when opponents hit hard, because hard is easy for her. Roberta didn't give her any pace. There was a moment when I knew that Serena was thinking about the Slam. I turned to my life partner, Ilana Kloss, and said, "She just thought about the record, and she's not going to beat Vinci because Vinci is playing her to a tee." This was a match Serena never should have lost, but Roberta played perfectly.

Roberta remained calm and made few unforced errors as the match progressed, while Serena lost her rhythm and showed signs of stress. After losing the second set, Serena smashed her racket on the ground. Roberta, serving for the match at 5–4 in the third set, won the game at love. The shock felt by more than 23,000 fans at Arthur Ashe Stadium was palpable. Roberta cried in her chair at courtside and called the victory "the best moment of my life."

The final featured two Italian women: Roberta and her friend Flavia Pennetta. Flavia, thirty-three years old and seeded twenty-sixth, had scored her own stunning semifinal upset over second-seeded Simona Halep of Romania. Italy's prime minister, Matteo Renzi, took an overnight flight to New York in order to see the final. "It's a great experience for Italian sport," he told the *New York Times*. "But particularly in this moment, the experience of Roberta and Flavia is the experience of great women who continue with pride, with strong approach, not only for tennis but for the life. Two girls from the south of Italy give a great message to every Italian."

Flavia won the final, 7–6, 6–2, and then surprised everyone when she announced in her victory speech that she would retire at the end of the year. Roberta would complete her career three years later at the 2018 Italian Open.

Above: At the unveiling of the statue of Althea Gibson at the USTA Billie Jean King National Tennis Center, from left, Renee Blount, Chanda Rubin, Zina Garrison, Sloane Stephens, Billie Jean King, Angela Buxton, Leslie Allen, Katrina Adams, sculptor Eric Goulder, Fran Gray (in wheelchair), Kim Sands, and Patrick Galbraith.

Serena's story, however, was far from over. She won her twenty-second major (and seventh Wimbledon) in 2016 and—while eight weeks pregnant— her twenty-third major (and seventh Australian) in 2017. Her longevity was stunning. She had won her first Grand Slam singles title at seventeen. Her most recent, at age thirty-five, made her the oldest Grand Slam title winner in the professional era.

After Serena and her husband, Alexis Ohanian, welcomed the birth of their daughter, Olympia, Serena returned to competition and her quest for Grand Slam title No. 24. But time was working against her, as was her legacy. The explosive power tennis that she and Venus had ushered in was now standard operating procedure for a new generation of players. Whereas Serena's opponents were once intimidated by her power, those who followed her considered it the norm. "I've really strived to be like her," said Bianca Andreescu of Canada, after defeating Serena in the final of the 2019 U.S. Open. "And who knows, maybe even better."

The new wave of talent included young women who had grown up idolizing Serena and were clearly ready to challenge her. They included four women who trained out of Florida: Naomi Osaka, Sloane Stephens, Madison Keys, and Coco Gauff.

The success of so many Black tennis players reawakened our appreciation for Althea Gibson, who in 1950 became the first African American to play in the U.S. Nationals at Forest Hills. For three decades I had lobbied the USTA to honor Althea in a significant way. Finally, in 2019, sixteen years after Althea's passing, the USTA unveiled a granite statue of her outside Arthur Ashe Stadium. Among those present was Fran Gray, Althea's dear friend and the longtime head of her foundation. Fran died only two weeks later.

Naomi Osaka won four Grand Slam titles between 2018 and 2021 and became a spokeswoman for racial justice.

None of the new stars showcased our sport's future more than Naomi Osaka. Her mother was Japanese, her father Haitian, making her at once Black, Asian, and American. She spoke softly and described herself as shy, but she flourished in the spotlight. She was at her best on our sport's biggest stages; three of her first six titles were in majors. And she was skillful with social media, which she used strategically to share her story with the world. She was profiled in a three-part docuseries on Netflix and featured in a multipage spread (including the cover) of *Sports Illustrated*'s 2021 swimsuit issue.

Naomi made her big breakthrough at age twenty in the 2018 U.S. Open. Tall, powerful, and with ground strokes whose consistency matched their blazing speed, she toppled Serena Williams in straight sets in Arthur Ashe Stadium to win her first Grand Slam title. But in one of our sport's unpleasant moments, Naomi was reduced to tears during the awards ceremony. Instead of relishing those first moments after a breakthrough triumph, she listened as the crowd booed its disapproval of a dispute between Serena and the chair umpire that had begun with a code violation for coaching and had escalated to a point penalty and then a game penalty. (Serena's coach, Patrick Mouratoglou, later admitted that he had been coaching with hand signals.)

The whole incident was a classic case of poor communication. Serena didn't hear the umpire give her a formal warning, and as her anger increased, so did the crowd's confusion over what was happening. Lost in the boos and the crowd's focus on Serena was Naomi's superb play and first major title.

I have always thought that tennis should allow coaching because it would help us grow our sport, would draw more coaches into the game, and would legitimize what was already happening. Coaches, everyone knew, were routinely sending signals to players during competition. The WTA has gradually relaxed its rules about coaching and as of 2022 allowed players to consult with their coaches when they were at the end of the court where their coach was seated.

NONE OF THE NEW STARS SHOWCASED OUR SPORT'S FUTURE MORE THAN NAOMI OSAKA.

Naomi won her second straight Grand Slam title a few months later at the Australian Open and also claimed the No. 1 WTA ranking. She was looking every inch like the next great champion in women's tennis when nature threw the world an unexpected curve: the severe acute respiratory syndrome coronavirus—SARS-CoV-2—a novel coronavirus that caused Covid-19. The highly contagious virus triggered a global wave of suffering and death that disrupted travel, business operations, and human interaction of every kind. It forced the cancellation of Wimbledon in 2020 for the first time since World War II. The French Open was postponed until September, and the Summer Olympics in Tokyo were postponed a full year. The U.S. Open would go on, but not as before. Officials implemented stringent safety measures that included regular Covid screening, mask wearing, capacity limits in the locker rooms, and—in a first that we hope never to see again—empty stands.

During the height of the pandemic, with tennis at a standstill, Naomi Osaka attended protests in Minneapolis sparked by the brutal police killing of George Floyd, a Black man. The experience, she later told Jason Gay of the *Wall Street Journal*, had given her "a chance to think about a lot about things, what I want to accomplish, what I want people to remember me by."

NAOMI OSAKA

A champion without borders

•

Naomi Osaka's tennis career was developed right out of the same playbook that, years before, Richard Williams had written for his not-yet-born daughters. Naomi's father, Leonard Francois, was awakened to tennis by a match at Roland Garros, coincidentally by a doubles match involving Richard's daughters, Venus and Serena! The plan called for serious tennis practice from a very young age. Naomi's parents—her Japanese mother, Tamaki, and her Haitian-born father—left Osaka, Japan, in pursuit of a more favorable tennis environment when Naomi was three years old. The family settled in Long Island, New York, and Naomi was soon playing tennis on the area's public courts. The Osakas later moved to Florida, an incubator of future tennis stars that allowed for year-round outdoor practice. Naomi honed her game playing against her older sister, Mari, who was also an excellent player. With financial support from the Japan Tennis Association, Naomi's game began to blossom. She won her first WTA matches at age sixteen but did not win a tour event until four years later, when she burst into stardom by winning both the 2018 Indian Wells Championship and the U.S. Open. The victories made her a celebrity across Asia and the most marketable woman athlete in the world. Her $60 million in earnings from June 2020 to June 2021 tied her with Tiger Woods at No. 12 on *Forbes* magazine's list of the world's one hundred highest-paid athletes. She personified the new woman—tenacious, multicultural, and, above all, successful.

SHE PERSONIFIED THE NEW WOMAN—TENACIOUS, MULTICULTURAL, AND, ABOVE ALL, SUCCESSFUL.

It was a changed Naomi who arrived at the 2020 Western & Southern Open, a tune-up to the U.S. Open that was normally held in the Cincinnati area but, because of the pandemic, had been moved to the National Tennis Center in New York so that players could remain in the city for both tournaments. Shortly after winning her quarterfinal match, Naomi joined a one-day strike that had been called by several professional sports teams following the August 23 shooting of another Black man, Jacob Blake, in Kenosha, Wisconsin. Naomi informed Western & Southern officials that she would withdraw from the tournament if she was forced to compete on the day of the protest. "I don't expect anything drastic to happen with me not playing, but if I can get a conversation started in a majority white sport, I consider that a step in the right direction," Naomi said in a Twitter post.

In response, the tournament suspended play for a day. And in that moment, Naomi became an internationally recognizable spokeswoman for racial justice. With this new mantle—and pressure—now on her shoulders, she won her semifinal match, then withdrew from the final because of an injured hamstring.

Naomi continued her advocacy during the U.S. Open that followed. When she walked onto the court for her matches, she wore a mask emblazoned with the name of a Black individual who had been killed during a violent encounter. The stands might have been empty, but the couches in front of televisions throughout the world were not.

Above: Iga Świątek of Poland on the run during her victory over Sofia Kenin of the United States in the 2020 French Open final. The tournament, which was postponed by the Covid-19 pandemic, concluded in October of that year.

EMMA AND LEYLAH

On the twentieth anniversary of September 11, a day of sorrow and remembrance dreaded by so many in New York, two unseeded teenagers – eighteen-year-old Emma Raducanu of Britain and nineteen-year-old Leylah Fernandez of Canada – gave a stunning and unexpected gift to fans in the final of the 2021 U.S. Open. The young stars epitomized the new diversity of tennis. Emma's mother is Chinese, her father Romanian. Leylah's mother is from the Philippines; Leylah's father was born in Ecuador. Emma and Leylah, with their youthful fearlessness and poise, awakened new audiences to women's tennis and signaled growth in a sport that had never been so competitive and unpredictable. The end result proved to be the biggest surprise since tennis was opened up to the pros, as Emma Raducanu became the first qualifier in history to win a Grand Slam championship.

Above: Leylah Fernandez, left, and Emma Raducanu after their unforgettable 2021 U.S. Open final.

Naomi Osaka won the Open—her third Grand Slam title—with a three-set victory over Victoria Azarenka of Belarus. When asked at the awards presentation what message she wanted to send with her masks, she replied, "What was the message that you got? The point is to make people start talking."

Tournament competition continued haltingly in a "new normal" in 2021. Naomi was again in top form as she won the Australian Open, her fourth major. But her resilience had begun to falter. At Roland Garros, where she had never performed her best, she stated in a Twitter post that in an effort to protect her mental health, she would skip the mandatory post-match press conferences. After winning her first-round match, she followed through with that promise and was fined $15,000. She then withdrew from the tournament.

When Naomi spoke openly about her anxiety and depression, she lent a public face to challenges millions of people have faced in silence. She forced tournament officials and fans alike to consider the human vulnerabilities of even the richest and most famous sports celebrities. Years ago, corporate sponsors might have abandoned Naomi. But not now. They supported her wholeheartedly. Once again, Naomi Osaka was a woman of the moment.

While Naomi and Serena drew the headlines, Ashleigh "Ash" Barty, an Indigenous Australian, quietly assumed the WTA's top spot in tennis. She was only 5 foot 5, but there was nothing small about her game. Ash reminded us that you don't have to be 6 feet tall to have the greatest serve in the world. Her serves routinely surpassed a hundred miles per hour, and they knifed into whatever sliver of the court she aimed them. She hit 325 aces in 2021, third most on the tour. Ash was also equipped with quickness, agility, a powerful forehand, and a variety of slices, including a one-handed backhand that skimmed the net and stayed low to the ground. She won four singles tournaments in 2019 (including the French Open and WTA Finals) and retained the No. 1 WTA ranking through the pandemic-truncated 2020 season.

Few tennis champions have performed better with the weight of history on their shoulders than Ash Barty. In fact, she seemed to relish the weight of history—the pressure of privilege. Ash came into the 2021 Wimbledon keenly aware that exactly fifty years earlier her role model and mentor, Evonne Goolagong Cawley, had become the first Indigenous Australian to win a Wimbledon title. On this historic occasion, Ash had a chance to become the second.

Evonne, who viewed Ash as a "little sister," is of Wiradjuri heritage; Ash traced her ancestry on her father's side to the Ngarigo people. "Evonne has guided the way," Ash said. "She's created a legacy like no other in Australia."

Wanting to honor Evonne's achievement in a highly visible way, Ashleigh asked Fila, her sponsor, to create an outfit for Wimbledon that mirrored the scallop-trimmed dress—designed by Ted Tinling—that Evonne wore during her victory. Evonne was deeply touched and gave her blessing to the plan. The result was an elegant fashion statement that linked two generations of Indigenous Australian women: a tank top and a skort with a floral pattern and scalloped hem.

As Ash Barty marched through the Wimbledon draw, she used the words "we" and "our" when discussing her matches. The victories, she believed, were never hers alone. In a throwback to tradition, she even thanked her umpires after her matches with a true handshake. She defeated Angelique Kerber of Germany in the semifinal and Karolína Plíšková of the Czech Republic in the final. Even during her victory speech, Ash was thinking of others. "I hope I made Evonne proud," she said. Evonne, who watched the match from her home in Queensland, was very proud indeed.

A few months later, history beckoned again, this time at Melbourne Park, home of the Australian Open. Ash was more than just the tournament favorite; she had a chance to become the first Australian to win since Chris O'Neil in 1978. It was a far different era in 1978. The tournament was still played on grass at Kooyong Stadium, and the women's singles had a draw of only thirty-two, the men's sixty-four. (The singles events did not expand to a 128 draw until 1988.) None of the top ten women in the world were entered in 1978, and Chris O'Neil was unseeded.

In an announcement that caught the tennis world flat-footed, Ash Barty announced her retirement in March 2022. Her prize money and endorsement earnings enabled her to quit and have other dreams. But I wish she had played another three years to help our sport.

Following Ash Barty's retirement, Iga Świątek, below, of Poland embarked on a thirty-seven-match winning streak—the longest of the twenty-first century—and captured her second Grand Slam title at the 2022 French Open at Roland Garros. The ribbon pinned to her cap showcases the colors of Ukraine's national flag. Iga, like thousands of Polish citizens, stepped up to support Ukrainians harmed by the invasion of Russia in 2022.

Ash Barty, twenty-five years old, reached the final round without dropping a set. There, she met Danielle Collins, a twenty-eight-year-old Floridian and two-time NCAA champion who fearlessly pounded her groundstrokes while positioned well inside the court. Danielle's ultra-flat forehands and backhands streaked over the net at speeds nearing seventy-four miles per hour. Imagine chasing down balls hit at highway speeds from one corner of the court to the other! Iga Świątek of Poland, who lost to Danielle in the semifinals, described her pace as "the fastest ball I have ever played against" in a match.

But Ash once again calmly fulfilled all the hopes and expectations—her country's and her own—to win her third Grand Slam title. Holding her nation's trophy high, she was a picture of joy and style and grace. Just two months later, while ranked No. 1 in the world and just a month shy of her twenty-sixth birthday, Ash stunned the tennis world by announcing her retirement. In a video posted to Instagram, she explained her decision. "I'm so grateful to everything that tennis has given me—it's given me all of my dreams, plus more—but I know that the time is right now for me to step away and chase other dreams and to put the rackets down."

We witnessed a very different evolution later that year, when Serena Williams, now 40 years old, bid farewell with a magical run at the U.S. Open. Buoyed by deafening, partisan crowds that cheered her every point—a record 29,402 fans watched her opening victory—Serena shimmered with the tenacity, ferocity, and shotmaking precision that marked her 27-year career. She reached the third round before losing a three-hour, three-set battle with unseeded Ajla Tomljanović, who grew up in Croatia and now plays for Australia. Afterward, Serena wiped away "happy tears" and told the crowd, "It's been the most incredible ride and journey I've ever been on in my life."

Serena's sublime career leaves an indelible mark on tennis history. She is a terrific role model for kids, especially girls of color. She was born to be a star—she has the *it* factor—and her skill, athleticism, and amazing emotional drive made her a champion. She is the all-time great because she belongs to the latest generation, and every generation gets better. The *next* generation, inspired by Serena, is already out there. Who Serena's successor might be, only time will tell.

As I reflect on the exceptional, yet vastly different, careers of Serena Williams and Ash Barty, I find myself reflecting on all the great women who came before them. From Charlotte "Lottie" Dod, who exhorted ladies to run their hardest; to May Sutton, who pushed up her sleeves and raised her hemlines; to Suzanne Lenglen, who brought thousands of fans to tennis and became our first professional; to Helen Wills Moody, who enchanted America with her skill and beauty; to Alice Marble and her explosive serve; to Pauline Betz, who dove for shots when necessary; to Maureen "Little Mo" Connolly, who won our first Grand Slam; to the Original 9, who risked their careers for a cause; to Chrissie Evert, who helped ignite the tennis boom; to Margaret Court, whose records set a coveted bar; to Martina Navratilova, who defied traditional views of femininity; to Stefanie Graf, who helped restore a proud German tennis tradition; and to Venus and Serena Williams, who transcended tennis and remade a once-elitist sport into a game that anyone and everyone could play.

Each one of these individuals, through her own unique qualities and skills, added something special to women's tennis. Each one brought us a step closer to our full potential as athletes and entertainers. Each one helped us come a very, very long way.

2022 AND BEYOND

○ - ○

As we celebrate the fiftieth anniversary of the Women's Tennis Association (WTA), so many of our goals have been achieved. Today's women pros routinely gain fame and wealth; their success is not dependent on how they look; they use their stature to start charitable foundations and speak out against injustice; and they have an organization—the WTA—that speaks for them, negotiates for them, advocates for them, and looks out for their health and well-being.

Today, 1,650 women from 85 nations compete in more than 50 tournaments on the WTA Tour. Women from well over 100 nations compete for the Billie Jean King Cup, the world cup of women's tennis. At the same time, our game continues its global spread. At the 2022 Australian Open, Angella Okutoyi of Kenya and Meshkatolzahra Safi of Iran became the first players from their respective countries to win a juniors match at a Grand Slam tournament. All of these women—our tennis sisterhood—are part of a continuum that began nearly 150 years ago. They are living the dream for which nine brave women risked their careers in 1970, just over 50 years ago.

The WTA's support for women has been unwavering. In November 2021, WTA Chairman and CEO Steve Simon voiced our support for Peng Shuai, a U.S. Open singles semifinalist, a former world No. 1 in doubles, and one of the most famous athletes in China. Peng, in a post on the social network Weibo, had accused a senior Chinese government official of sexually assaulting her in his home. Her Weibo post was soon deleted. When it appeared that Peng had been pressured into recanting her allegation, Steve put principle ahead of profit and announced the suspension of all WTA tournaments in China, including Hong Kong. The WTA's 2022 calendar was to include ten events in China, including the Wuhan Open and the WTA finals in Shenzhen.

And in March 2022, following Russia's unprovoked invasion of Ukraine, the WTA joined its male counterpart, the Association of Tennis Professionals, in suspending their combined event that was to be held in the fall in Moscow. Players from Russia and Belarus were allowed to continue competing in WTA and ATP tournaments, but without any identification of their nationality.

With slanted roofs that rise above the tree line, tennis clubs are perfect sites for solar arrays, as the Huron Valley Tennis Club in Ann Arbor, Michigan, demonstrates.

For me, personally, the rewards of the last fifty years have exceeded what I ever could have imagined. I saw our national tennis home named the USTA Billie Jean King National Tennis Center and the Federation Cup renamed the Billie Jean King Cup. And in 2021, the International Tennis Hall of Fame inducted the entire Original 9, the first time ever that a group of individuals was collectively enshrined.

In 2009, I became the first woman athlete to receive the Presidential Medal of Freedom, America's highest civilian honor. The award was not for my Grand Slam titles but for my role as an agent of change. As President Barack Obama placed the medal around my neck, a female military aide read my citation, which acknowledged my work to advance "the struggle for greater gender equity around the world" and my "unwavering defense of equal rights."

However, our work is not complete. Women tennis players still trail the men in overall prize money and endorsement income, so we still have a ways to go. But the fact that all four Grand Slam tournaments offer equal prize money to women and men has established a precedent and sends a positive message. That message was reinforced in 2020 when prize money at the Billie Jean King Cup rose

to the level of the men's Davis Cup. The International Tennis Federation (ITF), the global governing body of tennis, has established a program called Advantage All, which envisions tennis as "an equal advantage sport." Advantage All aspires to a future of "gender balance"—one in which every individual receives the same advantages and opportunities, both on and off the court. In an offshoot of Advantage All, more than one hundred women from national tennis federations are taking part in the ITF's new leadership development program, which seeks "to expand the pipeline of female candidates for future Board and Presidential elections, with the ultimate aim of achieving gender balance in the boardroom."

Because when a woman leads, she leads for everyone.

Our sport also faces challenges. Naomi Osaka reawakened us to the importance of mental health and the incredible pressure that comes with life at the top. Naomi seemed to have everything—titles, fame, and more money than she could ever hope to spend. But she expressed a sense of powerlessness when she lamented that she was like "a vessel that everyone's hard work is put into." Like earlier generations of young players, Naomi took time away from tennis to regroup.

The Covid-19 pandemic weighed on psyches, as well. Venus Williams championed the importance of mental health during this time and helped raise awareness as an ambassador of a $2 million initiative by the WTA and the BetterHelp therapy service to provide free therapy to the public. As Venus noted: "The challenge of taking care of our mental health through the ups and downs of life is something that all of us, no matter our background, can relate to." People must feel safe when seeking mental health therapy, and they should not be judged.

With the help of vaccines, testing protocols, and restricted attendance, tennis survived the Covid-19 era. Whether the pandemic will recede into the background or whether the world will face new hardships caused by Covid mutations—or even new viruses—remains to be seen.

We also must acknowledge the issue of climate change and what intensifying heat, floods, and fires mean for our future. Brush fires impacted the 2019 Australian Open qualifier, and excessive heat at the Tokyo Olympics left players gasping. Olympic quarterfinalist Paula Badosa of Spain, stricken with heatstroke, left the court in a wheelchair. How will rising temperatures and eroding coastlines impact junior tennis players who train at the famous centers in warm-weather parts of the world?

Major tournaments have implemented green initiatives, including Wimbledon's plant-covered "Living Wall" and the sustainably sourced containers for its famed strawberries and cream. The U.S. Open adopted dozens of sustainability initiatives in response to the Green Slam proposal made by Ilana Kloss, Pam Derderian, Nancy Decker, and myself, in partnership with the Natural Resources Defense Council. The Open recycles dozens of miles of racket string during the tournament, and its carbon-offset program replaces woodburning, particulate-producing indoor cookstoves in Africa with cleaner, healthier stoves.

But major events cannot solve our environmental challenges alone. More needs to be done in communities throughout the world, and we can start by advocating for solar panels on the roof of every indoor tennis facility.

Finally, how can we expand access to tennis so that more children have a chance to learn the game? I want us to reach more young players at the grassroots level so that we can identify more athletes whose raw talent and grit could make them future champions. I want it to be easier for families to "get in the system" of tournaments necessary to climb the ladder toward the pro tour. Whether you turn to tennis for fun or health or to become a pro, you should be able to get into the system quickly. The Mayo Clinic recently reported that tennis, which blends social interaction with cardiovascular demands, adds 9.7 years to life expectancy, more than any other sport. That's nearly *ten years*! I want more people to enjoy this magnificent activity! For that to happen, we must provide more free access and free coaching for young people who already love the game or simply want to learn to play.

Leadership in these areas and more continues to come from the WTA. I am proud of the WTA's evolution over the past fifty years and its leadership, both on and off the court. Women's tennis has set the bar in its quest for excellence, equity, and diversity in women's sports. I hope we continue to be the leaders in women's sports for the next fifty years. We have come a long way, to be sure, but continuous improvement is our goal. And that is a journey that never ends.

ACKNOWLEDGMENTS

The authors and their producers thank the following individuals and institutions for their invaluable assistance in the production of *We Have Come a Long Way* (published in 1988) and the revised and updated book, now titled *Trailblazers: The Unmatched Story of Women's Tennis.**:

Regina Ryan of Regina Ryan Publishing Enterprises, producer of the original book and editorial consultant for this revised and updated history.

The people of Virginia Slims, who made significant contributions to the game of women's tennis. Frank Van Rensselaer Phelps, who shared the results of his own personal research into the early history of tennis in England and the United States. Julia S. Morris, who researched hundreds of newspapers, magazines, and books and was there when we needed her, every step of a very long way. Sally Rousham, for her most professional research into the early history of women's tennis. Elizabeth Jochnick, who shared the results of her long and studious research into the life of Charlotte "Lottie" Dod. Patricia M. Barry, who shared the fruits of her voluminous research into the life of Mary Ewing Outerbridge and her family. Donn Gobbie, for sharing his detailed knowledge of the Original 9 and the early days of the Virginia Slims tour; and Kevin Fischer for his careful review of modern-era statistics.

The authors also thank the contributing researchers: Helen Russell, Karen Carpenter, Beverly Morris Ghesquiere, Carrol Robertsen, Joe D. Morris, Connie Miller, Marie Thole, Carolyn Rehder, Katie Canty, Karen Garloch, Marilyn August, Cindy Schmerler, and Robin Adair. We thank our translators, Ken Fisher and Marie Thole. Special thanks to the following individuals: Katrina Adams, Lesley Poch, and Jean Marie Daly of the United States Tennis Association; Amy Binder and Kathleen Stroia of the Women's Tennis Association; Nick Imison of the International Tennis Federation; Maureen Hanlon and Richard A. Remmert of the Women's International Tennis Association; Roxanne Aaron of the American Tennis Association; Alan Little of the Kenneth Ritchie Wimbledon Library; Sarah Frandsen of the All England Lawn Tennis Club; Valerie Warren of the Wimbledon Lawn Tennis Museum; Nicole Markham, Kacey Constable, and Jan Armstrong of the International Tennis Hall of Fame; Charles L. Sachs of the Staten Island Historical Society; Tobi Smith and Carol Miller of the Santa Monica Heritage Museum; Szilvia E. Szmuk of the William Fischer Library at St. John's University; Nancy Bolger, Annalee Thurston, Ina Broeman, Vicki Berner, and Diane Desfor of Virginia Slims; Jason Collins of Wilson Sporting Goods; Jutta Field of Loyola University; Sargent Hill; Tim Gregg; Bonnie Hagerman of International Management Group; Phil de Picciotto of Advantage International; Paul Deutschman and Maggie Higgins of Regina Ryan Publishing Enterprises, Inc.; Mary Witherell of World Tennis; Ingrid Burkart of Domino's Pizza TeamTennis; Marianne Delhaye of the French Tennis Federation; G. James Nicholls of Great Britain's Lawn Tennis Association; Larry King; Tip Nunn; William A. Starr; Greg Noble and Charlie Fry of the *Cincinnati Enquirer*; Richard Boydston. We thank the Kenneth Ritchie Wimbledon Library, the Ann Arbor Public Library, the Harlan Hatcher Graduate Library at the University of Michigan, the Public Library of Cincinnati and Hamilton County, and the Philadelphia Free Library.

We thank the women players, past and present, who provided interviews or pertinent information: Kitty McKane Godfree, Pauline Betz Addie, Shirley Fry Irvin, Doris Hart, Sarah Palfrey Danzig, Ann Haydon Jones, Maria Bueno, Dorothy Bundy Cheney, Louise Brough

* Individuals are identified with the names and titles they held at the time of their assistance, along with the organizations they represented at that time.

Serena Williams acknowledges the thousands of fans who cheered mightily for her at Arthur Ashe Stadium during her final appearance at the 2022 U.S. Open. Serena, who said she would evolve away from her tennis career sometime after the Open, lost in the third round to a resilient Ajla Tomljanović of Australia, 7-5, 6-7 (4), 6-1.

Clapp, Margaret Osborne duPont, Margaret Varner Bloss, Darlene Hard, Margaret Smith Court, Angela Mortimer Barrett, Christine Truman Janes, Althea Gibson, Kay Stammers Bullitt, Thelma Coyne Long, Rosie Casals, Betty Stöve, Evonne Goolagong Cawley, Wendy Turnbull, Nancy Richey, Olga Morozova, Stephanie DeFina Hagan, Valerie Ziegenfuss Bradshaw, Pam Teeguarden, Ilana Kloss, Cynthia Doerner, Peachy Kellmeyer, Ceci Martinez, Sylvia Hooks, Ann Koger, Bonnie Logan, Tracy Austin, Wendy White, Michelle Torres, Bonnie Gadusek, Terry Phelps, Carling Bassett-Seguso, Manuela Maleeva, Youlia Berberian, Peanut Louie, Zina Garrison, Lori McNeil, Rafaella Reggi, Susan Sloane, Martina Navratilova, Hana Mandlíková, Andrea Jaeger, Chrissie Evert, Pam Shriver, Helena Suková, Stefanie Graf, and Venus Williams.

Finally, we thank the following individuals for their interviews: Jimmy Evert, Lee Jackson, Merrett Stierheim, Pat Yeomans, Susy Jaeger Davis, Rex Bellamy, Brian Tobin, John Parsons, Rino Tommasi, Philippe Chatrier, Joseph F. Cullman III, Ellen Merlo, Donna Pallulat, Pancho Gonzales, Jeff Austin, Pat Sloane, Bill Talbert, Sandra Haynie, Gary Addie, Allan and Mumsey Nemiroff, Bud Collins, Bob Kelleher, Conny Konzack, Pavel Složil, Jerry Diamond, J. Howard (Bumpy) Frazer, Ron Woods, and Doug MacCurdy.

SOURCES

The following sources were used as important references in the production of *Trailblazers*.

Books and Other Published Works

Ashe, Arthur R., Jr. *A Hard Road To Glory: A History of the African-American Athlete 1919–1945*. New York: Warner Books, 1988.

Cleather, Norah Gordon. *Wimbledon Story*. London: Sporting Handbooks, 1947.

Clerici, Gianni. *The Ultimate Tennis Book*. Chicago: Follett, 1975.

Collins, Bud and Zander Hollander. *Bud Collins' Tennis Encyclopedia*. Detroit: Visible Ink, 1997.

Connolly, Maureen. *Forehand Drive*. London: MacGibbon & Kee, 1957.

Court, Margaret. *Margaret Court: The Autobiography*. Sydney: Pan Macmillan Australia, 2016.

Court, Margaret and George McGann. *Court on Court*. New York: Dodd, Mead, 1975.

Current Biography Yearbook. New York: H. W. Wilson, 1951, 1957, 1965, 1973, 1977.

Danzig, Allison and Peter Schwed. *The Fireside Book of Tennis*. New York: Simon and Schuster, 1972.

Davidson, Owen and C. M. Jones. *Great Women Tennis Players*. London: Pelham, 1971.

Dewulf, Filip and Wilfried de Jong. *Kim Clijsters: First and Only Official Career Overview*. Lanham, MD: Cannibal, 2012.

Engelmann, Larry. *The Goddess and the American Girl*. New York: Oxford University Press, 1988.

Frayne, Trent. *Famous Women Tennis Players*. New York: Dodd, Mead, 1979.

Gibson, Althea. *I Always Wanted To Be Somebody*. New York: Harper & Brothers, 1958; and New York: New Chapter, 2022.

Gobbie, Donn. *A Dollar & A Dream*. Brook, IN: Forty Love, 2021.

Goolagong, Evonne and Bud Collins. *Evonne! On the Move*. New York: E. P. Dutton, 1975.

Green, Geoffrey. *Kitty Godfree: Lady of a Golden Age*. London: Kingswood, 1987.

Hart, Doris. *Tennis with Hart*. Philadelphia: J. B. Lippincott, 1955.

Hart, Stan. *Once a Champion: Legendary Tennis Stars Revisited*. New York: Dodd, Mead, 1985.

Herrett, Elizabeth Louise. "A Thesis in Physical Education." Philadelphia: University of Pennsylvania, 1977.

Hillenbrand, Laura. *Seabiscuit: An American Legend*. New York: Random House, 2001.

International Tennis Federation. *World of Tennis*. London: HarperCollinsWillow, 1987.

Jacobs, Helen Hull. *Beyond the Game: An Autobiography*. Philadelphia: J. B. Lippincott, 1936.

King, Billie Jean and Frank DeFord. *Billie Jean*. New York: Viking, 1982.

King, Billie Jean, Johnette Howard, and Maryanne Vollers. *All In: An Autobiography*. New York: Alfred A. Knopf, 2021.

Koestler, Arthur. *Scum of the Earth*. London: Eland, 1991.

Lichtenstein, Grace. *A Long Way, Baby: Behind the Scenes in Women's Pro Tennis*. New York: William Morrow, 1974.

Little, Alan. *Dorothea Chambers: Wimbledon Champion Seven Times*. London: Wimbledon Lawn Tennis Museum, 1985.

Little, Alan. *Lottie Dod: Wimbledon Champion and All Rounder Extraordinary*. London: Wimbledon Lawn Tennis Museum, 1984.

Little, Alan. *Maud Watson: First Wimbledon Lady Champion*. London: Wimbledon Lawn Tennis Museum, 1984.

Little, Alan. *Suzanne Lenglen: Tennis Idol of the Twenties*. London: Wimbledon Lawn Tennis Museum, 1988.

Little, Alan and Lance Tingay. *Wimbledon Ladies: A Centenary Record, 1884-1984—Singles Champions*. London: Wimbledon Lawn Tennis Museum, 1984.

Marble, Alice. *The Road to Wimbledon*. New York: Charles Scribner's Sons, 1946.

Marchadier, Jarard. *Sixty Years of Tennis*. Lyon: La Manufacture, 1987.

Navratilova, Martina and George Vecsey. *Martina*. New York: Alfred A. Knopf, 1985.

Olliff, John. *The Romance of Wimbledon*. London: Hutchinson, 1949.

Schickel, Richard. *The World of Tennis*. New York: Random House, 1975.

Seles, Monica. *Getting a Grip: On My Body, My Mind, My Self*. New York: Avery, 2010.

Shannon, Bill. *USTA Official Encyclopedia of Tennis*. New York: Harper & Row, 1981.

Sharapova, Maria and Rich Cohen. *Unstoppable: My Life So Far*. New York: Sarah Crichton Books, 2017.

Tingay, Lance. *100 Years of Wimbledon*. London: Guinness Superlatives, 1977.

Tingay, Lance. *Tennis: A Pictorial History*. London: William Collins, 1977.

Tinling, Ted. *Love and Faults: Personalities Who Have Changed the History of Tennis in My Lifetime*. New York: Crown Publishers, 1979.

Tinling, Ted. *Tinling: Sixty Years in Tennis*. London: Sidgwick & Jackson, 1983.

Wade, Virginia and Jean Rafferty. *Ladies of the Court*. New York: Atheneum, 1984.

Williams, Serena and Daniel Paisner. *My Life: Queen of the Court*. New York: Pocket Books, 2010.

Wills, Helen. *Fifteen-Thirty: The Story of a Tennis Player*. London: Charles Scribner's Sons, 1937.

Wind, Herbert Warren. *Game, Set, and Match: The Tennis Boom of the 1960s and 70s*. New York: E. P. Dutton, 1979.

Periodicals

American Cricketer, American Lawn Tennis, Collier's Literary Digest, Forbes, Ladies' Home Journal, Lawn Tennis (American), *Lawn Tennis* (British), *Life, Newsweek, New Yorker, Pastime, Saturday Evening Post, Sports Illustrated, Tennis, Time, World Tennis*.

Newspapers

Boston Globe, Cincinnati Enquirer, Daily Telegraph, Guardian, London *Evening News, Los Angeles Times, New York Times, Philadelphia Evening Bulletin, Philadelphia Inquirer, Times* of London, *USA TODAY*.

Websites

www.ausopen.com, www.billiejeankingcup.com, www.britannica.com, www.instagram.com, www.itftennis.com, www.latimes.com, www.newspapers.com, www.nytimes.com, www.rolandgarros.com, www.tennisfame.com, www.twitter.com, www.usta.com, www.wikipedia.org, www.wimbledon.com, www.wtatennis.com, www.youtube.com.

A Note to the Reader

The source of the quote about paydays for men and women on page 8 is from "The World's Highest-Paid Athletes 2020: Behind The Numbers," by Kurt Badenhausen, *Forbes*, May 29, 2020.

Chapter One

The sources of quotations were: The quote about Margot on page 16, from *The Royal and Ancient Game of Tennis,* by Lord Aberdare, page 21. The quote about the Irish and white clothing on page 19, from *The Story of Women's Tennis Fashion,* by Ted Tinling. The All England Club Committee's quotes on page 19, from *Wimbledon Ladies: A Centenary Record, 1884–1984—Singles Champions,* by Alan Little and Lance Tingay, page 3. The observer's quote about Maud Watson on page 23, from *Pastime,* July 23, 1884. The Charlotte Dod quotes: about women running their hardest on page 24, from *World Sports,* "Great All Rounders—First Lady of Wimbledon," by Denzil Batchelor, October 1949; about the joy of games on page 24, from *Lottie Dod: Wimbledon Champion and All Rounder Extraordinary,* by Little, page 13. The quote about Charlotte Dod on page 24, from *Ladies of the Court,* by Virginia Wade and Jean Rafferty, page 23. The Grace Roosevelt Clark quote on page 25, from the *Sunday Courier,* Poughkeepsie, New York, 1940. The Dorothea Douglass Lambert Chambers quote about May Sutton's attire on page 32 and about the hazards of the challenge round on page 33, from the *Bradford Observer,* June 29, 1931. Elisabeth Moore's quote about five-set matches on page 32, from *Lawn Tennis,* February–March, 1902, page 116. The Chicago Prairie Club quote on page 35, from https://cptctennis.com/history/.

Chapter Two

The sources of quotations were: Elizabeth Ryan's quote about Suzanne Lenglen on page 41, from *Famous Women Tennis Players,* by Trent Frayne, 1979. The Lenglen quotes on pages 60 and 63, from "Why I Became a Professional," an article by Lenglen in her North American tour program, 1926; about her illness on page 46, "A Temperamental Jeanne d'Arc of the Tennis-Courts," *Literary Digest,* August 27, 1921. Molla Bjurstedt Mallory's quote on page 44, from *Literary Digest,* August 28, 1915. Grantland Rice's quote on page 43, from "Lenglen the Wonderful," by Grantland Rice, for *Vanity Fair / New York Times,* August 13, 1921. Robert (Bob) Kelleher's quote on page 44, from a 1987 interview with Cynthia Starr. The A. Wallis Myers quote on page 46, from *American Lawn Tennis,* November 15, 1921. Helen Wills's quote on page 55, from *Fifteen-Thirty: The Story of a Tennis Player,* by Helen Wills, page 84; Larry Engelmann's quote about Wills on page 55, from *The Goddess and the American Girl: The Story of Suzanne Lenglen and Helen Wills,* page 140. The Ted Tinling quote on page 56, from *Tinling: Sixty Year in Tennis,* by Ted Tinling, page 50. The quotes by Mary K. Browne on page 56, from "Fit to Win," by Mary K. Browne, *Collier's,* October 16, 1926, page 26. Hazel Hotchkiss Wightman's quote on page 58, from the *Boston Globe,* December 6, 1974.

George Lott's quote about Helen Jacobs on page 62, "The Greatest in Women's Tennis," by George Lott, *The Fireside Book of Tennis,* page 343.

Chapter Three

The sources of quotations were: Thelma Coyne Long's quote on page 73, from an interview with Cynthia Starr (c. 1987). The quotes from Arthur Koestler about Roland Garros during World War II on pages 73 to 74, from *Scum of the Earth,* by Arthur Koestler, 1941, page 73; the quote from Henry D. Fetter on page 74, from the *Atlantic,* May 2014. Doris Hart's quotes on page 76, from *Tennis with Hart,* by Doris Hart, page 52. Allison Danzig's quote on page 76, from *The Fireside Book of Tennis,* page 326. Bernard Destremau's quote about post-war tennis on page 78, from www.rolandgarros.com. Margaret Osborne duPont's quote on page 78, from a 1987 interview with Starr. The *Times* of London's quote about the American Wightman Cup stars on page 80, from June 15, 1946. The quotes from Pauline Betz on pages 81 and 86, Sarah Palfrey on 77 and 84, Gladys Heldman on 84, and Louise Brough on 82, from 1987 interviews with Starr. Ted Tinling's quotes about Gussy Moran on page 88, from *Tinling: Sixty Years in Tennis,* by Ted Tinling, page 121; about Moran's panties on page 88, from the London *Daily Express,* June 27, 1949. The quotes about Moran's sportscasting career on page 90, from "Glamour Girl of Sports," www.worldradiohistory.com, 1955.

Chapter Four

The sources of quotations were: Shirley Fry's quote about making ends meet on page 94, from a 1987 interview with Cynthia Starr. Althea Gibson's quotes about not dreaming of playing at Wimbledon on page 97; about her first match at Forest Hills on page 103; about serving ruthlessly, about lacking incentive to remain an amateur, and about the Globetrotters' tour on page 113; and about what she missed on page 116, from 1987 interviews with Cynthia Starr; about Dr. Eaton's court on page 100 and about being discouraged on page 110, from *I Always Wanted to Be Somebody,* by Althea Gibson, pages 44 and 83; her comments at 1957 Wimbledon on page 113, from the *New York Times,* July 5, 1957. Alice Marble's quotes about Gibson on page 98, from *American Lawn Tennis,* July 1, 1950. Allison Danzig's quote on page 99, from the *New York Times,* August 1, 1950. Angela Buxton's quote on page 103, from "Triumphing over Prejudice," by Jon Henderson and Matthew O'Donnell, the *Guardian,* July 8, 2001. Maureen Connolly's quotes about her dark destiny on page 104, from *Forehand Drive,* by Maureen Connolly and Tom Gwynne, page 3; about her concentration on page 104, from *Current Biography,* 1951; about fair pay on page 104, from *Forehand Drive,*

page 172; about retirement on page 109, from *World Tennis,* April 1955. Lance Tingay's quote on page 104, from the London *Daily Telegraph,* July 5, 1954. The quotes about Connolly from Shirley Fry on page 104, Pancho Gonzalez on page 110, and Chrissie Evert on page 110, from interviews in 1987 with Starr. Ted Tinling's quote on page 106, from *Tinling: Sixty Years in Tennis,* by Ted Tinling, page 145. Bob Kelleher's quote about under-the-table pay on page 109, from a 1987 interview with Starr. The *Time* magazine quote on page 110, from the edition of August 26, 1957. Doris Hart's quote on page 111, from a 1987 interview with Starr. The quotes about Gibson by Angela Mortimer and Darlene Hard on page 113, from 1987 interviews with Starr. The quote about New Yorkers' response on page 113, from the *New York Times,* September 6, 1951. Shirley Fry's quotes on page 114, from a 1987 interview with Starr. Fry's cable, on page 114, from *Sports Illustrated,* September 3, 1956. The quote about Gibson's experience on the LPGA tour on page 116, from "Pioneer Althea Gibson an Almost Forgotten Figure in Two Sports," by Steve Eubanks, www.lpga.com.

Chapter Five

The sources of quotations were: The quotes from Bob Kelleher and Shirley Fry on page 123, and from Rino Tomassi on page 126, from 1987 interviews with Cynthia Starr. The Maria Bueno quotes on pages 124, 125, and 126, from a 1987 interview with Starr; the (London) *Observer* quote on page 125, from the *Observer,* July 5, 1959; Wimbledon's quote on page 127 about all-white clothing, from www.wimbledon.com. Margaret Court's quotes, about playing right-handed on page 130, about fitness, confidence, and Bueno on page 133, and about playing at Wimbledon on page 234, from a 1987 interview with Starr. The Ann Haydon Jones quote about Margaret Court on page 133, from a 1987 interview with Starr. The *New York Times* quote about Court on page 133, from "Queen of All Courts," September 14, 1970. Darlene Hard's quotes about being an amateur on page 135, from a 1987 interview with Starr.

Chapter Six

The sources of quotations were: Bob Kelleher's and Bud Collins's quotes on page 149 from 1987 interviews with Cynthia Starr. Julius Heldman's quote on page 149, from *Sports Illustrated,* June 22, 1964. Bud Collins's quote about *World Tennis* on page 149, from *Bud Collins' Tennis Encyclopedia,* by Bud Collins and Zander Hollander, page 511. Rex Bellamy's quote on page 150, from the *Times* of London, July 4, 1970. The Rosie Casals quote on page 151 from a 1987 interview with Starr. The Ruth Bader Ginsburg quote on page 152, from the *Provincetown*